勝中得學習

失敗領教訓

"You may learn from victory; but you will learn from defeat."

Calligraphy by Shifu Hwang

From the Author's collection

OKINAWAN NO BUSHI NO TE

The Hands of the Okinawan Bushi

沖縄の武士の手

By

Ronald L. Lindsey

---

*Any photograph, drawing or quote presented in this book that is not identified as to the
source of this photograph, drawing or quote is part of the author's collection.
The illustration on the front cover was drawn by the author.
The Japanese sword tsuba pictured on the back cover was made of steel by the author.*

*"To those who carry the torch; in the past,
in the present, and in the future."*

Disclaimer and Warning

A Note to Readers and Parents

The information (techniques, ideas, strategies and attitudes) presented in this publication are the results of almost 50 years of practice by the author. The author obtained this information from Okinawan Karate Masters and other karateka both teachers and students over many decades.

This book presents to the general public, the fighting arts of the Okinawan Bushi (warriors). These arts were developed for self protection and for the protection of others; these arts are not to be used for sport or for any purpose other than protection.

Please use restraint when practicing all martial arts techniques including those presented in this book. Practice these techniques only under the supervision of a qualified martial arts instructor. The author and or publisher are not responsible in any way for injuries, accidents, fatalities or any other mishaps that may occur from the information presented in this book.

Parents seek only qualified martial arts teachers to instruct your children. Attend your child's classes and do not allow your children to learn dangerous techniques. Such training is for adults not children.

Instructors keep your classes safe.

INTRODUCTION

It is an honor to be allowed to do the introduction for Sensei Lindsey's book. At the time that I am writing this, I have been training with him for almost 33 years. He has a wealth of information to share based on his years of personal experience and research. I want to start out by explaining how I came to start training with him, as I hope that it will give the reader a "feel" for how he is as an instructor.

When I met Sensei Lindsey, I had already been training for 18 years. I say this, because I was not an impressionable novice when I met him. Rather, I had years of training and experience with a variety of other instructors. This made it impossible for me to empty my cup, as the Zen story goes. I studied Wado-ryu style for four years before I went to the United States Military Academy at West Point. After my first year at West Point, I was appointed as the Coach of the Karate Team. We were undefeated in intercollegiate competition during my last two years there. While at West Point, I had the opportunity to travel to New York City and study old style Tae Kwon Do, Goju-kai, Shorin-ryu, and Iaido. Once I was in the Army, I had the opportunity to study Goju-ryu, Isshin-ryu, Shotokan, and Moo Duk Kwan Tang Soo Do. I competed for years in tournaments in Texas and had become well-known for my Iaido, Sai, and Bo katas. However, I became weary of the tournament scene, and I began to lose interest in training. I was fast and flashy, but I wanted to learn the true fighting art of Karate.

Then, after severe injuries in an automobile wreck in 1978, I decided to return to tournament competition as a way to rehabilitate myself. It was at a tournament in Austin, Texas, where I was approached by Sensei Lindsey after he had seen me performing a Sai kata and an Iaido kata. I had previously been involved with another Okinawan Karate organization, but that had left me with a bad taste for organizations after the head of the organization absconded with the funds. So, when Sensei Lindsey approached me with an offer to join Master Fusei Kise's Kenshinkan Organization, which Sensei Lindsey was in charge of, I had no desire to take him up on this offer. However, I did have a burning desire to learn more Okinawan weapons katas, and Sensei Lindsey indicated that he had extensive training with all of the Okinawan weapons. He offered to teach me more about these weapons.

I went to visit him at his house in Bastrop, Texas, with the idea that I would learn more weapons katas. On my first visit, after we had warmed up, Sensei Lindsey gave me a practice Samurai sword and invited me to fight him freestyle while he defended with a pair of sai. As I mentioned, I had years of training with the sword and had done well in tournament competition doing Iaido katas. So, I thought that he must be pretty confident in his ability to use the sai. We sparred for almost 30 minutes. I could not believe that this man could block and defend against my attacks when they were not prearranged, and he had no previous experience sparring with me. I too had years of sparring with the sai, but I did not use the kind of techniques he was using so effectively against me. His principles of what he called "body change" allowed him to block and counter all of my techniques. Needless to say, I was very impressed with his ability and decided to train with him to not only learn more weapons katas but to also learn how to fight better with the weapons.

So, I began to travel to Bastrop to train with him on the Okinawan weapons. At the beginning of each workout, Sensei Lindsey would ask me to run through my empty hand katas. After each of my katas, he would then demonstrate how he did his kata. Again, I was there to learn Okinawan weapons. I had no desire to work on my empty hand katas, but he always insisted that we work on empty hand katas first. When I would do my katas, he would make some suggestions as to how I could do some of my techniques in the katas differently. I found his suggestions to be helpful, but I wanted to learn as much about weapons as quickly as I could, and this man would not leave the empty hand katas alone. Finally, I decided that the only way to get him to leave me alone about my empty hand katas was to learn his katas. My plan was to learn the Matsumura Seito katas and practice them over and over again until they were perfect (a sign of my youth and ignorance). Once I had perfected them, I thought that Sensei Lindsey would be left with no choice other than to just focus on teaching me weapons katas and weapons fighting.

As the months passed, I started noticing that my Karate was becoming more and more deadly. Without really being aware of my transition, I had become a Matsumura Seito practitioner. Sensei Lindsey never asked me to empty my cup. He simply spooned out a little of the tea at a time until my tea was completely replaced with a different brew. At that point, I understood that there is no separation of weapons training from empty hand training. The principles that are used for fighting empty handed are the same principles that are used when fighting with weapons. I did not understand until that moment that Sensei Lindsey had always been teaching me how to use weapons when he made me keep working on my empty hand katas.

We used to have a camp every year in La Grange, Texas. Because I helped Sensei Lindsey teach at the camps, I got to workout with the Okinawan masters of our organizations. At first it was Master Fusei Kise, and then later on it was Master Yuichi Kuda. One thing I observed when we worked out with the Okinawan masters was that Sensei Lindsey would always ask them about how Master Hohan Soken did certain techniques. As Sensei Lindsey discusses in his book, each one of the Okinawan masters who trained with Master Soken did some of their techniques a little bit different from how Master Soken did them. Sensei Lindsey would learn how each one of the masters wanted specific techniques done, but he would always verify with them exactly how Soken did his techniques to ensure that he did remember Master Soken's techniques correctly. It was not until many years later when Sensei Lindsey made the decision to teach his katas and fighting techniques as closely as Master Soken had done them that I realized what he had done all along. When I went back and looked at videos of Sensei Lindsey back when we were still associated with Master Kise and then with Master Kuda, I realized that Sensei Lindsey had always continued to practice the way that Master Soken did his techniques. He would learn how each of the Okinawan masters wanted techniques done, and he would teach others the way they wanted them done, but he always practiced and perfected the techniques that he had learned from Master Soken. It was only then that I could appreciate how hard Sensei Lindsey had tried to maintain the techniques of Matsumura Seito as faithfully as he could. Master Kuda appreciated what Sensei Lindsey was doing and even told Sensei Lindsey and I that he believed the day was coming when the only way a person would be able to learn pure Matsumura Seito would be to come and train in the United States rather than going to Okinawa. He stated this because so many karate practitioners are influenced by sport karate, and even on Okinawa there is a trend to move away from the old fighting arts and move toward the modern sport karate. Sensei Lindsey never criticized people for practicing sport karate. He just has a burning desire to practice Karate the old way.

There is an issue that comes up from time to time and that is that some people will say that Sensei Lindsey did not train with Master Soken as long as some others who were stationed on Okinawa. That fact is true, but there are two important mitigating variables that are involved with this. First, Sensei Lindsey was married and had already had training in Karate when he was stationed on Okinawa. So, he had a much more serious attitude than many of the young G.I.'s who were stationed there. Second, and most importantly, Sensei Lindsey continued to train almost daily after coming back to the United States and continued to train with Okinawan masters who had been students of Master Soken after he was back living in the United States. If a person spent more time training with Master Soken than Sensei Lindsey but then stopped training for 20 or 30 years, why would we expect that person to remember details of how they were taught? If a person spent more time training with Master Soken but never trained with another master after that, why would we expect that person to advance much further than the level he was at when he was on Okinawa? Sensei Lindsey has been almost fanatical about researching and studying Matsumura Seito. I have seen many masters of Karate in my life. They were excellent, but 5 or 10 years later, they were still at the same level. Because of Sensei Lindsey's constant striving to be better and learn a deeper understanding of the art, he is a better martial artist today than he was 10 years ago, and he will be an even greater martial artist 5 years from now. He is unique in how his ability and knowledge progress each year. I have watched countless 8mm films of Master Soken and his students doing kata and fighting techniques. I have looked at hundreds of pictures taken of Master Soken and his students practicing in his dojo, and I can state without reservation that what Sensei Lindsey is teaching is probably as close to what Master Soken taught as is humanly possible. That is not to say that no one else is doing this, but I can only speak of what I have seen with Sensei Lindsey.

My first Shorin-ryu instructor told me as I was about to leave on my career in the Army that I should look for someone that was better in Karate than I was. When I found a person like this, I should train with that person until I had learned all that I could and then move on and find someone else. I have done that all of my Karate career, but when I met Sensei Lindsey, I have not been able to empty that well of knowledge. For as quickly as I draw water from that well, he puts more water back in with his own training and understanding of Karate. I think that the reader will find the same thing.

Dr. Charles H. Tatum
Eighth Dan

"Ask and it will be given to you,
seek and you will find;
knock and the door will be opened to you."

Holy Bible
Matthew 7:7

AUTHOR'S PREFACE

Forty years ago if you would have told me that I would be writing a book about Okinawan Karate; I would have thought that you have taken leave of you senses. Thirty years ago if you told me that I would write a book about Okinawan karate I probably would have said that you were correct; and I had by that time started to collect pictures and information with the idea of using this material for a book.

Three years ago I started sorting through about five large card board boxes full of "stuff" to be used in my book. I had little bunches of material here and there all across my dojo floor. All in various stages of being sorted and organized in to subject matter groups.

During practice we just work around these piles of "stuff." After a month or so the five boxes of information or stuff had been reduced down to two large card board boxes and I started putting things in order and working on my text.

I never wrote an outline or followed any standard methods for writing this book. I did not want my book to be "prim and proper"; full of all the standard procedures that would be used as if I were writing an article for some professional journal. You see, I wrote this book to be what it is ....a 66 year old man, who has been practicing karate all of his adult life, telling a story. This story reflects on what I have seen, what I have been taught, what I have been told, what I have read and what I have experienced. This is my story.

I realize that my methods would make my college English professors turn over in their graves. However, I believe my method of writing is easy to understand and as such is "reader friendly." That is my principle reason for being so "unconventional".

I list my sources in the text where applicable; I also list them at the ends of each chapter under "Sources, Endnotes, and Explanations". I have accounted for the sources of all drawings and photos as best I could. The reader must realize that many of these photos and so forth have been in my possession for forty years or more. I could not remember the sources for many of the unlabelled photos and written notes.

The reader will find misspelled words and grammatical errors. There will be inconsistencies in the Table of Contents and other parts of the book. My work will have the mistakes of an old man who has been out of a class room for forty plus years. I apologize in advance for these mistakes.

It is my intention to write more books on Okinawan Karate, I hope to write about the Pinan Kata in the near future and to continue to write about the Shorin Ryu Kata of Okinawa.

Ronald Lindsey
Hakutsuru Kan Dojo
Bastrop County, Texas
January 16, 2011

*The Author demonstrating a posture from the Kata Rohai Jo in the
mountains of West Virginia.
October 2010*

ACKNOWLEDGEMENTS

It is difficult to know where to begin with acknowledging all of the people, who have helped, encouraged, supported and stood by me while I wrote this book. I will start off by express my gratitude and thanks to my family who have had to "live" this book day and night for the considerable time it took me to get the book finished.

My wife, Kathy, let me convert a spare bed room into my "production center," complete with resource books, notes, drawings and photographs scattered all over the place. My son, Brett had to endure my constant "belly aching" about computers and a thousand other things. Brett also did the "bird's eye view photos….he climbed on the roof of our house to do these. My son, Eric, served faithfully as the "model" for many of the photos used in the book; his wife, Tanya, was the chief photographer and served as one of my computer advisors. My daughter, Carmen, and her husband Bryan faithfully answered all of the "what do you think about this questions." Even my 5 year old grandson, Carson, and his three year old sister, Karlie, were involved. When they came over to play with their "Pawpaw", he was always writing his book and would tell them to "wait just a minute and I'll be there."

My students pitched in and helped in a thousand different ways. Charles Tatum wrote the introduction and served as one of my advisors. Charlie Dean, Mike Suber, Bill Ree, Mark Gracey, Jeff Walters and his wife Linea helped with the proof reading, and were there to help in any way they could. My student, Ronnie Locke, is the real hero in getting this book started and finished, he was responsible for all of the Japanese kanji calligraphy, as well putting up with all of my ranting and belly aching about computers and so forth, he helped in so many ways. Ron Carter and his wife, Michele, offered to write the Index. My friend, Shifu Hwang, was always there to write the classic Chinese calligraphy that appears in the book. I know I am leaving out others who assisted me with my book and I apologize if I have offended any one who I have not mentioned.

There were four of my students and one old friend who passed away while my book was being written. My students Chuck Chandler, Bill Muncy, Mark Wilson and Lee Mitchell died during the past year (2010). Their help and encouragement played a major role in my writing of this book. My friend, Willard Treadway, who I knew while I was going to college at Texas A&M University, also passed away. He was a black belt in Shorin Ryu Shorin Kan; he would have enjoyed my book.

The last group that I want to acknowledge for their help in assisting me in writing this book is the "Okinawa Karate GI's (the U.S. Army, Marine, Air Force and Navy Veterans) who served in Okinawa during the 1950's through the early 1970's). They learned karate on the island. They lent me their photographs, their stories, their advice and their support. I am proud to be a member of this group and I am glad these old veterans are my friends.

Ronald L. Lindsey
Bastrop, Texas ….June 2011

Logo for:
Kokusai Kobujutsu Hozon
Domei

Logo for:
Kokusai Shurite
Karate/Kobujutsu
Rengo Kai

Logos for the (Top)…Kokusai (International Kobujutsu (Old War Art) Hozon
(Preservation) Domei (Alliance) and on the (Bottom) Kokusai (International)
Shurite Karate/Kobujutsu Rengo Kai (Federation)

TABLE OF CONTENTS
Part 1

Page number

Okinawa: The History...the Culture...the Bushi...1

Chapter 1: Ancient History of the Ryukyu...5
    The Gempei Wars...12
    The Mongol Hordes teach Military Tactics to the Japanese.......................14
    The Tales of Tametomo no Minamoto...16
    Tametomo's son, Shunten, and his descendants...17
    The Kingdom of Chuzan...19
    Chapter 1 Endnotes, Sources and Explanations..28
Chapter 2: The Okinawan Bushi..29
    History of the Shaolin Temple...31
    Stories of the Shaolin Temple..34
    The Bushi who trained in China and their Lineages..................................39
    Kanga Sakugawa and Chatan Yara..39
    Ryukyu Kan..45
    Matsuda Tosabaru, Kanbun Uechi, Gokenki, and Seisho Arakaki..............46
    Nakaima Kenri...55
    Sakayama Ketoku...55
    Okinawa Kenpo..56
    Itoman village and the Dun Dun Gama (Cave)..59
    Itoman Bushi (Kinjo Matsu)...59
    Kanryu Higashionna...61
    Kojo Bushi..67
    Slapping the Rock at Tsuji...69
    Other Bushi..71
    Chapter 2 Sources, Foot notes and Explanations......................................84
Chapter 3: Okinawa's Greatest Warrior (Sokon Matsumura)....................87
    General Information..89
    Matsumura's Kata..91
    Bushi Matsumura the Man..93
    Matsumura and his wife...94
    Okinawa Whip Kick..97
    Matsumura and Kushigawa Uehara..98
    Matsumura the Weapons Master...98
    Matsumura and Nomura Clash..100
    The Bushi and the Rooster..101
    The Meiji Restoration...102
    Matsumura's Students..105
    Matsumura-Ha...107
    Anko Itosu and his friend Anko Azato..108
    Azato and Itosu's Students..111

Itosu-Ha..112
Kyan-Ha..117
   Chapter 3: Endnotes, Sources and Explanations.........................125
Chapter 4: Okinawa's Last Samurai..129
Hohan Soken's Early Life...134
The Training of a Bushi..138
Grandmaster Soken's Kata...139
Grandmaster Soken Seeks Other Teachers.....................................143
Moving to Argentina..147
Okinawan Tode..149
Defending Grandmaster Soken's Honor..158
Soken's Students..168
Fusei Kise's Dojo...170
Shisa Lions..174
A Tale of Five Swords...175
Kick Training...176
Testing His Techniques...176
Yuichi Kuda's Dojo...179
Grandmaster Soken's Kobujutsu..184
Hohan Soken's Death poem..188
   Chapter 4: Sources, Endnotes and Explanations.........................189

Part 2

My Walk with Matsumura..191

Chapter 5: Kokoro no Heiho (The Strategy of Mental Attitude)...........195
Wisdom..198
Nintai (Perseverance)...221
Loyalty...225
Integrity..230
Giri (Obligation)...234
   Chapter 5 Sources, Endnotes and Explanations..........................242
Chapter 6: Minari no Heiho (The Strategy of Appearance)..............243
Learning about Your Enemies...245
   Sensei Kise's Hitting Chart...248
   A Lesson in Atemi Waza from Hohan Soken...............................253
The Bushi's Secret (Developing Ki: The Key to Balance and Power.........254
   Tachi Kata of Shorin Ryu Matsumura Seito...............................255
     A Lesson from Seizan Kinjo..255
     The Dachi or Stances...256
     Strength and Weaknesses in Your Tachi and Kamae................262
Understanding and Projecting Your Power......................................267
   Make Every Step a Kick...269
   Sinking Power...270
   Shifting the Body Weight with out Stepping..............................271

     Using the Neko Ashi Dachi to Develop Power..........................272
     Power in the Front Hand-Power in the Rear Hand....................275
     Kicking Power...277
     Power Up-Power Down...278
     Gojushiho Introduces the Half Step..281
  Tsuru no Hane (Wings of the Crane)
     Developing Hands of Steel and Arms of Cotton.......................284
     The Awakening of Your Tendons..285
     Tendon Awareness and Strengthening Exercises.....................285
     Emulating Ancient Man..288
     Exploding Fist of Steel...289
     Gokenki Crane Wings...290
     Matsumura Crane Wings...291
     Kojo or Kogushiku Crane Wings..293
     He Tsuru Hane-Flying Crane Wings...294
     The Crane Beak...295
     Matsumura Nukite..296
     The Rake Hand..296
     Using the Thumb..297
     The Wrist...297
     Using the Matsumura Sanchin Crane Hands..........................298
     Putting Ki in Your Foot..299
    Chapter 6 Sources, Endnotes and Explanations.......................300
 Chapter 7: Maai no Heiho (The Strategy of the Combat Distance).......301
  Tokoshi no Heiho (The Strategy of Crossing a Great Distance).........305
     Understanding Irimi no Heiho..306
     The Maai..307
  Crossing the Maai with Gojushiho...311
     Shinkagi no Heiho...311
      Kaimon no Heiho...311
      Kiai no Heiho, Metsuki no Heiho, Kage no Heiho
      and Kashi no Heiho..317
      Hanashi no Heiho and Kado no Heiho...................................321
      Magiri no Heiho and Matsumura Hakutsuru..........................322
    Chapter 7 Sources, Endnotes and Explanations......................326
 Chapter 8: Chushin no Heiho (The Strategy of the Center)..............327
     The Invisible Wall...330
  Uke Waza/Blocking Techniques...331
     Practical Use of the Triangle or Wedge..................................333
     Kata Block/Honto Waza Block...334
  Suigetsu no Heiho (Change Body)...347
     If You Wish to Learn Suigetsu Study Rice...............................350
     Managing the Octagon..351
     Grandmaster Soken's Irimi...357
     Dealing with Multiple Opponents..359
     The Bus Driver...362

Glossary of Terms used in the Study of Bojutsu...*365*
Index of People's Names...*367*
Author's Contact Information..*372*

人生デ重要な事の
代価は実に小さい

"The important things in life cost very little."
A lesson from a Chinese fortune cookie.
Computerized drawing by the Author

PART I

OKINAWA

THE HISTORY...THE CULTURE...THE BUSHI

沖縄の歴史文化武士

The History, the Culture, the Bushi

Painting on the previous page is from
the author's collection

Millions of people all across the world practice a martial art that we now call karate. Out of those millions very few are familiar with the history of their art Most think that this martial art came from Japan, or Korea....most only know who their teacher is and assume that the art they are learning came from their teacher.

Most martial arts historians will tell you that the karate arts as we now know them came from the Ryukyu Islands of which the principle island is Okinawa. My goal in this first part of *"Okinawan no Bushi no Te"* is to create an awareness and an appreciation of the people who developed the art of karate.

The Okinawan people have endured a long history of hardship and disappointments. Yet through it all they have survived and prospered. They are among the most long lived and happiest people on earth. It was my good fortune to have lived among them and to have learned something about the Okinawan martial arts and culture. I invite the readers to join me as we explore part one of *The Okinawan no Bushi no Te*........

"The History....the Culture....the Bushi"

Ronald Lindsey

The White Crane
Okinawa's Ancient symbol of
Longevity.
Credit: Author's collection

3

Old Map of the East China Sea Area

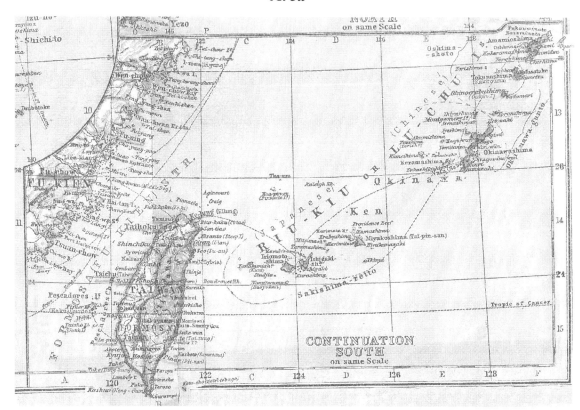

Map was found in a Flea Market in Warrenton, Texas
Author's collection

CHAPTER 1

ANCIENT HISTORY OF THE RYUKYU ISLANDS

流球島の古歴史

Ancient History of the Ryukyu Islands

Anthropological evidence and old folktales and legends point to the fact that the people who settled into the Ryukyu Islands traveled through three ancient routes. The people, who migrated to these islands came for many reasons; some were lost at sea, blown off course by storms or faulty navigation, and washed ashore never to return to their homes. Others came to seek their fortunes or to escape their enemies or maybe they came to escape diseases that often plagued ancient man. Still others came to satisfy a longing of "wanderlust". The ancient Asian people settled the for reaching areas of the Pacific Ocean for many reasons. If an island could support human habitation, people found it and carved out a living for themselves.

They came from a (1) northern route from the Asian mainland down through the Korean Peninsula across the sea to Japan. Moving through the islands of Japan then migrating on into the Ryukyu Islands. They also came from Siberia down into Northern Japan always moving southward until they reached the southern islands we now call the Ryukyus.

Some migrants brave the stormy waters of the (2) East China Sea and sailed directly eastward into the Ryukyu Islands. From the Southeastern Pacific areas they also came; moving north from Indonesia, the Philippines Islands to (3) Taiwan and then they moved northward into the Ryukyu Islands.

This migration was not a great flood of people; but rather it was a small trickle of individuals or small family groups that traveled from island to island always seeking the protection of an island harbor before nightfall.

The people, who settled into the "Nanto" or southern islands as the Ryukyu Islands, were called by the Japanese, found a land of few natural resources. They found rugged mountainous terrain with shallow, thin soils, little usable timber or mineral wealth. However, the islands offered the bounties of the sea, deep safe harbors, breath taking beauty, and a location along a string of islands that one day would be in the middle of one of the most profitable trade routes in the Pacific Ocean area.

As people learned about the safe routes to travel to the southern island; women and children soon came to establish settlements. Women and children bring the development of culture and the building of society. These developments took hundreds of years. Well into the 13th century the Ryukyu Islands were still a primitive society little removed from a Stone Age existence.

Drawing by Mike Roberts
Color productions

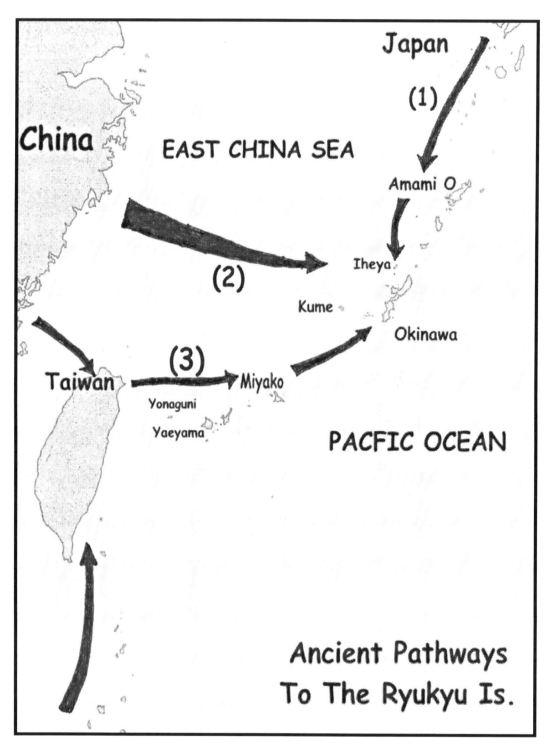

Credit: Author's Collection

8

Progress came slowly to the Ryukyu Islands. But simple facts worked to the best interest of the Ryukyu people. If you sail east from China, north from Taiwan, or south from Japan you have a good chance of bumping into one of the islands of the Ryukyu chain. This would eventually lead to trade, more settlements, and more people with more sophisticated skills that would improve the lives of the islanders.

It is recorded that the Chinese Kingdom of Yen had relations with the Wa; the Wa were a small tribe of people who live in the islands south of Japan. Most historic scholars agree that the people called "Wa" were the ancient Ryukyu people. The Kingdom of Yen fell due to internal conflicts; this resulted in Ch'in Shih Huang Ti becoming the first Emperor of China. He destroyed the feudal states and united the country. He reigned from 221-210 B.C. Emperor Ch'in was a builder. He began building the Great Wall of China and organized the country's great human resources.

Emperor Ch'in is of interest because he sent out numerous expeditions into the eastern sea looking for the secret by which base metals could be turned into gold. In 219 B.C. he sent out a mission of 3000 young men and women to seek the "Happy Immortals" who dwelt on islands in the eastern seas (again scholars believe this refers to the Ryukyu people). These Happy Immortals were alleged to know the secret of turning base metals into gold. The Emperor's ships never returned; legend has it that they reached Japan and went on to the Ryukyu Islands and made permanent settlements.

The career of Emperor Ch'in is very important to the history of the Ryukyus. His reign led to the establishment of the powerful Han Dynasty and a great expansion of China as the leader of the oriental world. Records of the Han Dynasty, state that the islands beyond Korea were divided into more than 100 provinces of which about 30 had contact with Chinese settlements in Korea. These records note that, in the 2nd century A.D., during a period of intense civil war, an old unmarried sorceress called Pimeku became very influential in the islands. She sent emissaries to the Chinese settlements in Korea to seek help in a local war. After Pimeku's death the war worsened. They subsided only when a relative of Pimeku, a girl of 13 years of age, was made ruler. Japanese traditions indicate that female rulers were often found in western and southern Japan.

In prehistoric Okinawa and in other Ryukyu Islands there developed a powerful group of female priestesses called "noro". The noro formed an almost cult like sub-society that worked closely with the local government a wielded considerable power over the Ryukyu society.

The importance of the noro was more than just simple influence. Since ancient days the noro had many duties; perhaps the most important was being the custodian of the fire. Fire was a precious commodity that was handed down from generation to generation. It was the duty of the noro to maintain the fire. The noro was expected to remain a virgin. Her duties required the care of the hearth fire, worship of the ancestors through ritual devotion, and to make arrangements for marriages, burials, travel and many other tasks. It should be noted that the Ryukyu Islands are made of coral and calciferous soil; stones such as flint or agate that spark when struck together are very rare. Therefore, it was difficult to build and maintain fire.

Noro Priestesses
(Photo Credit: Mike Roberts Color Productions)

The noro gradually lost their influence. However, the noro of Iheya Island retained their influence and responsibilities until the end of the 19th century. [(1-1)]

Also noted in early ancient Chinese records is the rise of a military group on the island of Kyushu in Japan. This was the rise of Jimmu, who was to become the first Emperor of Japan, thus founding a line of leadership that was to have great influence on the Ryukyu's and the world as a whole. As Jimmu sought to increase his influence through out Japan; many of the peoples he defeated sought refuge. Undoubtedly some moved south into the Ryukyu Islands thus increasing the influence of the early Japanese culture on the Ryukyu people. Defeated Japanese warriors who fled into these southern areas would have carried some of their warrior traditions with them. Although there is no record of Japanese martial skills arriving in the Ryukyus at this time; there can be little doubt that some of those fleeing Jimmu were defeated warriors and would have maintained their warrior skills. It must be remembered that Japanese warrior skills at this time were very primitive. However primitive that the skills of these warriors may have been, they were in all probability much more advanced than the fighting skills of the southern islanders.

The Legend concerning the birth and rise to power of Jimmu has long been a source of pride among the Ryukyu people. These legends put Jimmu's place of birth on one of the islands between Okinawa and Japan. It could be that one of history's most powerful groups of people, the Emperors of Japan, started their conquest for power on one of the Ryukyu Islands.

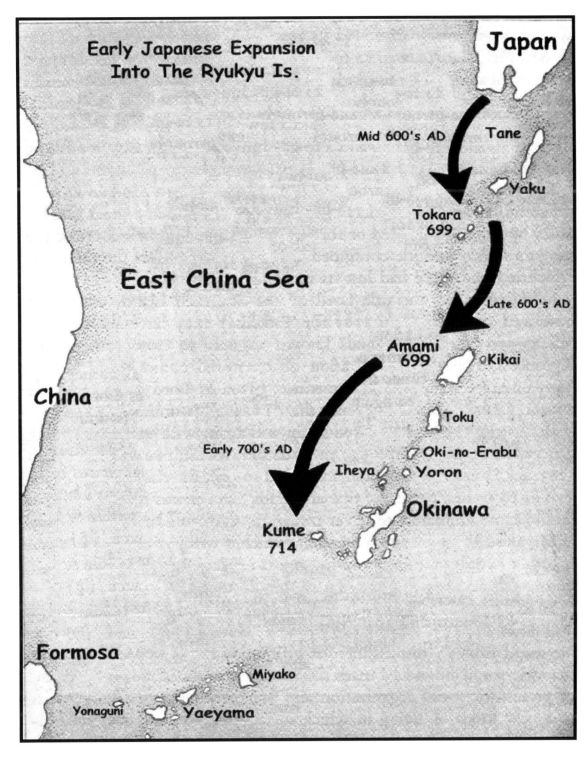

Credit: From the Authors Collection

In the late 500's A.D. the Japanese successfully increased their attempts to subjugate the islands to the south. By the mid 600's A.D. Japan had forced the islands of Tane, Yaku to submit. In 699 A.D. Tokara also submitted to the Japanese demands. The Ryukyu Islands fell like dominos, one by one they submitted. Amami and surrounding islands submitted in 699 A.D. However, Okinawa, Iheya, Toku, Yoran and others islands near by did not submit to the Japanese until much later.

By the late 800's A.D. Japanese expansion had run its course. Japan closed her diplomatic mission with China. The mission was too expensive to maintain. Japan turned inward to its own internal troubles and forced, through an almost constant civil war, all areas of Japan to submit to the Emperor's rule

THE GEMPEI WARS

In Japan starting as early as the 9th century there began the rise of three important and powerful families: the Taira, Minamoto and Fujiwara. The Taira family started by the grandson of Emperor Kammu was probably the first of these three families to begin its rise in power. The Minamoto family stemmed from a 10th century grandson of the Emperor Seiwa.

After several generations the Fujiwara family began to specialize in influence peddling between the Emperor and members of the royal court. The Taira and Minamoto families were left to compete for the influence and power to be gained by controlling the countryside. The real power of any country lies in controlling the rural and food producing areas. The rice production of ancient Japan was at stake and whoever controlled the rice production could rule the country.

Modern historians call the numerous conflicts brought about by this rivalry the "Gempei Wars". The name Gempei is a Chinese pronunciation of Gen or Gem for Minamoto and Hei or Pei for Taira. This was a period when the great military clans of the Taira and Minamoto played an increasingly more prominent role in the affairs of the country. As a result the power of the central government declined. Revolts were crushed by Minamoto no Yoriyoshi and Minamoto Yoshiiye in 1062 and 1091. In 1113 the warrior monks of Kofuku Temple were in open rebellion. By the middle of the 12th century the Taira Clan began to gain power over the Minamoto. By 1160 the Taira Clan under their ruthless leader, Kiyomaro, emerged supreme. However, after Kiyomori's death the fortunes of war began to favor the Minamoto after they emerged victorious at the battle of Dan no Ura in 1185. Yoritomo, the victorious leader of the Minamoto established the Shogunate or military governorship which became the real power in feudal Japan.

Yoritomo no Minamoto purged the country of his enemies. His depredations caused many deposed samurai to flee Japan. Even his brother, Minamoto Yoshitsune, fled his brother's wrath. Yoshitsune fled to the Asian main land; this brings up a very interesting theory that a number of oriental scholars support. There are those who claim that the great Mongol conqueror, Genghis Khan was none other than Yoshitsune no Minamoto. In certain Chinese dialects the kanji for Yoshitsune can be pronounced Genghis; isn't it strange that the Mongols had only limited success as warriors until the arrival of Genghis Kan? [1-2]

The turmoil of civil war in Japan sent many samurai and others into either forced or self imposed exile. These people fled Japan in all directions; some went south into the Ryukyu Islands. The warriors brought with them not only their military skills; they also brought civilian skills that were needed by the Ryukyu people.

The warrior class (Samurai) developed a method of warfare that was uniquely Japanese. By the 10th and 11th century horses had become increasingly available. Therefore, by this time the samurai had become a mounted warrior. The bow had become the weapon of choice. Battle lines soon degenerated into a melee with individual warriors issuing individual challenges to the warriors of the opposition. The warriors would charge each other mounted on their horses; shooting arrows at each other. The infantry or foot soldiers play only a minor role in battle. [1-3]

Individual fighting skills became very important. Actual battle strategy such as mounted mass cavalry charges, flanking moves or massed archers firing volley after volley of arrows played no part in these early battles. The 11th century Japanese warrior was a fierce brave fighter very skillful in the use of his weapons. However, their tactics and strategies were not very well developed.

Mounted Japanese Samurai
From the Author's collection

THE MONGOL HORDES TEACH MILITARY TACTICS TO THE JAPANESE

The Mongols under Genghis Kan introduced the military tactics in their conquest of most of Asia and parts of Europe that in the 1990's the U.S. Army called "Shock and Awe". They fought with mass use of horse cavalry in combination with massive use of archers that simply over whelmed their enemies with numbers and fire power.

In 1274 and again in 1281 combined Mongol and Chinese Armies under the command of Kublai Kan invaded Japan on the western coast of Kyushu on November 19, 1274. The size of the invading forces was estimate to be 15,000 Mongol and Chinese soldiers, 8,000 Korean soldiers, 300 large ships and 400 to 500 small ships.

The Japanese Shogun had mobilized all available forces in Northern Kyushu to meet the invaders. The Japanese commanders had little experience managing large forces and they were inexperience with conducting major battles since none had occurred in Japan during the last 50 years. The Japanese warriors were experienced only with the traditional warfare they had been conducting over the last few centuries. This consisted of individual combat between warriors. The Japanese had not learned the strategy of mass, surprise, and methods of war the Mongols had long practiced.

It appeared that the Japanese were headed for certain defeat. During the night a severe storm appeared, the Kan's forces re-embarked on their ships, they sailed out to sea and were destroyed by the storm. The second "Mongol" invasion of Japan occurred in 1281 with similar results.

Genghis Kan (Credit:
Mark Wilson Collection)

The Mongol invasions of Japan left the Japanese with an experience that had two major impacts on the Japanese people and leaders. They were forced to relearn their military tactics and they were left with a misguided sense of security that they were invincible. They thought the gods and the "Devine Winds" or Kamikaze would protect them. This attitude lasted until after Word war II.

Mongol Warrior (Credit Mark Wilson Collection)

Mongolian cavalry men (Credit: Mark Wilson collection)

THE TALE OF TAMETOMO NO MINAMOTO

The turmoil of civil war in Japan sent many samurai and others into either forced or self imposed exile. These people fled Japan in all directions; some went south and one person who did so was named Tametomo. He was a 5th generation member of the Minamoto clan. There are two legends that surround him. These legends were not written until 600 years after the alleged events took place; yet all of these legends are possible and the historic probability for them being true is quite high.

Both legends agree that in the 12th century, as the Taira Clan increased in power and wealth, among their most bitter enemies were members of Tametomo's own family. The legends go on to claim that the young Tametomo grew into a strong young warrior who excelled at archery. Yet he was stubborn and unruly. His father sent him south to Kyushu. Here, Tametomo associated himself with Ata, the Acting Governor of Kyushu. It wasn't long before Tametomo was appointed to the position of "Grand Superintendent." He also married Ata's daughter.

Tametomo took part in a Minamoto attack on the Taira-held capitol city. The Minamoto forces lost this battle and many of its leaders were either killed in battle or were executed. Tametomo was captured. As punishment for his part in the attack, the ligaments of his bow-arm were cut and he was exiled to the distant islands of the Izu Peninsula in eastern Japan in 1156. The Taira Clan remained in authority for the next 26 years.

It is at this point that the two legends surrounding Tametomo disagree. The first legend states that Tametomo died in Izu and had no connection with the Ryukyu Islands. The second legend says that he remained in exile for 14 years. He was said to have escaped his exile in 1165 to Oni-ga-shima (Devil's Island); which according to tradition is Okinawa. Needless to say it is the second legend that captures our attention.

Once in Okinawa the local Chieftain, Lord Osato, welcomed him. Tametomo married the chieftain's daughter and a son, Shunten, was born of this union. This marriage was a temporary arrangement as Tametomo was eager to get back to support the Minamoto Clan in the Gempei Wars of Japan.

He and his men soon left Okinawa and made their way back to Oshima in Sagami Bay. Here forces under the Vice Governor of Izu over whelmed them. Legend says that Tametomo hopelessly surrounded, chose to commit suicide (seppuku) rather than giving his enemies the satisfaction of killing him. Again legends state that this act by Tametomo set the precedent in Japan for the custom and tradition of seppuku or hara-kiri.

Tametomo's wife and infant son are said to have waited in vain for him to return. Their waiting place was in Urasoe Village just northwest of Shuri near small inlet that ever since has been called Machiminato, "Waiting Harbor".

After Tametomo's nephew Yoritomo no Minamoto defeated the Taira Clan at the Battle of Dan no Ura in 1185 it was the Taira's turn to run for safety. The defeated Taira Clan members and their supporters fled into the remote mountains, the Asian mainland, or to

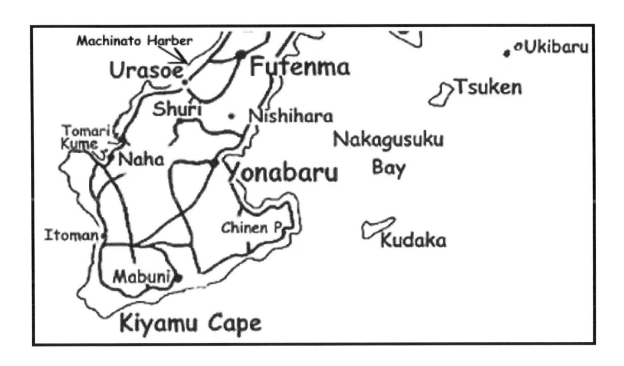

Machinato or Machiminato (Waiting Harbor) Credit: Author's Collection

the distant islands of the south. Today on several Ryukyu Islands there are strong traditions that support this historic probability. In the Sakishima Group for many years there was a strong memory of the Taira Clan. A shrine dedicated to Taira Kiyomori's second son still stands near Naze on Oshima Island. Graves, on Ishikagi Island in the Yaeyama Island Group and on Yonaguni Island, the southern most Ryukyu Island, are known as Yamato (Japanese) Haka (Grave) or Yashima-haka. Oral traditions link these graves to Sanuki province in Shikoku, Japan. This is the site of a battle lost by the Taira Clan in 1184. For many generations villagers on Yonaguni Island who claim to be decedents from the Taira refugees considered themselves superior to other island residents.

The reader needs to be reminded that the legends concerning Tametomo and other exiled Japanese who influenced Ryukyu History were not put into writing until the 17th century or in many cases even later. It is quite possible that Tametomo was a member of the defeated Taira Clan. When these legends were written the Tokugawa Shogunate was in power and they were decedents of the Minamoto Clan. It could be that in order to be "politically correct" the 17th century Okinawan writers chose to have Tametomo as a member of the winning clan.

TAMETOMO'S SON SHUNTEN AND HIS DESCENDENTS

The legends and history surrounding Tametomo although based on strong historic probability are hazy at best. However, with his son, Shuten, we are on "firmer ground" and have move beyond historic probability and into a clearer picture that is based on historic records.

17

Tametomo's son, Shunten, began to show leadership potential from an early age. When he was fifteen he was chosen by popular will to be the Lord of Urasoe village. This was a time of much political unrest. The local lords and chieftains were in revolt against the 24th overlord of the Tenson Dynasty. His immoral behavior brought about his eventual downfall and death. The overlord was assassinated by a political rival named "Riyu", who then moved to have himself declared overlord.

Riyu's ambitions were interrupted when the anji (local lords and chieftains) recognized Shuten as the overlord. Shuten was to rule wisely for 51 years and his descendents would continue to rule for many years.

Under Shuten's rule the Okinawan people enjoyed great political, social, and economic progress. Upon his death in 1237 his son Shumba-junki became King and like his father Shumba-junki proved to be an able leader. During his reign, a fine and impressive castle was built near Shuri. The use of a written language was introduced. New styles of dress were also introduced. Shumba-junki died in 1248 and at that time his son Gihon ascended to the throne.

Shuri Castle 1920's (Photo Credit: Author's Collection)

Famine and disease epidemics followed Gihon's reign. More than one half of the population died. Gihon appointed a young lord named Eiso to be regent. Six years later Gihon resigned as King, he with drew into the rugged mountains and forest in the northern part of Okinawa.

From 1235 to 1260, Eiso governed as regent. He reigned as king from 1260 until his death in 1299. He was a wise and able ruler; under his guidance Okinawa made great progress in foreign relations and in local development. Control was extended to other islands near Okinawa. Kume, Iheya and the Kerama Islands began to send in tribute to the Okinawan King. A system of taxation was initiated and put into practice. Okinawa began to grow in wealth; it became an Island Kingdom with wise leaders and a prosperous society.

18

In 1272 King Eiso received a demand from, the Mongol leader of China, Kublai Khan. The great Khan was about to invade Japan and demanded that Okinawa submit to his authority and to send support for the invasion. Eiso refused these and other demands. China answered King Eiso's action with a show of force. The Okinawans drove off the Chinese forces; however, 130 Okinawans were taken as captives. Eiso died at the age of 71. His son and grandson served well as kings. His great grandson, Tamagusuku's reign was marked by trouble. King Eiso established a system of grain storage to guard against famine. He also began other public projects to better the lives of his people.

The reign of Shuten through to the reign of Eiso covers the reigns of 8 kings (a span of 160 years). For the most part they provided wise leadership and Okinawa prospered. Thus it is that the civil wars of far off Japan set off a chain of events that let to Tametomo and his descendants having such a positive effect on the development of the Ryukyus Islands.

In 1393, China sent 36 families to Okinawa to settle near the port city of Naha. These migrants to Okinawa consisted of people who possessed certain skills that would benefit the Okinawan people. The "Thirty Six" Families settle in Kume village they were received with much gratitude by the Okinawans and were treated almost as royalty. For generations after the decedents of these Chinese settlers were considered as privileged citizens. It was this group of Chinese who introduced Kenpo to Okinawa. [1-4]

THE KINGDOM OF CHUZAN

The primitive scattered people that made up the population of Okinawa and the Ryukyu Islands in spite of a lack of natural resource prospered through trade with other nations. By the fourteenth century the island of Okinawa was divided into 3 Kingdoms, Hokuzan under the Lord of Nakajin Castle in the north, Chuzan the central Kingdom ruled by Satto

Drawing by the author
Credit: Author's Collection

Hokusan

Chuzan

Nanzan

Three Ancient Kingdoms of Okinawa

and Nanzan ruled by Lord Ozato in the south.

In China the Ming dynasty united the country in the 14th century. This gave Satto, the leader of Chuzan, an opportunity to become the one of the principle tributary states of China. This would give Satto the advantage over the other two Okinawan Kingdoms by enjoying greater trading privileges with China. In 1407 Lord Hashi over threw Satto's heir, Brunei, Hashi then set about to conquer Hokuzan and Nanzan, By 1429 Okinawa was unified under Sho Hashi and became known as the Kingdom of Chuzan.

In 1402 the Okinawa rulers began a system of sending an annual payment or tribute to China. This began a custom that lasted until 1873 and created close ties with China that insured that China would provide great influence on the Ryukyu people.

In the late 1400's the Okinawan King (Sho Shin) forced the owners of weapons (such as swords, spears and so forth) to turn these into a specified governmental warehouses to be stored. These type weapons bans took place several times through out Okinawan history and effectively disarmed the population of the country.

Also in the late 1400's there occurred a series of events in Okinawa that is still remembered and celebrate by festivals, and folk dances. This is the story of the Lord of Nakagusku, Gosamaru Seishun. The name Nakagusuku means "middle or central castle; (*Naka* meaning central and *gusuku* meaning castle). Lord Gosamaru was a famous warrior who was skill at building castles. He built the Zakimi Castle in Yomitan and was

The castles of the Gosamaru story
(Photo Credit: The Author's Collection)

a loyal servant of the King Sho Taikyu. The King had married Gosamaru's daughter.

Lord Gosamaru's enemy was the Lord of Kasuren Castle, Amawari. Lord Amawari was planning to lead a rebellion against the Okinawan King, Sho Taikyu. Gosamaru heard of Amawari's plan, and prepared his forces to defend the King against Amarwari's scheme. Amawari lied to the King and told him it was Gosamaru that was planning the rebellion. The King believed Amawari's lie and demanded Gosamaru's surrender and death. Gosamaru committed suicide rather than face his King. According to the folk dances and legends; Gosamaru's two sons disguised themselves as female dancers gained entrance to Amawari's camp during an outing that Amawari was enjoying. While dancing for Amawari, Gosamaru's two sons assassinated him and made good their escape.

A dancer portraying Gosamaru
(Photo Credit: Author's collection)

Zakimi Castle (Photo Credit: Peter Carbone Collection)

Nakagusuku
(Photo Credit: Mike Roberts
Color Productions)

22

Two Okinawan ladies, in formal attire, standing in front of the ruins of Nakagusku. Photo taken on or about 1965. (Photo Credit Mike Roberts Color Productions)

Another set of events that occurred in the late 1400's in the Sakishima Group (the southern most group of island in the Ryukyu Island chain) centers around the legendary chief of Yaeyama, Akahachi Oyakata. The Yaeyama people, under the leadership of Akahachi, resisted attempts made by the Okinawan government to intervene in local affairs. Untura the Chief of Yonaguni Island also resisted the Shuri Government's action.

The southern most group of island in the Ryukyu Chain drawing by the author.
Photo Credit: Author's Collection

Scene from Iriomote Island (Photo Credit: Mike Roberts Color Productions)

The forces of both Untura and Akahachi were over whelmed by Nakasone the Chief of Miyako who had sided with Okinawa. As a result Nakasone was appointed to be Okinawa's resident agent in charge of Miyako. Akahachi Oyakata is one of the first individuals in the Ryukyu Islands that is historically associated with the practice of martial arts. He is said to have been and expert with the Bo (staff).

I was taught an Eku kata about 30 years ago by Fusei Kise. He told me that the name of the kata was Akahachi no Eku/Bo. Sensei Kise said that his mother's people were from the Yaeyama Islands and the techniques found in the kata represented the techniques practiced in the Yaeyama Islands. The Akahachi no Eku/Bo kata is very smooth and relaxed and the kata is performed with continuous movement. It features sunakaki or sand throwing moves both by kicking the paddle of the eku upward putting sand in your

Akahachi no Eku Bo kata
Moving from upper left, high block;
sticking the tip of the paddle into the
sand; kicking the paddle to put sand
into the eyes of your opponent. Photo
credit: Author's collection.

opponent's eyes and flipping the paddle upward also to put sand in your opponent's eyes.

Another ancient kata that has survived from the "Sanzan" period of Okinawan history is "Shirotaru no Kun." *The Sanzan period refers to the time in Okinawan history to when Okinawa was divided into three kingdoms. King Sho Hashi unified the Island in 1429. Therefore, the Shirotaru Kata could date back to before 1429.*

Shirotaru was a Bushi who was involved in the many battles and wars of this time period. He was famous for his skill with the Bo and he was also involved in forming a settlement on Kudaka Island. [1-5]

Three photo of Shiro Taro no Kun Dai; which is alleged to be the older than the Shiro Taro no Kun Sho version of the kata.
The author is demonstrating the kata.
Photo credit: Author's collection

In 1609 the Okinawa/Ryukyu Kingdom of Chuzan was invade by the Satsuma Samurai of Southern Japan. The often troublesome and high spirited samurai of the Shimazu Clan of Satsuma Province, Kyushu, Japan were a constant worry for the new Tokugawa Government. The Shogun's reasoning was simple. "If I can't find something for the Satsuma Samurai to do, then they are going cause less trouble for me". So, the Tokugawa Shogun arrange for the Satsuma Samurai to invade Okinawa.

The Japanese force of 3,000 soldiers landed at Unten in northern Okinawa. The Okinawan population who had been disarmed generations earlier by their own king, could off little resistance. Nevertheless, the forces mustered by Okinawa at first put up a stiff resistance but they were soon over whelmed by the Japanese. The Satsuma Samurai were armed with all of the traditional weapons of the Japanese warriors. They also were armed with match-locked muskets. Fire arms were a weapon that was totally unfamiliar to the Okinawans. They soon were "brushed aside by the Japanese.

Rather than march south down the length of Okinawa, the Japanese returned to their ships and sailed down the west coast of Okinawa. They landed near Naha; here they were met with little resistance. They marched the short distance to the capitol of Shuri. They captured the palace, arrested the King and most of his court. They looted everything of value and took control of the Okinawa Government. King Sho Nei and many of his court were sent back to Japan where they would remain in exile for three years.

The Japanese would institute a harsh rule on the people of the Ryukyu Islands. They levied an annual tribute that Okinawa was forced to pay; it amounted to 1/8 of all revenues. This was equivalent to the sale of 482,000 bushels of rice. The islands of Amami, Yoron, Toku, and were forever removed from Okinawa's control. The economy of the Ryukyu Islands was devastated. The prosperous Kingdom Of Chuzan had endured for 300 years but it was now finished. [1-6]

Hidari Mitsudomoe

The Hidari Mitsudomoe was the crest of the Okinawa Royal family. The crest was adopted by King Sho Toku in the mid 1400's.

In 1609 after the Shimatsu Clan of Satsuma Province, Japan had conquered Okinawa; King Sho Nei along with many other high ranking Okinawans were taken as prisoners to Satsuma, Japan. There they were forced to sign oaths of allegiance to the Satsuma Clan. One Okinawan Tei Do, who was an Officer of the Okinawan Court, refused to sign the document. The Japanese sentenced him to be boiled alive in hot oil. As he was escorted to the vat of boiling liquid by two Satsuma Samurai; Tei Do suddenly grabbed his two escorts and with a shout of defiance jumped into the boiling oil taking the two Japanese with him. It takes very little imagination to see the three coma shaped object called the "Hidari Mitsudomoe" as three men wriggling in a dance of death in the vat of boiling oil.

Information comes from Robert Teller.

CHAPTER 1
ANCIENT HISTORY OF THE RYUKYU ISLANDS
Endnotes, Sources, and Explanations

General Sources: "Okinawa the History of an Island People" by George H. Kerr published by: Charles E. Tuttle Company; pages 1-159

"Living Crafts of Okinawa" by Hisao Suzuki, published by John Weatherhill, Inc.; pages 1-13

"Unante...The Secrets of Karate" by John Sells, published by W. M. Hawley; pages 1-15

"Arms and Armor of Weapons in Ancient Japan" I. Bottom and A. P. Hopson, published by Crescent Books: page 46

"Maishin Shorinji Magazine", published by Ronald Lindsey History in Bits and Pieces Article "Genghis Kan: a Legacy" by Mark Wilson

Foot Notes:

1-1.................................... *"Okinawa the History of an Island People"*
by George Kerr, page 37
1-2.................................... *"Arms and Armor, History of Weapons in Ancient Japan" by I. Bottom and A. P. Hopson, page 46*

1-3....................................*Website: www.wonder.okinawa*
"Brief Chronological Table Related to Okinawa Karate and Martial Arts Weaponry (1300- 1899)"

1-4...................................*General Okinawan Folklore*

1-5................................ *"Kobudo" by Nakamoto Masahiro*
Page 26

1-6................................. *"Okinawa the History of an Island People" by George Kerr, page 159*

"The study of the history of the Ryukyu people is a study of the enduring resourcefulness of the human species."

CHAPTER 2
"THE OKINAWAN BUSHI"

The Okinawan Bushi
(The Warriors of Okinawa)

*Picture on the previous page is gift
from Ronnie Lock.
Author's collection*

30

Since the 1850's there have been four famous Okinawan Karate Masters: these were: Sokon "Bushi" Matsumura (1797-1889), founder of Shurite; Nakaima Kenri (1819-1879), founder of Ryuei Ryu; Matsumora Kosaku (1820-1898), founder of Tomarite; and Higashionna Kanryo (1852-1915), founder of Nahate. Of these four masters all but one, Matsumora Kosaku, trained in China. *(2-1)*

The role that the Chinese Fighting Arts played in the formulation of the Okinawan Fighting Arts can not be over stated. We will begin our discussion of this role by studying the history of the Shaolin Temples of China, then we will learn about those Okinawan who trained in China and how these Okinawans took their art back to Okinawa where eventually American Military Servicemen and women took the art back to America and in many cases to other countries in the world.

HISTORY OF THE SHAOLIN TEMPLE

To understand the history of Okinawa Karate we must return to the point of origin. For the most styles of karate, this point is China, especially the various Shaolin Temples of China. There were several Shaolin Temples located in Northern, Southern and Central China. Much of the history concerning these temples has been lost.

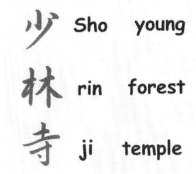

To start with it is necessary for the reader to understand that the term Shaolin is pronounced in the Okinawa/Japanese language as Shorin and the term Shorinji simply means Shaolin temple. The English translation is: *Sho* (Japanese) meaning *young*; and *rin* means *forest*. The term **ji** means temple. The term young forest temple describes a grove of young pine trees that stood near the original Shaolin Temple.

Over 1,500 years ago in the second year of the Taicho period during the reign of the Chinese Emperor Wei of the Northern Wai Dynasty (AD 478); an Indian "Holy Man" called Ba Tuo came to China. Also called Bodhidharma, Daruma or Ta Mo; he was the third son of King Sugandha in Southern India. Ba Tuo was a member of the Kshatriya or warrior class. He was said to be wise in the ways of dhyana or Zen practices. History does not record the reasons for BaTuo's travel to China. Perhaps he came to fulfill a death bed wish from his old master, Prajnatara, or perhaps he came because he was saddened over the decline of Buddhism in areas outside of India proper.

At the time, worshipping of Buddhism was in vogue in the palaces and with aristocrats, who took a fancy to building temples. In admiration of the Indian Monk, Ba Tuo, Emperor Wei built a monastery called "Zhi Hu" on a tall hill in 495 AD. Later it was named the Shaolin Monastery after the numerous pine trees growing in the area. The monastery was located in the Sungshau Mountains of Northern China. This was the first Shaolin Temple.

Bodhidharma
(Photo Credit: Author's Collection)

Bodhidharma instituted a training program for the monks as they were not physically fit enough to endure the rigors of long hour of Zen meditation. Being that he was of the warrior caste of India, he was well schooled in the bare hand fighting methods called Vajramushti, which means "the clinched fist as a weapon". He instituted a series of physical drills called "Shih pa lou han sho" or the Eighteen Hands of the Lo-han. Lo-han refers to "Monk Fist". It is believed that these drills were for physical development rather than for actual combat.

Some of these exercises are as follows: (1) Stand upright with your waist straight, eyes wide open and mind concentrating. Breathing fresh air in through the nose and exhaling through the mouth. (2) Stretch toward the sky… while pushing your Chi down to your lower torso. Raise the left hand and lowering the right hand; alternate raising the right and left hand. This is done as two actions. (3) Pushing the mountain: following the preceding exercise…stand with the feet about one foot apart, push your hands directly forward (palms forward). Strength is center in the middle of your palms, your Chi sinks to your naval, and this is done with four counts.

Paul Bystedt's Crane
Author's collection

Several decades after the deaths of Bodhidharma (he died sometimes between 529 and 535 AD) a monk named Chuen Yuan Shangjen expanded the original 18 hand and foot positions to 72. At this point it also became more of a combative art. He later met a master named Li. Together they expanded the exercises to 170 movements. It is said that all styles of Shaolin are derived from these original 170 movements. China obviously had martial arts long before the arrival of Bodhidharma; the influence of these Chinese styles also contributed greatly to the development of the 170 movements of Chuan-fa as it came to be called. However, Bodhidharma is credited with "Sowing the seeds" of Chuan-fa at the original Shaolin Temple.

It wasn't until the Tang Dynasty (618-907 AD) that the Shaolin Monastery saw its heyday. It became a resort of emperors and a gathering place for scholars. The monastery boasted over 1000 palaces and other facilities where as many as 1000 monks meditated. Outside of the walls were over 100 boarding houses where other monks lived. The security force numbered over 600 warrior monks. In the wars that led to the establishment of the Tang Dynasty, the Shaolin Monks contributed greatly to the Tang Army. These monks assisted in crushing the army led by Wang Schichong.

The Manchus took over China and established the Ching Dynasty (1644-1911). They placed most of the Chinese people under a form of servitude and required that the people wear long pony tails hair style as a symbol of this servitude. Many secret societies sprang up to over throw the Manchus...Shaolin Monks actively supported these societies and supported other efforts to reestablish the Ming Dynasty (1386-1644).

Emperor Yung Ching (1723-1735 AD) took steps to eradicate the Shaolin Monastery and other Anti-Ching elements. An Army of 3,000 cavalrymen and infantry launched an all out attack on the monastery. In the darkness of the night they used heavy guns to knock down the walls and storm the monastery, killing all but 13 monks. These 13 escaped and fled to other parts of the country.. Eight of the 13 went south into what is now the Fukein Province. This is how the Shaolin art spread to Southern China.

A monastery was established in Fukein Province and probably in other areas as well. Five of the monks remained in Northern China and soon began teaching the arts to monks at the original

Nio Guardian of the Heirin Temple in Japan. This is similar to the statues that guarded the Chinese Shaolin Temples.

Photo credit: Wikimedia Commons

Shaolin Monastery. Therefore, from the middle of the 1700's on, there was more than one Shaolin Monastery.

In 1829, a high official from the Ching Dynasty came to the Northern Monastery and discovered that martial arts were still being practiced. They were given permission to continue the practice since their purpose was only self protection, not political.

Shaolin Monks in secret societies were active in the Boxer Rebellion of 1900. This rebellion was crushed. It resulted in the Ching Government taking steps to abolish all Shaolin Temples and other martial arts training halls. Under the Chinese Communist Government the Martial Arts of China became more of an acrobatic-gymnastic activity. It has only been since the last two decades that the interest in the original Shaolin Arts have returned to China.

STORIES OF THE SHAOLIN TEMPLE

The Suzan Shaolin Temple was located near a holy mountain some 1500 years ago. Contrary to popular belief, Daruma did not found this temple. The Suzan Temple had existed 20 years before Daruma arrived in China. In the Suzan temple, the 18 skills of "Fist Arts" were taught. The "Yokin Kyo" which was a book used as a guide to teach the 18 skills was developed in the Suzan Temple.

The Suzan Temple was located in Kanan Province. Later the Zozan Temple was located in Kosei Province; even later the Kuryo Temple was located in Fukein Province. As the years passed, the Suzan Temple fell into disfavor from governmental officials. All monks in this temple feared for their lives. They escaped by fleeing in all directions. Fleeing to the south some built the Zozan Temple in the Kosei Province. Other went north to found another temple in the Kahoku Province. Some monks under the leadership of Gabai Zenni went west and started the Gabai Shaolin Temple.

During the reign of Emperor Kouki; a monk of the Kosei Province, named Ikunzenzi traveled through out China learning various Shaolin exercises. During his travels he was often in danger of being attacked by gangs of thieves and other criminals. An old man named "Rison" spoke of a Shaolin priest called "Hakugyo Ku Hou." It was through this contact that Ikuzenzi gained acceptance into the Zozan Shaolin Temple.

In the Zozan Temple, Ikunzenzi, Rison, and Hakugyo developed famous Shaolin Five Arts., better known as the Shaolin Five Animal Fist. This style made the Shaolin Temples famous through out the orient and was based on the Tiger, Leopard, Snake, Dragon and Crane.

Around the same time the monks of the Northern Shaolin Temple developed another Five Animal Style. This was based on the Tiger, Leopard, Lion, Elephant and Dragon. This style was called Butuo Go Kei Kan. Other Chinese Styles soon followed similar patterns.

Most Okinawan Karate styles have been influenced in modern times by the Fukein Shaolin Temple. It was here that Bushi Matsumura studied; therefore, it is important that we now focus our interest on the Shaolin Temple in the Chinese Province of Fukein.

There exists an old tale that is well known among the practioners of the Fukein Shaolin Temple Style:

Once upon a time during the reign of the Chinese Emperor Kan Ryoi (1726) the Shaolin Temple was attacked by "soldiers of misinformation". After learning of this mistake the Emperor tried to apologize to the monks for the action of his soldiers. However, the monks did not accept the apology. Instead the monks moved to the Province of Fukein and established another temple.

Fukein Kyuryu Shaolin Temple
1. Old Temple
2. Shaolin Temple
3. Women's Quarters
4. Kyuryu San
   (9 Dragon Mt.)

Photo Credit: Author's Collection

The first temple was a small structure built near Sensu Province. Soon another temple was built near the middle of the Kyuryu Mountain. This temple produced many famous martial artists; among these were Suida, Myoch, and Badoto Ku. Some of the monks became famous political activists protesting against the government.

During the Chinese Min Dynasty, Shaolin Kenpo was introduced to Okinawa. This Kenpo came from Fukein Province, China. The Kyuryu Shaolin temple was located in the southwestern part of Fukein Province in the heart of the Nine Dragon Mountains from which the Temple gets its name.

There were three gates that allowed access to the temple grounds and buildings. Only the Grandmaster and his assistant could come and go as they pleased. There were 3 main outdoor exercise areas. Training was done in all types of weather. There was also a large cave that was used for training with special wooden dummies. The Kaiki room was used to punish those students who did not conform to the rules of the temple.

An average day in the Kyuryu Temple would start at 4:00 am when a wooden drum would sound wake up call for all of the trainees. A short time later a bell sounded the signal for all trainees to go to their assigned areas and exercise. A bell was also used to inform the trainees of meal times and other aspects of training. It was said that one left the temple only after mastering the art.

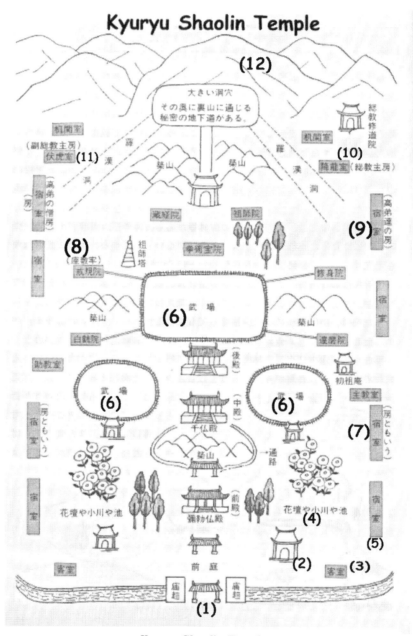

Kyuryu Shaolin Temple

Kyuryu Shaolin Temple
1. Main gate, 2. Front garden, 3. Guest House, 4. Garden and Pond, 5. Miscellaneous Room, 6. Exercise Areas, 7. Misc. Room, 8. Punishment Room, 9. VIP Room, 10. Grand master's Room, 11. Assistant Grandmaster's Room 12. Kyuryu Mountain

Picture Credit: Author's Collection

Kyuryu Shaolin Temple
Credit Author's Collection

Okinawa

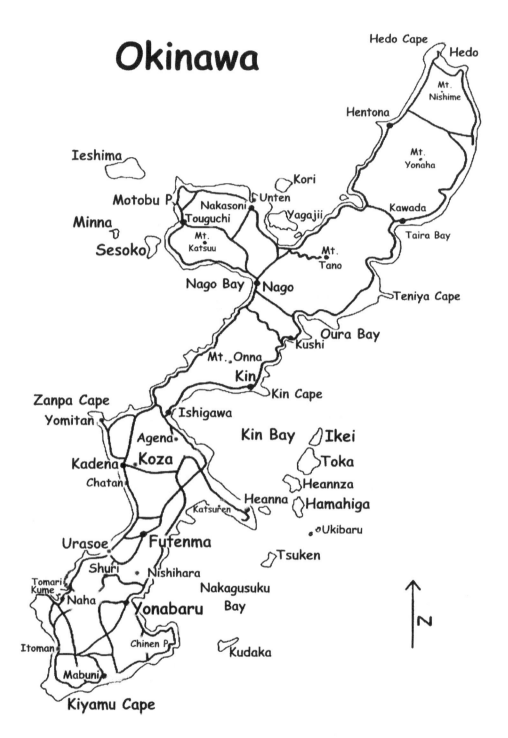

Map of Okinawa showing location of major towns' cities, village and near by island that play a role in the history of Okinawa's fighting arts.
Picture credit: Author's collection

THE BUSHI WHO TRAINED IN CHINA AND THEIR LINEAGES

The Okinawan martial arts throughout history have been greatly influenced by Chinese martial arts masters. Many of these masters were Chinese governmental envoys sent to Okinawa for diplomatic purposes. Some 36 Chinese families founded the Okinawan community of Kumemura in 1393. It is said that the Chinese families in Kume maintained ties with China for many generations. However, it was Okinawans traveling to China who were to bring the greatest martial influence from China. Most of the Okinawans traveled to China to learn Chinese medicine, literature and calligraphy or for diplomatic reasons; after the1870's one of the principle reasons was to avoid the Japanese Military draft. The study of the fighting arts was never the main reason for Okinawans to travel to China. [2-2]

KANGA (TODE) SAKUGAWA AND CHATAN YARA

Kangi Sakugawa the son of Kanga (Tode) Sakugawa. The son Kangi was said to have borne a close resemblance to his father. (Photo Credit: Author's Collection)

History does not record the name of the first Okinawan who went to China to study martial arts. However, we do know that Sakugawa studied on Okinawa under Kusanku and returned with him to China. Historians disagree on the date of Sakugawa's birth and death. Some historians place Sakugawa's birth and death dates as 1733 to 1815. Others say that these dates are about 50 years too early. Much of the modern martial traditions on Okinawa go back to Sakugawa. It is safe to say there were Okinawans who trained in China before Sakugawa but their names are not known. [2-3]

Kanga Sakugawa was born as Teruya Kanga in the Akata community of Shuri the capital city of old Ryukyu Kingdom. At the age of 17, he began his training in "te" under the tutelage of an old Bushi named Takahara Peichin. Takahara was famous as an astrologer and maker of maps.

We just do not have much information on Chatan Yara except for the fact that he must have been about the same age as Sakugawa and that Yara (1740-1814) was born in the village of Chatan located on the west coast of Okinawa just south of Kadena Village which is now the site of Kadena Air Force base. It is said that in 1756 a Chinese military attaché named Kusanku-zuiko came to Okinawa. It was approximately this time that Sakugawa and Chatan Yara began their study of the Kenpo under the military attaché Kusanku.

Historians disagree on just what type of art Kusanku brought to Okinawa. However, Kusanku is credited with introducing the technique of chambering the punch and pull on hand back while the other hand extends forward to increase power.

Punching from the chamber; introduced to Okinawa by Kusanku
Both photo credits: Author's collection

Kusanku remained in Okinawa for 4 years when he returned to China it is believed that both Yara and Sakugawa accompanied Kusanku back to China were they remained to study with the Chinese Master for many years. Some say Yara trained in China before Kusanku came to Okinawa.

Returning to Okinawa Sakugawa became an administrator for the Shuri Government. He became known as "Tode" (Chinese Hand) Sakugawa and developed the Dojo concept still used on Okinawa.

Photo alleged to be of Toude Sakugawa. I am not sure of the origin of this photo; I have had it in my collection for over 20 years.

Photo credit: Author's collection.

Sakugawa was given the title of Satonushi and sent to the Yaeyama Islands as the Chief Shuri officer. After many years, as a reward for his services; the Okinawan King gave Sakugawa a small island. Sakugawa was a famous Okinawan Samurai. His influence on the Okinawan is still felt today. He is said to have developed the Kusanku Kata that today is called "Shiho" Kusanku.

Shiho Kusanku
Both photos from
the Author's

Sakugawa also passed on to the future his "Sakugawa no Kun"; which is based on the staff or Bo technique he learned from Kusanku. This may be Okinawa's most famous Bo kata as it has influenced many Okinawan master of kobujutsu.

Author demonstrating
Sakugawa no Kun
Chu
Both photos are from
the author's
collection.

41

Sakugawa Lineage

Takahara Peichin   Kusanku

Kanga "Tode"
Sakugawa

Aburaya Yamagushiku
1797-1881

Kogushiku Shinunjo 1780-?

Bushi Ukuda

Bushi Sakumoto

Makabe Chokun

Bushi Matsumoto

Ginowan Donchi

Bushi Matsumura 1797-1889

Sakugawa is better known to the modern day martial artist than is ***Chatan Yara (1740-1812);*** yet, Yara was an accomplished artist that left his mark on the karate world. Chatan Yara is remembered for several kata that were developed by him. These are Chatan Yara no Kun, Chatan Yara no Sai, and Chatan Yara no Kusanku.

The tonfa kata called "Yara Gua no Tonfa" was developed by Chatan Yara's step son. The word Gua means small and usually refer to one's nephew; in this case the Yara Gua Kata is in reference to Chatan Yara's step son and means "Little Yara's Tonfa Kata." [2-4]

Chatan Yara was of Chinese ancestry he was the first of his clan to be accepted into the service of the Okinawan King. He was in charge of managing the king's horse stables which were located near Yomitan Village.
.

There are several old tales about Chatan Yara; the first one starts out when Yara was 12 years old. According to the story this is when Yara's uncle approached the parents of Yara to suggest that the strong young man be sent to China to obtain a proper education which would include learning the fighting arts.

Yara is alleged to have spent 20 years in China studying under Wong Chung-Yoh. Upon his return from China, Chatan Yara found Okinawa greatly changed. Japanese Samurai from the Satsuma Province seemed to roam the island at will.

Once while walking near the beach near the village of Chatan. Yara came upon a Japanese Samurai who was ravishing a young Okinawan woman. Yara quickly found himself fighting for his own life as the swordsman drew his sword and attacked. Yara ran to the beach where there several were fishing boats. Yara quickly picked up an Eku (boat oar) and leaped high into the air jumping over the Samurai's low cut and brought the eku down shattering the skull of the swordsman.

Drawing by Ken Penland
Author's collection

Below: an aerial view of Naha in the 1960's looking north.
Photo credit: Mike Roberts Color Productions

Typical Okinawan Ships that traveled from Okinawa to China and other Asian Ports during the time if Sakugawa and Chatan Yara. Photo Credit: "Uechi Ryu Karate-Do Master Text" by Kanei Uechi and other Uechi Ryu Seniors

Early 1960's view of a Northern Okinawan farming village. Photo credit: Mike Roberts Color Productions

A farmer and his water buffalo
Photo credit: Mike Robert's Color Productions

Above: Ryukyu Kan Constructed in 1873 and
ended its operations in 1945.
On the left: Andaya Masaharu
Photo credit: Photo Credit: "Uechi Ryu Karate-Do
Master Text" by Kanei Uechi and other Uechi Ryu
Seniors

RYUKYU KAN

In the Chinese province of Fukein, there existed a large dormitory to house Okinawa visitors. This building was called "Ryukyu Kan;" it was constructed in 1872 and remained in use until 1945.

In 1879, the Japanese Governor on Okinawa, Matsuda Michiyuki, with the help of Japanese troops took control over the Okinawan government. The Japanese tried to prevent Okinawans from going to China, but they were not successful. The Ryukyu Kan remained in operation until 1945. It was a large building with a floor space of a large gym. The last managers were Gima Seichu and Nakagoshi Chogo. The Ryukyu Kan housed many Okinawan visitors and served as a refuge until the people could adjust to the Chinese way of life.

Anya Masaharu, an Okinawan, who owned the Anya Yoku trading company from 1931 to 1945, assisted many Okinawans with their travels to China and with their stay at the Ryukyu Kan. Anya was a student of the famous Chinese White Crane Master, Go Ken Ki. Like Go Ken Ki, Anya was a tea merchant and was recognized as Master Go's leading student.

MATSUDA TOSABURO, KANBUN UECHI, GOKENKI, AND SEISHO ARAKAKI

Uechi Kanbun (1876-1947), Matsuda Toksabudo (1876-1931) and *Seisho Arakaki (1840-1920)* also called Sanda Unchu and Kamade Unchu, traveled to China together. For a short time they lived in the Ryukyu Kan, later they went to about 10 different places in China. They found the language to be difficult and their purpose for traveling to China was to learn the Chinese fighting arts and to avoid the Japanese Military draft.

From Left to right Matsuda Tosaburo, Kanbun Uechi, Go Ken Ki, and Seisho Arakaki
Photo Credit: "Uechi Ryu Karate-Do Master Text" by Kanei Uechi and other Uechi Ryu
Seniors

They left Yonabaru, Okinawa bound for China on March 29, 1897. The voyage took 10 days. It is believed that Arakaki had been to China several times previously. Both Matsuda and Uechi were good friends, they were from the Motobu area of Okinawa and they traveled to China to learn the martial arts and to escape the Japanese Military draft.

Matsuda Tosaburo, Uechi Kanbun and Seisho Arakaki were descendents of Shuri and Naha area Bushi who had been granted farm lands located on the Motobu Peninsula, Okinawa. Uechi had studied Bojutsu under his father, Kantoku Uechi, and from other Motobu Area experts, Taru Kise and Kamato Toyozato. Seisho Arakaki was a well established martial artist from the Kumemura area of Naha.

At this time in our story we will concentrate on activities of Matsuda and Uechi as history does not mention the activities of Arakaki during this trip to China. We will discuss Arakaki's history a little later. Upon arrival in Fukein Province, China: Matsuda and Uechi went to the dojo of Kojo Kaho, some historians believe this dojo was at the Ryukyu Kan.

Eventually Kanbun Uechi started studying under Shushiwa and Matsuda Tosaburo studied a similar style of Kenpo under another teacher. Shushiwa concentrated on teaching the kata Sanchin, Seisan and Sansei Ryu. Matsuda's teacher taught more kata to include Suparinpei. Under Shushiwa Uechi studied a few kata very deeply; were as Matsuda learned more kata but none as deeply as Uechi learned. Uechi did not learn the Suparinpei Kata. In later life Matsuda often said that Uechi's art would be different if he would have learned Suparinpei. While in China both Matsuda and Uechi met a Chinese Crane Fist Master named Go Ken Ki. Master Go would move to Okinawa by 1910 and would become a friend of Matsuda and Uechi for many years.

Both Matsuda and Uechi learned Chinese medicine as well as the fighting arts. It was his skill with Chinese Medicine that led to Kanbun Uechi gaining acceptance into Shushiwa's Kenpo School. It seems that Master Shushiwa became very ill and his students were concerned about their teacher's health. The students were aware of Kanbun Uechi's skill in the use of Chinese Medicine. Uechi was sought out by the students and began to treat Shushiwa. Soon the Kenpo Master had been cured of his illness and as a result Kanbun Uechi was accepted as a student of Shushiwa.

Uechi's training under Shushiwa was very severe. He also worked in the gardens near Shushiwa's school. Hard work and severe training developed young Uechi's body and mind. This type of training and development would form the foundation of toughness that would become the trade mark of Uechi Ryu Karatedo decades later.

By 1904 Kanbun Uechi had become an assistant to Shushiwa. Uechi continued to practice martial arts and Chinese medicine. In 1907 he moved to a town called "Nansei" and opened a dojo calling his style Pangainoon Kempo (half soft, half hard kempo).

Matsuda came back to Okinawa in 1901 at this time he was 33 years old. He would always say in his later life that he needed another 10 years of practice in China. His style was old Chinese Classic Kenpo, it was Sanchin based and very similar to what Kanbun Uechi brought back to Okinawa. Uechi came back to Okinawa in 1909. Matsuda moved to Okuhento Village and Uechi moved to Motobu Chatan. Seisho Arakaki who apparently did not stay in China very long also moved to the Motobu peninsula near the village of Chatan near the island of Sesoko. Matsuda was found guilty of avoiding the Japanese military draft and served one year in prison.

"The pen is useless without the sword; the sword is useless without the pen."
A lesson from a Chinese fortune cookie.

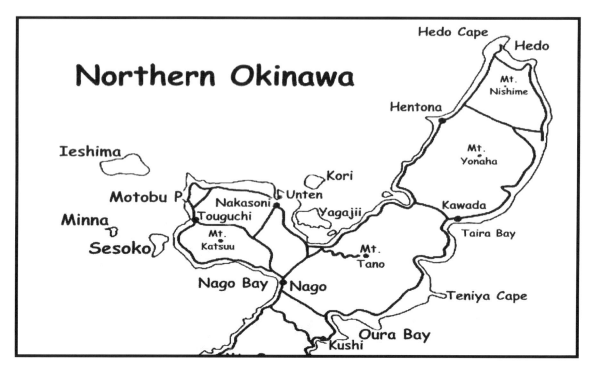

Northern Okinawa and principle Villages of the Motobu Peninsula: (Photo Credit: Author's Collection

Matsuda was an expert with the Chinese walking stick and with the Chinese halberd. He brought his expertise with these weapons as well as his Kenpo to Okinawa. By 1914 the Chinese halberd was no longer used by the Okinawans.

Matsuda trained every morning with the Iron geta. Matsuda referred to Uechi as "Bushi" and Uechi also called Matsuda "Bushi". The lived close to each other. Often at the festivals held in Okuhento Village they would demonstrate their kata and technique.

Matsuda's leading student was Tongushi Kansaburo. Matsuda's teaching style was very rapid he taught kata after kata very quickly. Later Matsuda moved to Osaka, Japan. He died in 1931 at the age of 54. He was a great teacher; his style is believed to have died out on Okinawa.

Computer generated drawing by the author

Kanbun Uechi moved from Okinawa to the Osaka area of Japan in 1924. Poor economic conditions in Okinawa forced him to leave. A short time later he moved to the Wakayama Province of Japan where he began working in a large clothing mill.

In 1925 Uechi opened his first dojo in Japan. He limited the number of people who trained with him by carefully screening prospective students and forbade his students from practicing out side of the dojo.

In 1932 Kanban Uechi relocated his dojo to a site 2 miles from the original dojo. He called his new dojo "Pangainoon Ryu Karatejutsu Kenkyu-jo".

After World War II, Kanbun Uechi returned to Okinawa. He left his dojo in Wakayama province in charge of his student, Ryuyu

Kanbun Uechi
Photo credit: Author's collection

Tomoyose. Shortly after Kanbun Uechi returned to Okinawa, he became ill with a kidney ailment called Bright's disease; he died in late 1948. He was 71 years old.

Kanbun Uechi was an amazing karateka. He was capable of many unbelievable physical feats. Yet he was a quiet good natured man and was like by all who knew him. In his son's (Kanei Uechi) dojo in Futema, Okinawa there is a large bamboo pole hanging over the door. It is said that Kanban Uechi would stand in sanchin dachi and ask two strong students to place the end of the pole against his stomach. The students then tried to push against Uechi's stomach with the bamboo pole. In spite of pushing as hard as they could they were unable to move Uechi. No one since Kanbun Uechi has been able to duplicate the feat.

Kanbun Uechi left a great legacy. His student Ryuyu Tomoyose was his leading student and is generally recognized as his successor. Later Kanei Uechi Kanbun Uechi's son became the master of Uechi Ryu.

"Not having a goal is more to be feared than not reaching one"

A lesson from a Chinese fortune cookie.

Senior Students of Kanban Uechi in Wakayama Japan 1937
Front row: left to right Ryuyu Tomoyose, Kanbun Uechi, Susumu Tamamura
Back row: Kaei Akamine (Photo Credit: Author's collection)

KANEI UECHI was born in 1911 on Okinawa. He was the eldest son of Kanbun Uechi. When Kanbun Uechi left in 1924 for Japan; he left his family behind in Okinawa. When Kanei reached the age of 16 (1927); he joined his father, Kanbun Uechi, in Wakayama, Japan. It was at this time that Kanei started training under his father. This training would continue until 1937 when he received permission to open his own dojo. At this time he moved to Osaka were he taught for two years.

Kanei Uechi
Photo credit: Author's
collection

In 1941 Kanei Uechi was promoted to Go Dan and in 1942 he returned to Okinawa after his students in Osaka were drafted into the Japanese Military. Kanei moved to the Nago area of Okinawa where he began teaching in his mother's yard. His students consisted of his brothers and a few neighborhood youths.

"The secret of happiness is not in doing what one likes, but in liking what one does."
A lesson from a Chinese fortune cookie.

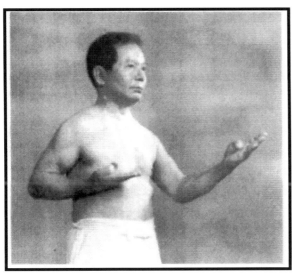

In 1944 Kanei Uechi and his students were called off to war with the Japanese Army. The Nago dojo was closed; however, it opened up again in 1947 when Kanbun Uechi returned to Nago, Okinawa from Japan. The elder Uechi died in January 1948 and was buried on the Uechi lands near Nago.

In the late 1940's Kanei Uechi moved his dojo to Ginowan, Okinawa. The son of his father's top student, Ryuko Tomoyose became the assistant instructor at this dojo. The dojo was called "Uechi Ryu Karate-jutsu Kenkyu-Jo. Kenkyu-Jo means training hall.

Kanei Uechi performing Sanchin. Photo Credit: "Uechi Ryu Karate-Do Master Text" by Kanei Uechi and other Uechi Ryu Seniors

The dojo again was moved in 1957 to its present location in Futema, Okinawa. In 1967 both the All Japan Karatedo Federation and the newly formed All Okinawan Karatedo Federation awarded Kanei Uechi the 10th (JU) Dan Rank. It is interesting to note that in 1957 the Uechi art was called Karatejutsu but by 1967 it was called Karatedo.

Uechi Ryu Karate Dojo Futenma, Okinawa. Photo Credit: "Uechi Ryu Karate-Do Master Text" by Kanei Uechi and other Uechi Ryu Seniors

Credit: Author's collection

51

During the 1950's Kanei Uechi and his senior students created 5 additional kata. Bring the total number of kata taught in the system to 8; the names of the new kata are called (1) Kanshiwa, (2) Kanshu, (3) Seichin, (4) Seirui, and (5) Konchin.

In 1958 Kanei Uechi held the first dan test held in Uechi Ryu Karate. Seiko Toyama and Seiyu Shinjo were promoted to Go Dan and others were promoted to a lesser rank. In 1959 Ryuyu Tomoyose awarded Kanei Uechi a Shihan or Master Instructor Certificate. In 1967 Kanei Uechi was awarded the Ju dan rank by the Japanese Karatedo Federation. Kanei Uechi died in 1991 at the age of 80. He was a kind and gentle man and a superb martial artist. Under his leadership Uechi Ryu Karatedo became an art practiced by tens of thousands of people throughout the world.

Ryuko Tomoyose (10 Dan), son of Ryuyu Tomoyose, a student of Kanban Uechi.
Both father and son rose to the rank of Ju (10) Dan
Photo credit: Rick Langenstein collection.

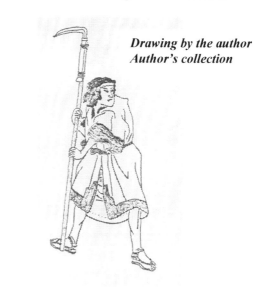

Drawing by the author
Author's collection

Gokenki (1886-1940) was a Chinese tea merchant who befriended Kanban Uechi during his long stay in China. In 1911 or 1912, Gokenki moved to Okinawa to work for the Eeiko Chako Tea Company.

Thus far we have discussed Okinawans who went to China to learn the Fighting Arts; with Gokenki we have one of the few Chinese who went to Okinawa and taught the fighting arts. Gokenki taught a style call *"Kingai Ryu"* which was based on Hakutsuru Ken (White Crane Fist). Kingai actually translated means "Golden Chicken"; little is known as to the origin of this style.

On technique…. "Only simple things are worthwhile; if it is complicated…discard it. If it does not work…discard it"…a wise saying!

Gokenki and students Photo Credit:" Uechi Ryu Karate-Do Master Text" by Kanei Uechi and other Seniors

After several years on Okinawa, Gokenki open a Tea Shop and Tea Import Company called Sen Shun Kai. At night his tea shop served as a karate dojo. Master Go's top student was Anea Shosho (Anya Masaharu). Anea lived in Naha and worked for a trading company owned by Anea Yoko, who may have been Anea Shosho's father. Anea Shosho was 12 years younger than Master Go; he lived in Naha and often traveled to Shanghai, China. Other students of Master Go were Yabe, Metorima, and Sagara.

Around the time of World War I or a little later (about 1920 to 1925) Gokenki was involved in the formation of a study group called a "Kenkyu-Kai. This group consisted of a number of the Okinawan karate leaders; these included Chojun Miyagi, Kenwa Mabuni, Chomo Hanashiro, and Hohan Soken plus others. It was during this Kenkyu Kai's activity that Gokenki became famous through out Okinawa and his Hakutsuru Ken played a role in influencing Okinawan Karate. It is through this influence that certain kata such as Hakutcho, Paiho, Naipai and others became known to some Okinawan styles.

Japanese sword tsuba
From the Authors collection

Seisho Arakaki (1840-1920) also known as Kamade Unchu was born in Kumemura near Naha. He was an interpreter of the Chinese language for the Okinawan Royal Court. His duties for the Okinawan King took him to China on several occasions.

During these visits he often had the opportunity to study the Chinese fighting arts. History is unclear as to whom he studied under while in China. There is a record of Arakaki having studied under Waishinzan and there is a general assumption among historians that he may have studied under others; however, official records are lacking.

In 1867 Seisho Arakaki was among several Okinawan Karate masters who demonstrated Okinawan karate for the visiting Chinese Ambassador. After the Japanese take over of Okinawa in 1879; Arakaki and many other of the Okinawan aristocracy move from the southern part of Okinawa and settled in the Motobu Peninsula area of Northern Okinawa.

O'Sensei Tsuyoshi Chitose and Bill Dometrich 1967 Photo Credit Bill Dometrich collection

It is believed that once in the Motobu Peninsula area Arakaki developed the Sesoko no Kun kata based on the Bo techniques of Sesoko Island. His other kata were Unshu, Seisan, Shihahai, Niseishi and Arakaki no Kun.

He did not create a specific style; nevertheless, his technique influenced many of the modern styles of karate. He taught many Okinawans among these are Kenwa Mabuni and Tsuyoshi Chitose (1898-1984). Perhaps the Chito Ryu style founded Grandmaster Tsuyoshi Chitose follows the teachings of Seisho Arakaki closer than any other style.

The Chito Ryu Karate style was brought to the United States and to other countries by American Military personnel and later by Japanese Instructors. One of the first American service men to teach this style was William Dometrich who started teaching Chito Ryu in 1955. Sensei Dometrich has live up to his obligation to his teacher.

Drawing by Mike Roberts Color Productions

54

NAKAIMA KENRI (1819-1879)

Nakaima Kenri was born in Kume village and was a descendent of one of the original Chinese families who settle in Kume. He left to Okinawa at the age of 19 to study kenpo in the Fukein Province of China. He returned with the confirmation of a full mastership in Chinese Kenpo. He passed his knowledge to family members and this eventually led to development of the Nakaima family style of Okinawan karate called Ryuei Ryu.

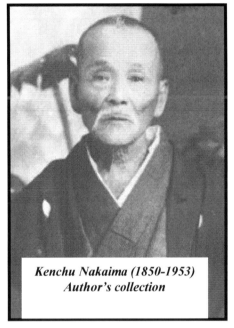

Kenchu Nakaima (1850-1953)
Author's collection

In 1869, Norisato Nakaima went to China to study under Ruruko. He returned to Okinawa in 1879. He passed his knowledge on to Kenchu Nakaima (1850-1953). Who then passed the system on to Kenko Nakaima. After Kenko the style was passed on to Tsuguo Sakumoto, Kenji Nakaima and Takayuki Kinjo.

The ancient kata of Sanchin, Seisan, Niseshi, Sanseru, Seyonchin, Ohan, Pachu, Anan, Paiku, Heiku, and Paiho as well as the weapons kata as learned and practiced by the Nakaima Bushi are preserved in Ryuei Ryu for the present and future generations.

SAKAYAMA KETOKU (WAKUDA TARU)

Sakayama Ketoku is not a well known to the modern karate historian. But to the people of Nago he is well known as the teacher of Shinkichi Kuniyoshi. Sakayama know as Wakuda Taru or Bushi Wakuda had studied with Ruruko in China.

In the early 1900's, Bushi Kuniyoshi had a dojo in the Nago area of Okinawa. Kuniyoshi was one of the teachers of, *Shigeru Nakamura (1892-1969)*, the founder of Okinawa Kenpo.

So it is that each practitioner of Okinawan Kenpo keeps some of the Wakuda Bushi's technique alive.

Shigeru Nakamura
Author's collection

OKINAWA KENPO

When I was stationed in Okinawa in the late 1960's one of the first things I did after I got settled into my military job was to seek a karate teacher. Many people suggested that I seek this famous instructor up north in Nago. Most did not know his name they only knew his reputation. Nago was too far away for me to travel several days per week. But I did remember the instructor's name....**Shigeru Nakamura**. I also remember people describing how he could "bust" the bark of trees off by punching the trunk with his fists.

Nakamura Sensei studied under several instructors beside Kuniyoshi Shinkichi; He studied under his uncle Teiichi Nakamura, Choki Motobu, Kensu Yabu and Chomo Hanashiro.

Okinawan Kenpo Group Photo 1960's
Grandmaster Shigeru Nakamura front row seated in chair to left is Seikichi Odo and to the right is Kina San. Photo credit: Author's collection

Nakamura Sensei taught the following kata: Naihanchi Shodan, Nidan, and Sandan....Pinan Shodan, Nidan, Sandan, Yondan, and Godan.....Kusanku Sho and Dai....Pai Sai Sho and Dai....Gojushiho, Chinto...Niseshi....Sesan....Anan...and Seipa. He also taught the following kobudo kata: Tokumine no Kun, Choun no Kun, Sakugawa no Kun, Chikin no Bo, Shishi no Kun, and Ko Bo.

Grandmaster Nakamura's students are: Shian Toma, Teru Higa, Hiroshi Miyazato, Seikichi Odo, Seiyu Oyata, Taketo Nakamura, Toshimitsu, Kenko Chibana, Kenichi Kinjo, and Seijiro Maehara and many others.

56

Left… Seikichi Odo applying a technique… Photo credit: Roy Jerry Hobbs collection. On the right Seiyu Oyata …Photo credit Author's collection

Seiyu Oyata born in 1926 is descendent of an old Okinawan samurai family. One of his ancestors was Zana Oyata an important Okinawa court official in the early 1600's. Seiyu Oyata's father was the middle weight Sumo Wrestling Champion before World War II

Just after World War II ended **Seiyu Oyata** observed an old man, who still wore a top knot, practicing with a pair of nunchaku on the other side of a stone wall from where Oyata was standing. The old man, known as **Uhgusuku (Ogusuku or Oshiro) no Tanmei,** was the last Bushi of the Ogusuku family.

Ogusuku no Tanmei was about 90 years old at the time; he agreed to teach Seiyu Oyata the Ogusuku family art; thus this ancient art of the Ogusuku Bushi was saved from extinction. The old warrior also introduced the young Oyata to an old Bushi named Wakinaguri no tanme. This old bushi was of Chinese decent and taught Seiyu Oyata the art of hitting vital areas of the body. . Today it is possible to learn the Ogusuku art from Sensei Oyata or from his students in the USA and in many other countries; but, it is almost extinct in Okinawa.

The **Ogusuku** or **Uhgusuku** clan was for many generations were the gate guards of Shuri Castle. Since this was a job that was "outside;" these gate guards had plenty of room to wield the Rokushaku (6 foot) Bo. As a result the Ogushiku (now more commonly called Oshiro) people were among Okinawa's best Bo experts. There are those who say that Shiro Taro no Kun is also called Ogusuku no Bo.

After the death of the old warriors Uhgusuku no Tanme and Wakinagiri no Tanme: Seiyu Oyata began studying under Grandmaster Shigeru Nakamura, the founder of Okinawa Kenpo. Oyata Sensei studied under Grandmaster Nakamura until Nakamura's death in 1969.

In the mid to late 1970's Grandmaster Oyata named his style of Okinawan Kenpo....***Ryukyu Kenpo.*** A few years later he re-named his art Ryu-te and in 1977 he moved to the United States to found the International Headquarters of his Karate organizations **[Oyata Shin Shu Ho(an organization of Oyata's senior students) and Ryu-te (the name of his martial art.)}**

Grandmaster Oyata has contributed much toward the preservation of the old fighting arts of the Ryukyu Islands. He has trained students all over the world; but more important he has trained a core of seniors that can continue teaching his art long into the future.

Seiyu Oyata in 1964 with a Grand Championship Trophy he won in a tournament in Japan. Photo credit: Author's collection

ITOMAN VILLAGE AND THE DUN DUN GAMA (CAVE)

The following story comes from the book *"Ryu-te no Michi....The Way of Ryu Kyu Hands (Classical Okinawan Karate)" by Taika Seiyu Oyata, published by Oyata Enterprises Inc. Independence, Missouri...pages 2-3 and 2-4.*

Itoman today is a fairly large city that caters to fishermen and serves as a port of call for trade ships. Itoman is probably Okinawa's second busiest port. The people of the Itoman area have a somewhat different appearance from the other Okinawan people. Their noses a more prominent than others; in general the people of Itoman have some physical features that are common to the European race.

Our story begins in the 14th century when Okinawa was heavily involved in prosperous trade businesses with other nations. As a result there were many people from other lands visiting and living in Okinawa.

There is a cave near Itoman that is called "Dun dun Gama". Today the cave is about one mile from the shore. However, prior to various "land reclaiming projects" on Okinawa (that have occurred after the turn of the last century) the cave was once about 40 feet from the shore line.

During the ancient days an English trade ship was destroyed by a storm near the present town of Itoman. The eight survivors were rescued and took shelter in a large cave near the town. It is said that the eight survivors were from London, England and the cave was called "London Gama" which over the years London change to "Dun dun Gama"

It is also said that the original name for Itoman came from the words meaning "eight men" which over time became "Itoman." The eight survivors lived their lives in the Itoman area; they married Okinawan women, they fathered children and over time the people of Itoman acquired some Caucasian features.

THE ITOMAN BUSHI

Kinjo Matsu was one of the descendents of the eight shipwrecked English sailors. He was known as the strong man of Itoman village.

He was also known as "Itoman Bunteku, and was made famous by Richard Kim's book "The Weaponless Warrior" as the

Kinjo Matsu, drawing by the author. A photo of Kinjo son was used as a model for this drawing. Matsu's son resembled his father. Credit Author's collection

Itoman, Okinawa 1950's Photo by Mike Robert's Color Production
Credit Author's collection

character "Itoman Bunkichi." Itoman Bunkichi was very powerful and is said to have been able swing under a bridge from one side to another by gripping the bridge timbers with his fingers. He did not teach many people; if he left a lineage of students it is a well kept secret. It could be that he took all of his great knowledge to his grave.

Itoman fisherman from the 1960's, the style of boat seen in the back ground has been used in Okinawa for hundreds of years. Photo by Mike Roberts Color Productions.
Credit: Author's collection

KANRYO HIGASHIONNA (1853-1916)

When Higashionna went to China with Kinjo Matsu and Akamine no Umae, he had no idea how his life and his legacy would be affected by his decision to go to China. He had begun his karate training under Bushi Matsumura in Okinawa. Later he trained under Arakaki Seisho. It was Arakaki who probably encouraged Higashionna to travel to China and made the arrangement of where to go …who to see and so forth.

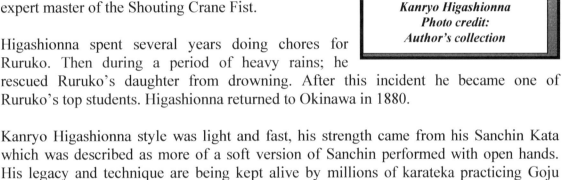

Kanryo Higashionna
Photo credit:
Author's collection

In China, Kanryo Higashionna studied with Kojo Taitei, Waixinxian, and Ruruko. Ruruko's real name remains some what of a mystery. It is said that his actual name was Xie Zongxiang and that he was an expert master of the Shouting Crane Fist.

Higashionna spent several years doing chores for Ruruko. Then during a period of heavy rains; he rescued Ruruko's daughter from drowning. After this incident he became one of Ruruko's top students. Higashionna returned to Okinawa in 1880.

Kanryo Higashionna style was light and fast, his strength came from his Sanchin Kata which was described as more of a soft version of Sanchin performed with open hands. His legacy and technique are being kept alive by millions of karateka practicing Goju Ryu and Toona Ryu.

Kanryo Higashionna's students:

Jhuhatsu Kyoda…..founder of Toona Ryu*   **Seito Higa**
Chojun Miyagi……founder of Goju Ryu   **Shimpan Shiroma**
Kenwa Mabuni ……founder of Shito Ryu*   **Koki Shiroma**

*Toona is the Okinawan Hogan (Dialect) for Higashionna
*Shito is the Okinawan Hogan combination of Shisu (Shi) for Itosu
and Toona (to) together forming Shito giving recognition to Mabuni's teachers
Anko Itosu and Kanryo Higashionna

Crane Tsuba made of steel
Author's collection

Kanryo Higashionna and students
Higashionna is second from the right, front row. Chojun Miyagi is in the middle second
Photo credit: Author's collection

Chojun Miyagi
Credit: Author's collection

Juhatsu Kyoda
Credit: Author's collection

Chojun Miyagi, founder of Goju Ryu, and one of Kanryo Higashionna's students also studied in China. Miyagi went to China several times during the 1920's. On some of his visits to China; Miyagi would stay with Shigeru Tamaya.

Tamaya Sensei lived in China until the political tension between Japan and China deteriorated near the beginning of World War II. He studied martial arts under a Chinese Master named Sohaku.

Two of Higashionna's students went on to found their own systems. The first of these, Juhatsu Kyoda, founded the Toona Ryu system. This system has a small membership and is found mainly in Japan.

Chojun Miyagi founded the Goju Ryu style which is now practiced by millions of people all over the world. Chojun Miyagi was born in to Okinawan aristocracy in 1888 and he died in 1953.

One of my students, Mark Gracey, who in the past had studied with Seiyu Oyata; said that Oyata Sensei knew Chojun Miyagi and may have been his kin.. According to Mr. Gracey, Oyata Sensei described Miyagi's technique as being light and fast, yet very powerful.

Miyagi Sensei was a gentleman, he passed on his teacher's technique to a number of students, and some of these are as follows:

Jinan Shinzato, Seiko Higa, Meitoku Yagi, Jitsuei Yogi, Saburo Uehara, Kei Miyagi, Echi Miyazato, Koshin Iha.

Shigeru Tamaya
Photo credit: Author's collection

Left: Eiichi Miyazato
Right: Meitoku Yagi
Roy Hobbs collection

Grandmaster Miyagi passed on to his students the legacy of Kanryo Higashionna. Today this legacy is carried on by millions of Goju Ryu Karatedo practitioners through out the world. Important as this may be; Miyagi Sensei also passed on the legacy of the Okinawan Bushi being gentleman as well as warriors. Chojun Miyagi was Okinawa's "gentle giant." He was large and powerful yet he never harmed anyone….this part of his legacy is too often forgotten.

Seiko Higa (1898-1966)
Last living student of Kanryo
Higashionna….a student of
Chojun Miyagi and teacher of:
Seiko Fukuchi
Seikichi Toguchi
Yasuhide Tamaki
Kimo Wall
and others

Painting of Seiko Higa from the
Kimo Wall collection. Sensei
Wall credits all members of the
Shodokan Dojo as being his
teachers and family.

The following story is from the "Karate Illustrated Magazine" I do not know which volume of the magazine in which this story appeared. I have quoted the article exactly how it appeared in the magazine….this article speaks highly of the character of its author, Seikichi Toguchi.

"Conceit"

"Once, in a city in Okinawa; there lived a man who claimed to be a karate master. Actually, he was just a bully who was strong enough and clever enough to beat up anyone in the surrounding area. Like all bullies, he was arrogant, insolent and everyone hated and feared him. However, everyone knew how useless it was to resist his wishes because the bully could always use his strength to force his will upon them. So the people let the bully act the way he pleased and stayed out of his way as much as possible. He took this as a sign of respect and his conceit grew ever greater.

In the same city there lived a wise old fisherman. Every time he saw or heard about the activities of the bully he felt angry. He waited and waited for some one to teach the bully a lesson. But, because no one did and the

Seikichi Toguchi
Roy Jerry Hobbs collection

bully's ego continued to grow, the old man decided to take up the task himself.

One day the old fisherman invited the bully to go fishing with him in his boat. The bully, convinced that the fisherman acted out of fear and respect, accepted the invitation. As the old man rowed his boat far out to sea, he quietly listened to the bully's boasting and bragging. Finally, the boat was so far from shore that the bully could not possibly swim back. Now, it was time thought the old man for the lesson to begin.

Suddenly the fisherman stood up, he put his feet on the sides of the boat and holding his oar; he began rocking the boat violently from side to side. The bully was completely helpless for the sea was not his element. All he could do was grab the sides of the boat tightly and with his face white with fear, he held on for dear life.

Then the old fisherman…never stopping his rocking…raised his oar in his hands and made out as though he was going to smash the bully's head with the oar. By now, the bully thoroughly terrified, turned whiter than ever and cringed back into his seat. Weakly and miserably, he apologized for his ways and misdeeds.

The bully never forgot this incident. From that point on, he behaved himself; he helped other people and was truly a changed man. In time he became a real master, loved by all.

Conceit, like that of the bully, is a common thing. There is hardly anyone who does not have a little conceit. Can you imagine a young woman who doesn't think she is pretty, or at least interesting looking; or a young man who doesn't believe he is handsome?

There is nothing wrong with conceit as long as it doesn't go too far. Conceit is simply self-confidence and self- confidence can often serve as a source for energy in life when it arouses a person's vitality and desire to excel or improve one's self.

However, conceit, like many things, can get out of hand. When it does, it weakens a person's ambition by making him think he is better than he actually is and that he does not need to improve himself. It takes discipline and self-criticism to keep one's self confidence from becoming conceit.

Strong conceit prevents the growth of one's character or ability. To reach any goal, one must be modest, always maintain self control and strive hard to reach the goal. This is the long cherished desire of one that lives by the code of Okinawan karate-do."

Seikichi Toguchi
(1917-1998)
"The last Okinawan Master to be given the title of Bushi"

後に続く者たちは良き
手本を求めている

"Young eyes are watching, set a good example."
A lesson from a Chinese fortune cookie.

Drawing by Albert Lucio

KOJO BUSHI

There is an old Okinawan saying "To speak of karate is to speak of the Kojo family; to speak of the Kojo family is to speak of karate." The Family of Kojo or Kogushiku (Okinawan Dialect) goes back in family records to the 1600's.

There were three main groups or family clans that provided the chief body guards to the Okinawan Kings. Firm written history is lacking so specific dates for this do not exist.

The first chief body guards came from the Motobu Clan. The second clan that carried out this responsibly was the Kojo Clan. The third and last clan to serve in this capacity was the Matsumura clan.

Matsu Higa
Credit: Robert Teller collection

The Kojo family descends from the original thirty six Chinese families to settle in Kume, Okinawa in the late 1300's. Their name was Cai in Mandran Chinese. The first member of the Kojo Clan to study the fighting arts was Kojo Shinpo Uekata. He was born in the late 1600's and learned Gongfu in Fuzhou, China. He died in the mid to late 1700's. He passed his art to his oldest son, Shinunjo.

Kojo Shinunjo Peichin (born in the late 1700's) studied under his father Shinpo Kojo. He is also alleged to have studied under Tode Sakugawa. There are those that say he was also called Matsu Higa. Like his father, he also studied in Fuzhou, China. Shinunjo passed on his knowledge down to his son, Saisho.

Kojo Saisho (1816-1906) studied in Fuzhou China where he learned the art of the Yon Shaku Bo (4 ft. staff).It seems that this weapon usc morc uscful to the Okinawan King body guards since the palace in Okinawa had low ceilings which made it difficult to use the Rokushaku Bo (six foot Bo) indoors.

In 1848 Saisho took his son, Isei and his nephew Taitei to train with Iwah. Iwah was also one of Bushi Matsumura and Maezato Ranho's teachers. Taitei also studied with Waixinxian. Upon his death Kojo Saisho left his art to his son, Isei.

Kojo Isei (1832-1891) took over Iwah's dojo in 1862. Iwah also visited Okinawa in the 1860's accompanied by Kojo Isei and Bushi Matsumura. In 1868 Isei returned to Okinawa. He began teaching his art to family members He was called Isei no tanme. He passed his art on to his son Kaho Kojo.

Kojo Kaho (1849-1925) born in Fuzhou, China; began studying under Iwah and his father in 1855. In he returned to Okinawa with his family in 1868. In 1880 he returned to China where he learned two more Crane kata from Waixinian. Under the leadership of Kojo Kaho the development of the Kojo Ryu system was completed. He returned to Okinawa in 1900. He passed his art to his grandson; Yoshitomi Kojo (1909-1995) also called Kojo Kafu. Yoshitomi maintained the family art and was teaching his family art and in keeping with family tradition. He was preparing his son Kojo Shigeru (1934-1991) to take over the family art. However, Shigeru Kojo died in 1991 of cancer.

Kojo Shigeru
Photo credit: Resources Unlimited

In 1958 *Irimaji Seiji (b. 1941)* began studying Kojo Ryu under Yoshitomi Kojo. In 1995 Yoshitomi Kojo promoted Irimaji Seiji to 9th Dan. After the death of his teacher Yoshitomi Kojo in 1995, Irimaji Seiji founded the Koshin Ryu Kohokan Karate/Kobudo Organization. His leading student is Takaya Yabiku. The technique of the Kojo family long maintained with in the family is being continued through the activity of Irimaji Seiji and Takaya Yabiku.

L to R Irimaji Seiji andTakayaYabiku
Photo credit: Resources Unlimited

"Slap the Rock at Tsuji if you wish to test your skill at Ti."

"Slapping the rock at Tsuji"
Computer generated drawing by the author....author's collection

SLAPPING THE ROCK AT TSUJI

Tsuji Machi was and probably still is the" Red Light" district of Naha, Okinawa. For over 100 years this was the place that the Okinawan bushi, bar room brawlers, street fighters, and karate "want to be's" came to test their fighting skill and gain a reputation as a fighter. Both the gentry and commoner made use of this custom and came to Tsuki to test their skill.

Tsuji was a place that slept during the day and played at night. There existed a large rock in Tsuji that protruded from the ground. For generations this rock was the meeting place for those who wished enjoy a "good fight" either as a spectator or as a participant.

A challenge was made to all comers simple by walking up to the large rock and slapping or just laying your hand on the rock. Your challenge was accepted by the same gesture. No one really knows how this practice started; we do know that the custom of "slapping the rock at Tsuji lasted until World War II.

Drawing by the Author

69

The most famous and perhaps the most successful of all of the Tsuji Machi fighters was *Choki Motobu (1871-1944)*. You might call Motobu Choki the *"Star of Tsuji."*

Choki Motobu was born into the *"Motobu Udun"*, this high ranking Bushi family descended from a sixth son of the Okinawan King Sho Shitsu.

Choki Motobu is often depicted as a semi-educated common brawler. But the fact is that Motobu trained under several prominent Okinawan Masters these include Bushi Matsumura, Anko Itosu, Tokumine, and Kosaku Matsumora. The simple fact is that Choki Motobu was well educated; he wrote some of the first books on Okinawan Karate. He like most Okinawan Master of his day lack a command of the Japanese language; this fact mark him as uneducated by the Japanese.

Choki Motobu
Credit: Sid Campbell collection

Both Photos are of Choki Motobu. Photo credit: Author's collection

Choki Motobu like many of Okinawa's Bushi class loved to fight. Bushi Matsumura at the age of 17 years traveled all over Okinawa fighting other Bushi to test his skills and to build a reputation which led to his employment as a body guard to the Okinawa King. Motobu's love for fighting was not unusual among Okinawan Bushi.

Sensei Fusei Kise told me an interesting story about Choki Motobu. I realize that by telling this story I may be offending some readers. Nevertheless, this is history and all stories of Okinawan Karate need to be told so they will not be forgotten.

I ask Sensei Kise about Choki Motobu's reputation as a fighter. He answered back that Motobu defeated some people by locking them in a closet in his home and not feeding them so they would become weak. He then fought them and easily defeated his "house guests." Of course it is impossible to gauge the reality of this story.

OTHER BUSHI

Many of Okinawa's finest samurai are scarcely remembered today. The follow are bits a pieces about just a few of these old warriors. Some were weapons experts others were karate experts; most were skilled in both arts.

We will start off with discussing **Chikin Seinori Oyakata.** *Chikin is the Okinawan Hogan (dialect) for the kanji that is pronounced "Tsuken" in the Japanese dialect.* The information for this story comes from three sources; (1) a book titled "Karate and Ryukyu Kobudo" by Katsume Murakami, (2) a book "Okinawa Kobudo by Nakamoto Masahiro and (3) conversations with my Okinawan teachers.

First from Murakami's story: Chikin was a Shuri samurai who was born in 1624. It seems that some time after his birth he was given the task of taking care of the King's mute son. This must have been a boring task for a "young up and coming' samurai. But nevertheless it was his task and Chikin made the best of it. Over a period of time Chikin taught the child to make vocal sounds. The King was pleased and promoted Chikin to a higher rank.

Some other samurai became jealous of Chikin and decided to drown him in the swift tidal currents of Nakagusku Bay. He was taken to the tidal flats between the main land of Okinawa and a large island located on the east side of the bay. He was tied to some large stones and thrown into the water. When the tides came in, he would drown.

Now Nakamoto's story; Chikin was part of a plot to over throw the mute king of Okinawa, Sho Gen, and replace him with his brother. However, the plot was discovered and those who had plotted against King Sho Gen were punished. Chikin was tied to several large stones and thrown into the swift tidal current.

In both stories; nearby fishermen rescued Chikin and took him to the island on the east side of the bay. Here Chikin hid in a large cave; he emerged from his hiding each day at dawn and dusk to practice his Bo Kata. Chikin had sort of ruddy complexion that resulted in him being called "Akahito" or Akacho both meaning "Red man." Over the years the island was called Chikinjima (Chikin's Island).

Today several Okinawan Bujutsu styles have a Chikin or Tsuken Bo kata. These are as follows: Shorin Ryu Matsumura Seito, Matayoshi Kobudo, Bugeikan, Okinawan Kenpo and the Ryukyu Kobudo Hozon Shinkokai Today the old fighting technique from Chikin Seinori are being maintained by thousand of modern martial artist that follow the teachings of these styles or organizations.

There are other samurai named Chikin that have left their mark on the Okinawan fighting arts. Tsuken or Chikin Kora (Korugawa) lived before 1850. His Sai and Bo technique are today widely practiced in the kata Chikin Hantaguwa no Sai and Urasoe no Kun. There exist a famous and widely practiced sai kata called **Chikin (Tsuken) Shitahaku**. The kata is very old. I was told by a Japanese man that the name of this sai kata translates as the sai kata of Chikin, an old man of Tomari. I have not made any attempt to verify this.

Soeishi Ryotoku (1772-1825) was a famous Shuri samurai who develop three Bo kata that are widely practice throughout the world. Shuji or Shiushi no Kun (Koryu) is the modern name of one of the kata developed by Master Soeishi. He also developed the Choun no Kun. These two were combined by the master to create the Soeishi no Kun kata that was taught only to family members before 1900.

Sueyoshi is a famous Okinawa Bushi name. There were several Okinawan martial artists named Sueyoshi. One was Anyu Sueyoshi. He was also known as the Chief Magistrate of Naha. One Sueyoshi formulated the famous Sueyoshi no Kun kata. He is alleged to have died after 1900.

Sueyoshi Anyu….Shuri Bo Master Photo taken in 1853 by the Perry Expedition. Credit: Author's collection

Many kata and technique have been lost with the passage of time; in other cases, old names are no longer used. *Toyama* was the name of an Okinawan Bushi who lived in the late 1800's. His teacher and technique are unknown. Yet it may be that he is remembered under the name of *Oyadomari.* The Oyadomari family members were among the most famous Tomari village Bushi.

Yamachi was a Samurai who cut off his top knot and became a farmer after 1879. He used a very heavy Bo and his technique was very powerful. Today the Yamachi Bo technique is either lost or very rare.

Bushi Takemura or Tokumura is an almost forgotten Okinawan Samurai yet in the closing days of the Okinawan Kingdom he was one of the most famous Bushi on the island. He developed the *Takemura Kusanku*.

Bushi Takemura is alleged to have studied under Bushi Matsumura; however, his name does not appear on most lineage charts. Takemura taught his art to *Soko Kishimoto (1862-1945).* Kishimoto was born on the Motobu Peninsula of Okinawa. He lived in Nago and was famous in that area for his fighting skills. He was known as *"Nago no*

Seitoku Higa Photo credit: Author's collection

Agarie." Kishimoto was one of the teachers of a modern genius of the martial arts known as *Seitoku Higa*. Sensei Higa studied under; Miinshin Higa, Kankan Toyama, Chibana Choshin, Soko Kishimoto, Seikichi Uehara, and Masami Chinen. He founded the Bugei Kan in 1968.

Seitoku Higa played a major role in developing and founding some of the Okinawan Martial Arts organizations. In 1961 he helped found the Okinawan Kobudo Association. He played a major roll in the organization of the All Okinawan Karatedo Federation in 1956.

In 1985 I asked Sensei Yuichi Kuda who he had been studying under since Hohan Soken died. Sensei Kuda said that he studied under Seitoku Higa and was in fact Sensei Higa's number two student. When I ask Sensei Kuda about Sensei Higa's skill level he said that Higa could be the best in Okinawa and described Higa's skill with the Bo as equal to Hohan Soken's skill.

The *Motobu family* descended from Okinawa kings and they were the king's bodyguards. They held this position for many generations. The last of the Motobu Clan to study the ancient *Motobu Udundi* (Motobu family hand) was *Choyu Motobu.* It was the tradition of the Motobu Bushi to keep this art with in the Motobu family.

The fighting arts of the Motobu family were headed for extinction when in 1916 Choyu Motobu broke with tradition and began teaching Seikichi Uehara, (a non family member) the Motobu Udundi. Uehara was a school friend of Choyu Motobu's son.

Choyu Motobu (1857- 1926)
Robert Teller Collection

Seikichi Uehara and Shian Toma
Photo credit: Roy Jerry Hobbs
collection

When the son of the senior Motobu showed little interest in learning his family art; Choyu Motobu devoted his teaching to Seikichi Uehara; and in 1926 young Uehara was designated to be the successor to this ancient art. Thus saving the ancient Motobu Udundi from extinction.

Seikichi Uehara (1904-2004)
Robert Teller collection

Seki Toma applying a typical Motobu
technique on Roy Hobbs
Credit: Roy Jerry Hobbs's collection

Grandmaster Seikichi Uehara was a superb martial artist and a real gentleman. He had tremendous hand strength and would often demonstrate this strength by crushing raw apples with his finger tips.

Perhaps his greatest demonstration of skill occurred when Grandmaster Uehara was 96 years old. He demonstrated his art on national television by fighting in a match against a 30 year old former boxing champion.

Seikichi Uehara
demonstrating a throw from
Motobu Udunti
Roy Jerry Hobbs collection

During the televised match Sensei Uehara defeated the boxer and then apologized to him because Uehara felt that he had taken advantage of the boxer who was only 30 years old and lacked the maturity need to over power some one like Uehara! [2-4]

The Motobu Udunti is an old and very effective art. Uehara taught many people among these are: Seitoku Higa, Seki Toma and Shian Toma.

"There will always be a stronger one amongst the strong."
A lesson from a Chinese fortune cookie.

Chokuho Agena (1859-1911) is often called the "strong man of Agena." He was one of the many Okinawan karate masters of the Meiji Era that did not teach many people. Yet today his influence has greatly impacted thousands of karateka through out the world.

Richard Kim in his book "The Weaponless Warrior," published by Ohara Publications in 1974 made the general martial arts public (out side of Okinawa) aware of Agena.

In Kim's book there are several tales that attests to the physical strength and martial prowess of Agena. One such tale involves Agena saving water from a number of barrels which contained emergency water supply for his village.

As the story goes the village officials became aware of the fact that the water barrels were rapidly loosing water. There was not enough time to send for the local cooper smith to repair the barrels. The officials came to Agena for help. Agena answered the call of his village and with the strength of his fingers tightened the clasps of the barrels and stopped the leaks until the repairs could be more permanent.

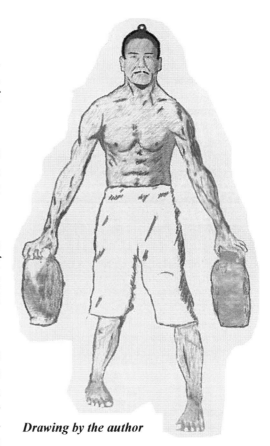

Drawing by the author

General Okinawan folklore states that Chokuho Agena was a student of Sokon Matsumura; yet his name is not found on most lineage charts. So some what of mystery remains as to the idenity of Agena's teachers.

Mike Muller gave me the following story about Chokuho Agena. Mike was a Staff Sergeant in the U.S. Army Special Forces stationed at Fort Hood Texas in the late 1990's and practiced Hakutsuru techniques and kata with me for about one and half years.

Some may find this story offensive, but the reader must realize that the oriental culture is different than the cultures of many other nations and places. Do not be too hasty in judging these people.

The story was typed by Seiko Chinen and given to Mike Muller in the 1980's. She is the granddaughter of Chokuho Agena. She also wrote by hand some "last minute" details that she remembered after the typing was finished. I did not re-write this story; rather I left the story just as Mike gave to me. I hope the reader appreciates the fact that Mrs. Chinen is self taught when it comes to speaking and writing English. I find her letter to be charming and unique.

Mini Story of TERA-Gwa (BUSAR) Warrior

CYOKUHO AGENA(Child Name, KAMA) was born at Tera-gwa(the name of house)

of Gushikawa Villiage in 1859 (Ansei-6)

He dead in 1911 (Meiji-44)With Disease of Asthama, age was 52.

Two (2) Son and a Daughter were born from he and his wife, named macchi

Agena. His gentleness and a mild mannered personality is stil loved by

present World people.

He named his first son YAMATO, His first Daughter USHI and second son

Seiei.   He married with MACCHI when his age was 20 and was living

as general Farmer.

one day His wife MACCHI asked him to buying a machine for Cloth make

He complied with wife's requests and out of home to Naha to obtains it.

He was thinking that it is great fine chance to have pleasure at Naha

Yumachi (Four town of Naha Where were most of beautiful prostitute)

on his way, He stoped by at one of KARATE School and looked hard the

KARATE practices of some other person, His standing watches was discovered

by DOJOO'S house maid and reported about it to a Karate Dojoo Master,

a Master of Dojoo called this young man in to Dojoo and asked many

questions like his address, that where he from, tittle of Job, age etc.

a Karate teacher allowed him to stay the place to watching the practice

of KARATE and asked again that may stays here as long as he wants.

A young man staied there for a while and watced hard the practice of

Karate, and told teacher that he recollected his business at Naha this time

and he has to leave here and made promise with teacher to meet again

at this Karate DOJOO,   after he brought his wife's requests back his home

got wife's agreement to go back to Naha for Karate Jutsu practice.

when he made his second attendance of Karate Dojoo of naha, There

were many his freinds already entered the Dojoo Who named like

MOTOBU-UME, MOTOBU-AKAR, NAKIJIN-TARA, TOMIBARU-YAMA and HEIGWARA-KAMATA

etc. Warrior Agena's oldest Son was already entered Japanese Army in

located Bassed in Fukuoka City.

He already had attended to a War of Japanese and Rosia, but his Father

Cyokuho Agena had no any karate practice given to him.

his son Yamato has Learned Karate at service time.

 after he discharged his service, he was employed to Fukuoka Police Dept.

as a Teacher of Karate, there for he could not comes back to his wife and

childen of gushikawa villiage.

he dead at Fukuoka after the end of the world War.

a Daughter Ushi Agena age 94 1808-1885 is stil living at lshikawa city

with good Health with her family. second son also passed away by the

last second world War, but many of Cyokuho Agena Warrior's Grand families

lives well at present time at many where.

Continue.

Later Chokuho became Acting master of Dojoo
and when Daughter Ushi has Enough age.
She was Taught Self-Defense Karate Jutsu by her
father.
1. Chokuho, Agena had several One's pupil.
2. many great Actual fact stories around his young life.
3. He entered public Service as master of Karate.
   (teaching Karate for public Service members)
4. 91 descendants are being in the present.

77

P.S.

My name is Seiko, Chinen
I am working at Camp Butler
Fire Department, Zukeran Station
phone: 635-2566 or 635-4203,
every other day 24 hrs on duty.
I am a grand child of Agena
warrior

I have heart that you know
about the story of my grand father.

your house maid mrs Agena
is my relation, who has connection
with agena warrior.

There is another very interesting story concerning the death of Agena. This story was first told to me by Greg Lindquist, who is a student of Seiyu Oyata and if my memory is correct Mr. Linquist received this story from Sensei Oyata.

Drawing by the author

Mike Muller confirmed this story when he trained with me in the 1990's. Mike received the story from Grandmaster Eizo Shimabukuro in the 1980's. Mr. Muller was a student of Sensei Eizo Shimabukuro.

It seems that Chokuho Agena had a disagreement with Chotoku Kyan. The argument and disagreement was very serious and led to Agena's death.

Carrying the Sewing Machine home.

Chokuho Agena took the same path home at the same time each day. The path went under the branches of a large tree. Chotoku Kyan climbed up in to the tree and centered himself on a large limb directly over the path on which Agena would travel to his home. When Agena came along Kyan jumped down on Agena's neck. The attack broke Agena's neck and he died several days later. This act started a feud that lasted for many years.

Today Chokuho Agena's legacy can be found in the Kobudo system founded by Shinpo Matayoshi after World War II. Shinpo Matayoshi's father *Shinko Matayoshi (1888-1947)* primarily learned martial arts from three Okinawan Masters, these are: Ukikata (Chokuho) Agena, Shinchin Matayoshi, and Oh Irei. We can say that Chokuho Agena passed his "torch of learning" to Shinko Matayoshi; who passed the torch on to his son *Shinpo Matayoshi (1921-1997).*

Shinko Matayoshi
Photo credit: Author's collection

Shinko Matayoshi learned his art from the following:
Chokuho Agena.........Shinchin Matayoshi........Oh Irei

Shinpo Matayoshi learned from the following:
Shintoku Matayoshi....Shinko Matayoshi.....Shingi Matayoshi

Shinpo Matayoshi founded the Ryukyu Kobudo Renmei in 1970; today this organization has thousand of members scattered throughout the world. The technique of the various masters who taught Shinko Matayoshi and Shinpo Matayoshi are being kept alive by these members.

Shinpo Matayoshi

Photo credit: Author's collection

"You will never know your full potential until you try."
A lesson from a Chinese fortune cookie.

Aburaya Yamashiro (1797-1881), also known as Chinen Pechin or Yamagusuku Andaya, was a student of Chinen Shichanaka and Tode Sakugawa. Yamashiro did not develop any kata on his own. He served as a link by which many of the kata of the past survived through the 1800's to the modern times. Yamashiro had several students; these include Sanda Chinen, Tawada no Megantu and Sanda Kanagushiku (Kinjo).

Tawada Megantu (1814-1884), was a student of Bushi Matsumura and Yamashiro. He was also called Tawata Shinboku Chikudun Pechin. He was kin by marriage to Anko Itosu and Choshin Chibana. Tawata was an expert in the Pai Sai Kata and developed his own Tawata Pai Sai kata. He also developed his own sai technique that is found in the kata Tawata no sai. His sai kata has some moves that resemble the Matsumura no Sai kata which adds to the speculation that Tawata may have studied sai technique under Bushi Matsumura.

Sanda Chinen, also called *Yamane Usumei*, son of Aburaya Yamashiro died in the 1920's. He passed on his knowledge to his son, *Masami Chinen (1898-1976).* Masami Chinen founded Yamane Ryu and developed the

*Masami Chinen
Author's collection*

*Sabuburo Kochinda and wife,
Mekiko Photo credit:
Resources Unlimited*

*Sanda Kinjo
Robert Teller collection*

Yonegawa no Kun Kata. Masami Chinen had many students; these include Choki Oshiro, Yabiku Moden, Higa Nisuburo, Higa Raisuke, Higa Seichiro, Akamine Yohei and Sabuburo Kochinda. These individuals maintained the art of old and passed it on to modern times.

Sanda Kanagushiku (1841-1920), Sanda Kinjo, was Okinawa's first police inspector; this led to his nickname *"Uhuchiku"* ("big police man" in the Okinawan dialect). His style was very practical and based on real technique and experience. Kinjo Sanda may have been the premier Okinawan sai technician. His kata Uhuchiku no Sai and Uhuchiku no Nunte kata are still practiced today.

Around the turn of the last century Sanda Kinjo started teaching *Shosei Kina (1883-1981)*. Kina studied under Kinjo for about twenty years. It was Shosei Kina that passed the teachings of the old Uhuchiku on to the modern day.

Sensei Kina passed his knowledge on to *Shinyei Kyan (1912-1997)*, and *Shinyu Isa*. Shinyei Kyan taught *Nakamoto Kiichi (born 1928)*.

Shosei Kina
Robert Teller's collection

Above: Shinyei Kyan…. on the right Shosei Kina and Kiichi Nakamoto
Photo credit: Peter Carbone and the Weapons Connection

Isa may have been the first to use the name Uhuchiku Kobudo. Nakamoto Kiichi founded the Okinawa Denko Kobujutsu Hozon Budo Kyokai. Thanks to the activities of Shosei Kina, his students and grand students the art of the old Uhuchiku is being practiced and preserved by dedicated students throughout the world.

Group photo of Okinawan Kobudo practitioners 1933
Front row …in the middle Moden Yabiku, on the far left Shinken Taira.
Photo credit: Author's collection

Yabiku Moden (1882-1945) and his student ***Shinken Taira (1897-1970)*** probably did more to preserve the kobujutsu arts of Okinawa than anyone. Moden Yabiku studied karate under Anko Itosu, and Bojutsu under Chinen Sanda, and Saijutsu under Kinjo Sanda. He researched and saved 40 old kobudo kata from extinction. Moden Yabiku founded the Ryukyu Kobujutsu Kenkyu Kai. He passed on his knowledge to his student Shinken Taira.

Shinken Taira continued the work of Moden Yabiku by researching and preserving the kobudo techniques of his teachers and the kobudo techniques of many others through out Okinawa.

Taira was born on the Island of Kume which is west of Okinawa. His family name was Miyazato, but he often used his mother's name which was Taira. Shinken Taira studied karate under Gichen Funakoshi. From his grandfather, ***Gimu Kanegawa (1862-1921)***, he studied techniques with the Kama, Suruchin, Tekko and Tinbe. Taira learned Bo, Sai, Tonfa, and Ekujutsu from Moden Yabiku. From ***Kamiya Jinsei (1894-1964)*** he learned Chatan Yara no Sai, Choun no Kun and Soeishi no Kun.

82

Kamiya Jinsei was a physician who lived in Itoman village. He was the president of the "All Sports Association of Itoman" and contributed money to aid Taira in his Kobudo research and preservation.

Shinken Taira became the second president of the Ryukyu Kobujutsu Kenkyu Kai and in 1955 changed this organization's name to "Ryukyu Kobudo Hozon Shinkokai." He taught many people on Okinawa and in Japan among his students are:

*Eisuke Akamine (1925-1998...*from Okinawa ...became the second president of the "Ryukyu Kobudo Hozon Shinkokai"
*Motokatsu Inoue (1918-1993)....*from Japan
*Ryusho Sakagami (1915-1993)...*from Japan and kinfolk to Moden Yabiku.

Left to right...Eisuke Akamine...Shinken Taira
Bo tai Tonfa (Bo vs. Tonfa)
Photo credit: Author's collection

Tsuba (Japanese Sword Guard) from the late 1500's Author's collection

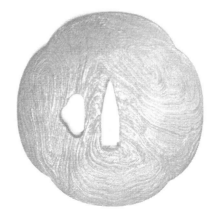

83

SOURCES, FOOTNOTES AND EXPLANATIONS

CHAPTER 2

2-1   *Source: Okinawa Karate Folklore*

History of the Shaolin Temple

Source: "Shaolin Temple" by Charles Tatum…Kenshin Kan Newsletter

Stories of the Shaolin Temple

Source: "Gate to the Fukein Shaolin Temple" by Akio Kinjo

The Bushi Who Trained in China

Source: Okinawan Karate Folklore and conversation with my Okinawan karate teachers.

2-2   *Ibid*

2-3   *Explanation: There are no official birth and death dates for Sakugawa Tode and Chatan Yara. For years the accepted dates for Sakugawa were 1733-1815 which were the   dates found in Richard Kim's book the "Weaponless Warrior". The recent book by Nakamoto Masahiro " Okinawa Traditional Old martial Arts…Kobudo" offer the following birth and death dates for Sakugawa (1786-18670 and for Chatan Yara (1740-1812).*

Ryukyu Kan

Source: Most of the information for this sub-chapter is from "Uechi Ryu Master Text" by Kanei Uechi and Uechi Ryu Seniors

Matsuda Tosaburo, Kanbun Uechi, Gokenki, and Seisho Arakaki

Source: Ibid
In addition information on Seishi Arakaki comes from information given to me by William Dometrich nearly 30 years ago.

Nakaima (1819-1879)

Source: "Okinawan Karate…Teachers, Styles, and Secret technique" by Mark   Bishop
Additional information is from conversations with my Okinawan teachers.

Okinawan Kenpo

Sources: Conversations with Greg Linquist, Nick Flores and Yuichi Kuda

Itoman Village and the "Dun Dun Gama" (Cave)

Source listed in text

The Itoman Bushi

> *Source: Ibid*

Kanryo Higashionna (1853-1916)

> *Source: General Okinawan Karate Folklore; information about Shigeru Tamaya comes from Fusei Kise.*

Kojo Ryu

> *Sources: Chuck Chandler who received this information from Takaya Yabiku and Irimaji Seiji*

Slapping the Rock at Tsuji

> *Source: General Okinawan Karate Folklore*

Other Bushi

> *Sources: Ibid....other sources consist of general Okinawan Karate folklore, Okinawan Karate Teachers, Styles and Secret Techniques by Mark Bishop, Kobudo by Nakamoto Masahiro and conversations with my Okinawan teachers.*

> 2-4   *Conversations with Yuichi Kuda*

Okinawan lady weaving
Drawing by the Author

守分忠誠 暴風狂颶我心

止如嬰兒之熟睡

"Be steadfast in your duty.
Be unswerving in your loyalty.
Know both the tempest of the storm
and the gentle innocence of a sleeping child."

Calligraphy by Shifu Hwang
Poem by the Author

86

CHAPTER 3

OKINAWA'S GREATEST WARRIOR
SOKON MATSUMURA

Gift from Ronnie Locke
Credit: Author's Collection

沖縄の最も偉大な武士

Okinawa's Greatest Warrior

GENERAL INFORMATION

In spite of being famous and well known, much confusion and controversy remains concerning Sokon Matsumura. First of all, there is confusion concerning his birth date. Information concerning his birth date that has been handed down through Shorin Ryu Matsumura Seito Karate/Kobujutsu practitioners that state he was born in 1797 and died in 1889. [3-1]

Other sources place his birth date in the year 1796. Some say that written records exist that dispute these dates. In Okinawa, when man reaches the age of 88 years, a special ceremony is held to celebrate what the Okinawans consider to be a special and lucky day. It is alleged there is a written record showing that a woman took her child to Matsumura for a "lucky embrace" on the

Sokon "Bushi" Matsumura
1797-1889
Author's collection

date of and celebration of his 88th birthday. This was in 1896; therefore, some historians state that Sokon Matsumura was born in 1809 and died at the age of 92 years in 1901. [3-2] It is safe to say that Bushi Matsumura was born near the beginning of the 19th century and died near the beginning of the 20th century.

Bushi Matsumura's name or names are often confusing to both the martial historian and the karate practitioner. Matsumura's original surname was Kiyo. [3-3] Later in life, when he was appointed to the position of "Body Guard" to the Okinawan ruler (Shoko); Sokon Kiyo was allowed to change his name to Matsumura (Machimura in Okinawan Hogan) meaning "pine village".

Sokon Matsumura was known by many names during his long career. His Chinese name was "Bu Seitatsu". He was also known as "Unyu". During his many years of faithful service to 3 generations of Okinawan Kings he accomplished many brave feats; he was famous in Japan, China and Okinawa. [3-4]

When Sokon Matsumura was awarded the title of "Bushi" he was given a great honor. The title "Bushi" was awarded only to a member of Okinawa's Samurai class. The title "Bushi" held a special meaning for the Okinawan people. In Japan, the title "Bushi" was given to every male born into the Samurai class; but in Okinawa the title had to be earned. In Okinawa, those who held the title "Bushi" were superb martial artists and were also gentlemen. King Sho Tai conferred the title "Bushi" on Sokon Matsumura. Sokon Matsumura was also called "Bucho" which meant head samurai. [3-5]

History provides precious little information concerning the teachers of Sokon Matsumura. It is generally accepted by most historians that Sakugawa Tode was

89

Sokon "Bushi" Matsumura
Painting by Chuck Chandler
Author's collection

Matsumura's Seven Virtues of Bu

Bu prohibits violence.
Bu keeps discipline as in soldiers
Bu keeps control among the population
Bu spreads virtues
Bu gives one a peaceful heart
Bu helps keep the peace between people
Bu makes the people of a nation prosper

Matsumura's first teacher. Most historians maintain that Sakugawa lived from 1733 to 1815. If we accept Matsumura's birth date as 1809 and Sakugawa's death as occurring in 1815; then, there is not much time for Matsumura to have studied with Sakugawa. Therefore, it is clear that Sakugawa must have died at a later date or Matsumura could not have studied with him for any appreciable amount of time.

There are legends that Makabe Chojun (1728 - 1823) was one of the early teachers of Sokon Matsumura. It can be verified that Sakugawa was the teacher of Makabe Chojun; so, it is quite probable that both Sakugawa and Makabe were teachers of Matsumura. Sokon Matsumura's great-grandson, Hohan Soken, maintained that his great-grandfather, Sokon Matsumura was well traveled. Legends state while in Satsuma province, Japan, he studied and mastered the Jigen Ryu, a method of Kenjutsu under Yashichiro Ijuin. [3-6]

Master Soken also states that Matsumura traveled to Fukein province in China and studied in the famous Shaolin Temple for 26 years. [3-7] Others maintain that his Shaolin study was only for about 10 years. Legend has it that Matsumura studied with military attaché Ason and Iwah; still other legends say that a master of one of Fukein Province's fighting traditions named Wai Shin Xian was Matsumura's teacher. [3-8]
.

MATSUMURA'S KATA

Hohan Soken stated that, when Matsumura returned to Okinawa from Fukein China's Shaolin Temple, he was a master of Shaolin and was appointed as "Bucho" or head body guard to the Okinawan King. Oral legends passed down from Takaya Yabiku place the dates for Matsumura's return from China at around 1845.

It was Matsumura's connection with the Shaolin Temple that eventually led to the Karate system that Matsumura founded to be called Shorin Ryu. Hohan Soken stated Sokon Matsumura, brought back to Okinawa the following kata from the Shaolin Temple: "Pinan from the Shaolin Tiger, Naihanchi from the Leopard, Pai Sai from the Snake, Gojushiho from the dragon, Hakutsuru from the Crane, and Kusanku from the dragon with some crane techniques mixed in." [3-9]

Information dating back to the 1990 and coming from Takaya Yabiku states that Bushi Matsumura brought back three kata from China in 1845 and that it is from these three kata that many of the kata of Suide or Shurite were developed. These kata are *(1) Matsumura Hakutsuru Sanchin (2). Matsumura Hakutsuru Mai or "the wife's Hakutsuru and (3) Matsumura-ke tode or the Matsumura Family Chinese's Hand Hakutsuru (this is the kata Hohan Soken practiced on a raft on a lake near Shuri, Okinawa.* [3-10]

Drawing from the "Little Pictures of Japan" published by The Book House for Children

91

The ***Pinan kata*** are said to have been developed after the turn of the last century by Anko Itosu. In the late 1970's I asked Anthony Sandoval who was studying on Okinawa at that time under Seiki Arakaki about the relationship between the Pinan kata and the Channan kata. Sandoval asked Sensei Arakaki about this and wrote back to me stating that Sensei Arakaki had said ***"during the days of Bushi Matsumura Pinan Sho Dan was called Channan Sho and Pinan Ni Dan was called Channan Dai."*** Sandoval went on to say that Sensei Arakaki said these were Bushi Matsumura's kata. Later, I asked this question to Fusei Kise and Yuichi Kuda. Chuck Chandler in the late 1990's asked Takaya Yabiku about the Pinan/Channan Kata controversy. All replied with answers confirming what Anthony Sandoval told me.

I believe that when Anko Itosu brought karate in to the public school system of Okinawa during the early 1900s. He wished to use the Channan kata as introductory kata for beginning students. I believe that the term Channan suggested a Chinese origin for these kata and that it was politically unpalatable for the Japanese /Okinawan School officials to accept the name Channan. Itosu used the name Pinan instead.

Pinan

 pin or hei meaning calm

 an meaning restful

Channan

 Cha in Chinese or Cho or Naga meaning long lasting

 an meaning restful

Pinan meaning calm and restful...,Channan meaning long lasting rest
The definition for both terms are practically the same.

Drawing by Katherine Sturges from "The Little book of Japan" published by The Book House for Children

Author's collection

Channan is the name of a town just west of Hong Kong; could it be that the source for this kata? Is Pinan Kata some how connected to this town? It is possible that Hong Kong, being a busy port, would have been used by the Okinawan traders. Any way according to Hohan Soken and his students Pinan Sho Dan and Ni Dan are Bushi Matsumura's kata and the other three Pinan Kata were developed by Anko Itosu.

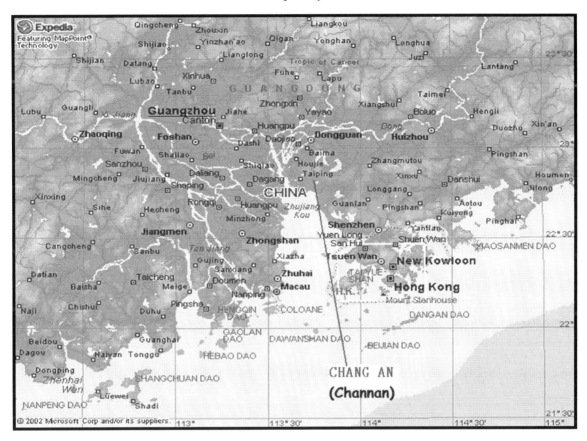

Chang An a village in China located between Hong Kong and Canton; could this be there source of the Channan Kata?
Credit: Jeff Walters's collection

BUSHI MATSUMURA, THE MAN

Matsumura was a tall, thin, wiry individual. He was often described as being skinny with very long legs. When he squatted, his knees would be over his head. Some historians state that he stood about 5'7", which was very tall for an Okinawan of the 1800s. He was said to be of Chinese decent.

Matsumura had a "beetle brow" and was considered quite ugly. He was very limber and from a squatting position would practice roundhouse kicks to the front and over his shoulders. All of his techniques emphasized speed and balance. He believed that only through speed came true power. From the techniques learned at the Shaolin Temple, he used his hips to develop torque or twisting power. He stressed that torque + speed =

power. It is this principal of twisting the hips for power that became a major power source for all styles. Matsumura favored jumping techniques and the people of Shuri would say that he could run up a tree. He would often use a tree for a training aid. He would hang from a tree limb for hours to develop his arms and legs. He could jump up and grab or pinch a ceiling beam and hang there like a monkey. His height, quickness, strength, and knowledge enabled him to develop an effective fighting style. [3-12]

MATSUMURA AND HIS WIFE

Sokon Matsumura was a very well educated man and entered into the Okinawan king's service fairly early in his life. Matsumura married a beautiful girl named Yonamine Tsuru. She was an excellent martial artist in her own right.

Yonamine contributed much to Bushi Matsumura's knowledge and skill. *Oral legends passed down through Hohan Soken's students (both Okinawan and Americans) state that Yonamine Tsuru was Kusanku's grand daughter. It is said that the kata "Kusanku no Mai" was developed by Kusanku and maintained by his family members. This kata may very well be the original Kusanku Kata.*

A drawing by Bob Frazer depicting Yonamine Tsura's fighting skills. Photo Credit: Author's collection.

Again oral traditions handed down by Hohan Soken and his students state that Bushi Matsumura inherited the Kusanku Kata practiced by Sakugawa; today this kata is believed to be called Shiho Kusanku (4 directional Kusanku). Matsumura is said to have developed his own version of Kusanku which today is called Matsumura no Kusanku; this kata is very rare and is the kata Hohan Soken used to teach the use of the jiffa (hair pin). [3-13]

Credit "Little Pictures from Japan" Edited by O.B. Millar pictures by Katharine Sturges

94

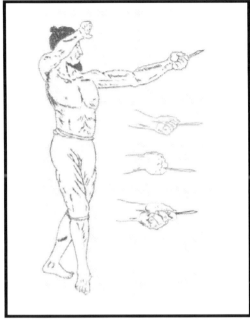

To the left, Matsumura Kusanku Kata teaching techniques with the jiffa; Drawing by Bob Frazer, below are six types of Jiffa. Both photos or drawings are from the Author's collection.

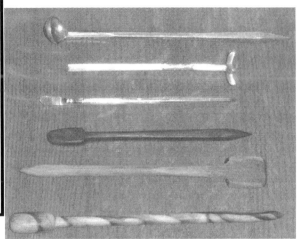

Teenage Okinawan girl carrying her baby brother showing the typical Chinese-Okinawa-Japanese method of carrying babies.
Drawing by Author

Oral traditions told to Shorin Ryu Matsumura Seito members by their Okinawan Sensei states that **Seisan** is one of the kata Matsumura brought back from China and that he altered the kata to instruct his wife to defend herself while carrying a baby on her back.

Fighting with a Seisan Kata technique. Drawing by the Author. Credit Authors collection

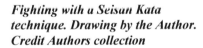

Okinawan karate has numerous variations of the Seisan kata. These variations all have a series of three moves that teaches a woman to defend her self with one hand while securing the baby with the other hand.

95

Seisan Kata also teaches the use of the tessen (iron fan). The Seisan practitioner is taught to draw the tessen from the obi (belt) and strike the opponent much the same as a swordsman swiftly draws his sword and cuts down his advisory. [3-14]

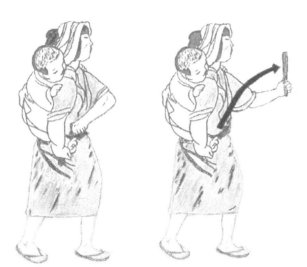

Drawing the tessen (iron fan) from the obi and striking you opponent on the head. The Shuri Seisan kata is very old and comes from Bushi Matsumura

Drawings are by the Author.
Credit Author's collection

"Be aware of your suroundings"
A lesson from a Chinese fortune cookie

OKINAWAN WHIP KICKS

A specialty of Bushi Matsumura was the whip kick. This was the style of kicking before the turn of the last century. The kick was performed by using either the tip of the toes or the outer edge of the foot as the striking surface. Sensei Kuda said the style of kicking

Okinawan of the samurai class wearing long robs. Photo Credit: Chuck Chandler collection

executed by chambering the kicking leg, bringing the knee up and then snapping the foot outward was not taught until the Okinawan men stopped wearing the long robes. The long robes would affect the efficiency of the more modern style of kicking.

These lighting fast whip kicks are kept low and are part of the Hakutsuru or White Crane influence found in Matsumura's karate system and was once part of Okinawan karate in general.

Often this kick as practiced in the Matsumura Hakutsuru kata uses two directional whip kicks (to the front and to the side). Matsumura is alleged to have killed three men by whip kicking them in the liver.

Whip kick drawing by Bob Frazer Author's collection

97

MATSUMURA AND KUSHIGAWA UEHARA

This version of the famous clash between Uehara and Bushi Matsumura was told to me by Seizan Kinjo. Kushigawa Uehara was a village tough guy who had a reputation as a good fighter; he challenged Matsumura's position as the King's chief bodyguard. As was the custom of the day, the dispute was to be settled through combat in the presence of the King. Each man threw only one punch or strike; Matsumura won by striking Uehara's punching hand and breaking it. Simple and quick Matsumura won the match.

Breaking the bones of the punching fist....technique taught
by Grandmaster Hohan Soken. Drawing by Albert Lucio
Author's collection

MATSUMURA THE WEAPONS MASTER

Matsumura was an expert at using everyday implements as weapons. He was also a renowned Sai and Bo expert and developed his own kata for each weapon. On several occasions, he defeated his opponent with a tessen (iron fan). Matsumura was also an avid pipe smoker. Once, while walking through the streets of Shuri enjoying his favorite pipe, he was suddenly attacked by a sword-wielding Samurai. In spite of the sudden attack, Matsumura avoided the razor-sharp sword and dispatched the swordsman by striking him in the head with the bowl of his pipe. Matsumura developed his own Bo Jutsu or staff fighting arts. His influenced is seen today in the Bo fighting methods from the village of Nishihara, Okinawa.

Drawing by Bob Frazer
Credit Author's collection

There is today some what of a debate among karate historians as to whether or not Sokon Matsumura was a weapons or kobujutsu practitioner. It is a debate that is well supported on all sides. First of all, in the 1960's American practitioners of the Shorin Ryu Matsumura Seito Style were given a handout about the system. The handout contained a brief history of the style; this history mentioned that Bushi Matsumura was an expert with the traditional weapons of Okinawa. A set of three books "Ryukyu Kobudo" by Motokatsu Inoue mentions Bushi Matsumura as being a weapons practitioner. There exist a somewhat rare kata called Matsumura no Sai that allegedly comes from Bushi Matsumura. More importantly Matsumura was a professional soldier of his day. It would have been in his best interest to be proficient in the use of weapons.

Bushi Matsumura is said to have been taught the Jigen Ryu Bujutsu system of the Satsuma province of Southern Japan. This was the sword fighting system of the Satsuma (Shimazu Clan) Samurai. This legend like so many other Okinawan karate legends has been handed down orally from generations to generation and is difficult to confirm. This information about Matsumura's study of Jigen Ryu was told to me by Sensei Fusei Kise as he examined my collection of Japanese swords.

This drawing was given to me by Gary Catherman.
Author's collection

"The true purpose of Kobujutsu is to protect yourself, your family, your country and others from those that would inflict harm upon them. There is no other purpose more noble than this."

A composite statement taken from many sources by the Author.

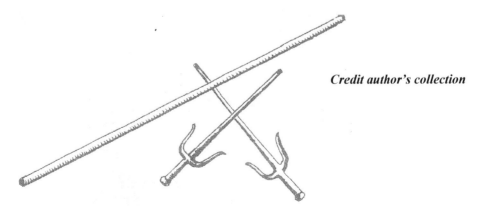

Credit author's collection

99

Nomura and Matsumura playing the sanshin.
Drawing by Albert Lucio....Author's collection

It was common for the Samurai class to play a musical instrument called the "Sanshin". It is a three stringed banjo-like musical instrument, the strings being plucked with a large bone plectrum. Sokon Matsumura was a very good sanshin player. Nomura was an Okinawan Samurai recognized as the island's best sanshin player. Even today, there is a style of the sanshin playing called Nomura Ryu.

Both Matsumura and Nomura studied and practiced Karate. Nomura was a gentleman; however, he wanted to find out if he could beat Matsumura in a shiai (fighting contest). One day he asked Matsumura for a shiai and Matsumura agreed. Now they had not decided on a date; and as time went by, Nomura figured that if he waited long enough Matsumura would forget about the shiai.

After six months or so, Nomura and Matsumura met to play sanshin music. When songs are played with the sanshin one usually sings at the same time. Okinawan songs last a long time and vocal pitch can be quite high. Nomura was to use this to his advantage; he sat on Matsumura's right hand side. He and Matsumura were to sing in tune together, and when they were both at a high note with the air exhausted from Matsumura's lungs he would attack. Nomura thought he would be able to overcome Matsumura at this point because he was younger and his lungs were in better shape.

Patiently, he waited until the last high note of the song. As soon as Matsumura hit the top of the high note, Nomura stood up on his right leg and at the same time thrust his sanshin towards Matsumura's head. Now, Matsumura was always cautious and reacted instantly to the attack. As soon as he saw the sanshin coming he jerked his head back and out of the way, at the same time he slapped the sanshin with his right had and deflected it. He was successful; had he moved any other way or tried to stand up, it would have been too late. He immediately countered with a back fist to the face of Nomura. But, instead of hitting him, he held back, his fist was the width of a hair from Nomura's face. At that instance Nomura froze and knew he had lost. He slowly backed away from Matsumura and bowed deeply then said, "I am no match for you. You have won". Matsumura was a gentleman and showed mercy by not attacking. For he thought it better for Nomura to learn from the incident rather than to kill him outright.

THE BUSHI AND THE ROOSTER

Sensei Seizan Kinjo once told me a story about an Okinawan Bushi whose life was saved by his fighting rooster. I was told this story about 41 years ago and I believe this story was about Bushi Matsumura; but to tell the truth I may be mistaken about this. I hope the readers understand that my memory is not as good as it once was and also Sensei Kinjo's English was not very good so I may err as to the actual characters of this event. This incident shows the resourcefulness of the Okinawan Bushi.

"Cock Fight"
Author's collection

Rooster fighting was and I guess it still is a pastime enjoyed by many oriental cultures. This fact was certainly true of the Okinawan culture. Many of the warrior class were avid fans of rooster fighting and many would wager large sums of money on a cock fight.

As the story goes, Bushi Matsumura had spent the afternoon pitting his favorite rooster against others at the "rooster fighting pit in the Nominoue area of Naha, Okinawa. Matsumura's rooster had been successful and had won a tidy sum of money by defeating all challengers. Many at the rooster fight had seen Matsumura put the silver coins he won in a small bag and tuck the bag into his obi. It goes without saying a number of the people watching Matsumura were sore losers and wanted their money back. As the afternoon gave way to the evening and the evening turned into night Matsumura left Nominoue by walking back to his home in Shuri.

Matsumura's route home would take him along the Azato River into a forested area that was a bit dangerous yet it was some what out of his way and he reasoned that anyone who knew he was carrying a lot of money would be waiting for him along the shortest route to Shuri. The night was well lighted by the moon and Matsumura hurried home as fast as he could walk.

As he was leaving the most dangerous area three men stepped out from the shadows and demanded that Matsumura hand them his money. Matsumura quickly saw that one man was armed with a pair of sai. Matsumura was carrying the rooster under his left upper arm. As soon as he was aware of his situation he grasps the chicken with two hands and held it in front of his chest. Almost immediately the bandit armed with the sai threw his right hand sai with a power 'flick "of his wrist at Matsumura's chest. In the blink of the eye, Matsumura instinctively used the rooster as a shield; the sai hit the rooster in the breast and the entire blade or shank of the sai stuck deep into the rooster. Quickly Matsumura pulled the sai out of the breast of the chicken and threw the weapon into the chest of his attacker still armed with another sai. Matsumura's aim was true. The sai hit the bandit's heart killing him instantly. The other two bandits fled in fear for their lives.

THE MEIJI RESTORATION

The late 1860s and through the 1870s was a very difficult time for both Japan and Okinawa. For those of us who are greatly interested in the history of both Okinawan Karate and the Japanese Martial Arts; we must understand the political and social situation of this era.

In 1864, Okinawan envoys traveled to Peking, China, carrying Okinawa's annual tribute and pledges of loyalty to Peking from the young Okinawan King Sho Tai. Two years later, Chinese ambassadors came to Okinawa court to confirm these loyalties. The ambassadors were the last to perform these rites. This diplomatic activity had continued in unbroken tradition for five hundred years. In November, the ambassadors returned to China, the ancient relationship between Okinawa and China was finished. [3-15]

In February 1867, the Emperor of Japan died. Japanese Crown Prince Mutsuhiro, then fifteen years of age, succeeded his father as Emperor of Japan. Mutsuhiro was crowned Emperor Meiji and would reign until his death in 1911. Thus the Japanese Empire (and all of her provinces (including Okinawa) entered into the time era known as the Meiji Restoration. This signaled the end to the Samurai Class of both Okinawa and Japan.

On October 3, 1867, representatives of some forty feudal lords met at Kyoto to discuss the resignation of the Shogun. A letter was sent to the Shogun at Edo (Tokyo), advising him to relinquish his control of Japan to the Emperor Meiji. The Shimazu clan of Satsuma Province in Southern Japan was the first to sign this letter. [3-16]

This coalition of feudal lords was too powerful for the Shogun to defy. A short time later, the Shogun submitted his resignation. This marked the end of the Tokugawa military government and change Japan forever. The Tokugawa Shoguns had controlled Japan for 267 years. In January 1868, the reign - name of the Japanese Empire was changed to "Meiji", meaning "Era of Enlightened Government". Japan was on the road to modernization. This was the beginning of intense nationalistic attitudes that eventually led to Japan's total defeat at the end of World War II. The old feudal order of Japan had ended; for the Okinawa Bushi it was the beginning of the end of their way of life.

Technically, the Tokugawa Clan had surrendered control of only those territories over which it exercised direct feudal control. The new imperial government now had to call upon each feudal lord individually to surrender his province and other lands that he controlled.

In August 1869, the Shimazu Clan, overlords of the Satsuma province took the lead. All the Clan's territories including the Ryukyu Islands were placed under the control of the new government. Within two years all of the feudal lords of Japan had surrendered their lands to the control of the Meiji Government.

The Shimazu Clan had gained control over Okinawa in 1609. Their "rule" over Okinawa was not extremely strict. The Okinawans were allowed to keep their king, their ancient social order, customs, and their autonomy. As long as the Okinawans paid their annual tribute to the Shimazu Clan; they were allowed considerable freedoms. The Okinawans also paid an annual tribute to China. Although the Okinawans were discreet about their payments to China; the Shimazu officials were aware of this activity and somewhat reluctantly allowed it to go on.

The Meiji Era arrived with a "crash". The social order of Japan changed rapidly. The Samurai class was abolished; they were made to cut off their topknot hairstyle. The wearing of swords was made illegal. In Japan, as much as possible, dispossessed samurai and aristocracy were used to fill newly created government jobs. Many formed the core of the newly created military.

Nevertheless, there was resistance. Samurai revolts were commonplace. The last of these revolts occurred in Satsuma in 1877, the samurai rebels were defeated by government troops. The Meiji government's control of Japan was complete. Now she could turn her attention to the islands south of Japan.

The Last Okinawan King, Sho Tai
Photo Credit:
Wikipedia Commons

In 1875 a Japanese Imperial Decree was sent to the Okinawan King with numerous demands that had to be met. The Okinawan King and feudal lords were expected to acknowledge and carry out these demands made by the Meiji government, as had all of the Japanese feudal lords. Sho Tai was to travel to Tokyo for consolation with the Japanese Emperor. Sho Tai ignored these demands; he feigned illness and would not leave Okinawa.

Sho Tai fully expected China to come to his rescue. The Japanese on the other hand were jealous and fearful of Okinawa's long relationship with China. If the Meiji government wished to solidify its southern border; Sho Tai must be forced to conform to the demands of the Japanese Imperial Government.

On March 30, 1879; Sho Tai was forced to withdraw from Shuri Castle. The castle was quickly occupied by Japanese troops. The demand for Sho Tai to visit Tokyo was again made; again, he feigned illness to avoid the trip. On May 18, the Japanese steamship "Tokai-maru" arrived at Naha with the first Japanese Governor of Okinawa, Nabeshima Naokira. Also on board was an imperial court physician Dr. Takashima. Over the protest of Sho Tai and Okinawan court officials Dr. Takashima certified the King to be physically fit for the journey to Tokyo.

Finally, Sho Tai gave in and abdicated his throne. On May 27, 1879, the last King of the Ryukyu now thirty-six years of age set sail for exile in Japan; accompanied by a group of ninety-six courtiers. Sho Tai and his courtiers docked at Yokohama on June 8 and traveled by train to Tokyo. The King, his family and many of his attendants would never see Okinawa again.

Bushi Matsumura was among these ninety-six courtiers. He was near 80 years of age. His grandson, Nabe Matsumura, who was a scribe for the Okinawan Court was slated to go to Tokyo as one of the courtiers. However, the old "Bushi" advised against this; Nabe was urged to remain in Okinawa and to go into hiding. [3-17]

Bushi Matsumura had offered his grandson wise advice. To complete their mastery over the Okinawans; the Japanese police arrested large numbers of Okinawan leaders. They were held in jails, subjected to long persuasive lectures and threatened with physical violence.

The Okinawan gentry were no longer masters in their own land. Japanese filled most of the newly created government posts. The new comers took precedence over the old aristocracy, and formed a new elite. The Okinawa Samurai Class was in ruin and many were left destitute. The Matsumura family, like most of the Okinawan Samurai Class, had lost their fortune and their high rank in society.

The old "Bushi" with no king to serve was retired. Many of the Okinawan gentry received a stipend that lasted for a short time. It is reported that Bushi Matsumura never regained his fortune and died in relative poverty. Nabe Matsumura moved from Shuri to Nishihara Village. The Meiji Restoration was difficult for the Okinawan people to accept. It created anti Japanese feelings among the Okinawan people that lasted for generations. Anti Japanese feelings were strong among several of the Okinawan karate masters that I knew. [3-18]

MATSUMURA'S STUDENTS

The Bushi taught many famous students, among these were:

Anko Itosu (1832-1915)   Ishimine Shinchi (1812-1892)
Anko Asato (1827-1908)   Tawata Shinboku (1814-1884)
Kensu Yabu (1866-1937)   Chinen Mahsanra (1842-1925)
Chomo Hanashiro (1869-1945)   Kobashigawa Kyosho (1854-1922)
Sakihara Pechin   Kiyuna Pechin no Tanmei
Nabe Matsumura (grandson) (1860's -1930's)
Ryosei Kuwei (1863-1920's)
Chotoku Kyan (1870-1945)

Matsumura taught each of his students differently. Many of his students went on to develop their own style of karate. Today, styles such as Kobayashi Ryu, Shobayashi Ryu, Shorinji Ryu, and others can be traced back to Bushi Matsumura. These styles are all members of the original Suide (Shuri-te) Family. Bushi Matsumura left the "hands" of his teachings to his grandson, Nabe Matsumura. Karateka all over the world owe a debt of gratitude to Bushi Matsumura and his students.

The following is a copy of Bushi Matsumura letter to Ryosei Kuwae, this document has been in the Kuwae family since the 1880's:

Reproduction of the Matsumura Bucho Ikku; Credits: Author's collection

Drawing from Little Pictures from Japan

Author's collection

"To Kuwae Ryusei:

These are my teachings that you must understand and make your own. You must firmly resolve to study deeply if you wish to understand the truth of the Martial Arts. This resolve is very important. Fundamentally, the literary arts (Bun) and the martial arts (Bu) are the same. Each has three elements.

As far as art is concerned there are Shishu no Gaku, Kunko no Gaku, and Jussha no Gaku. Shishu no Gaku is the act of creative writing and reading; in other words, the study of literature. Kunko no Gaku means to study the past to gain an understanding of ethics by relating past events to our way of life. Both Shishu no Gaku and Kunko no Gaku are incomplete until supplemented by Jussha no Gaku, the study of the moral aspects of Confucius.

Have a tranquil heart and you can prevail over a village, a country or the world. The study of Jusshu no Gaku is the supreme study over both Shishu no Gaku and Kunko no Gaku. They are then the three elements necessary for the study of the arts.

If we consider Budo, there are three precepts. They are Kukushi no Bugei, Meimoko no Bugei, and Budo no Bugei. Kukushi no Bugei is nothing more than a technical knowledge of Bugei. Like a woman, it is superficial and has no depth. Meimoko no Bugei refers to a person who has physical understanding of Bugei. He can be a powerful and violent person who can even harm his own family. Budo no Bugei is what I admire. With this you can let the enemy destroy himself, just wait with calm heart and the enemy will defeat himself. People who practice Budo no Bugei are loyal to their friends, to their parents and to their country. They will do nothing that is considered unnatural or contrary to nature. We have the seven virtues of Bu and they are:
1 Bu prohibits violence
2. Bu keeps discipline as in soldiers
3. Bu keeps control among the population
4. Bu spreads virtues
5. Bu gives one a peaceful heart
6. Bu helps keep the peace between people
7. Bu makes people of a nation prosperous

Our forefathers handed these seven virtues down to us. Just as Jussha no Gaku is supreme in the arts, so Budo is supreme in the martial arts. Mon-bu (art and martial arts) have the same common elements. We do not need Kukushi no Bugei or Meimoko no Bugei; they are not necessary. We do need Budo no Bugei...this is the most important thing.

I leave these words to my wise and beloved student Kuwae.
Matsumura Sokon"

MATSUMURA-HA

An entire book could be written about Matsumura-Ha (Matsumura linage). However, there are only perhaps four of Matsumura's students whose legacy greatly influenced karate world wide and whose legacy can be found in dojo all over the world. Anko Itosu, Anko Azato, Chotoku Kyan, and Nabe Matsumura, all left their mark on the karate world. We will discuss the first three in this subchapter (Matsumura-Ha); Nabe Matsumura is not as well known than the other three; his legacy will be discussed in Chapter 4.

Computer generated photo of Bushi Matsumura standing in front of the Engaku-ji. Computer generated photo by the Author. Photo credit: Author's collection

Bushi Matsumura was alleged to have conducted his classes either at his home or in the Shuri Castle complex. It is said that one of the places within the castle complex where Matsumura would often teach was in the courtyard in front of the main gate of the "Engaku-ji." This was a Buddhist Temple within the castle grounds. [3-19]

Drawing from "Little Pictures of Japan" Published by The Book House for Children pictures

Masters Itosu and Azato had many things in common. The first of which were their given names. Both were named Anko, which in the Okinawan dialect is pronounced "Yasutsune". Both were born into the privileged class; and they were approximately the same age. Master Azato was born in 1827 in the village of Azato and died in 1906. Master Itosu was born in Shuri Village in 1830 and died in 1915. The name Itosu in Okinawan Hogan is pronounced "Shishu" and Azato (Okinawan Hogan) would be pronounced as "Yazusato" in Japan. [3-20]

The Azato Clan of Okinawa was among the "Tonochi" class, which were the hereditary chiefs of towns and villages. They had been the leaders of the Azato village for many generations. The Azato family had been treated as the equal of the Governor of Okinawa. The social position of both Masters Azato and Itosu afforded them the opportunity to receive an education in the traditional Four Chinese Classics and the Five Chinese Classics of Confucius. This education also included the learning of martial arts.

Masters Itosu's training is alleged to have started at the age of seven, when his father would tie him to a pole and poke at the young boy with a stick to develop his fighting spirit. In 1846, Itosu's father asked Bushi Matsumura to accept the boy as a student to learn Matsumura's style of "Ti". Itosu was also quite well trained in Bo Jutsu.

The young Azato also became a student of Bushi Matsumura. Master Azato's training also included horsemanship, kenjutsu and archery. Master Azato became one of Okinawa's leading swordsmen. He was extremely well schooled in Jigen Ryu, the sword or Kenjutsu style of the Japanese Samurai from Satsuma Province. Both Masters Itosu and Azato studied with not only Matsumura; but, also with a master named Gusukuma (Shiroma in Japanese). Gusukuma was said to have studied under a Chinese man who had drifted ashore on Okinawa. Itosu also studied with a Nahate master named Nagahama

Modern tsuba made of brass with a carved dragon for decoration. Credit: Author's collection

The greatest strategic asset possessed by both Masters Itosu and Azato was the value they placed on education. They were both brilliant scholars and were tolerant and open minded. These character traits served them well during the political unrest, which Okinawa experienced, in the late 1800's.

Physically the two masters were very much different. Traditionally the Okinawan karate masters taught their students according to the student's physical attributes. Matsumura and Gusukuma following this custom, they taught Itosu and Azato differently.

Anko Itosu...Credit: Robert Teller collection

Azato was tall with broad shoulders. Azato possessed a very athletic build. Itosu on the other hand was of average height with a massive barrel chest. He developed somewhat of a large belly as he grew older. Itosu stood about 5'2" and was said to weigh over 220 pounds which was very heavy for an Okinawan. Itosu possessed great strength in his arms and hands. He would often entertain on lookers by crushing large bamboo staves with the strength of his handgrip.

Yoriyuki Yasuzato (Grandson of Anko Azato) James Knoblet collection

Azato was taught to think of his arms, hands and feet as swords. His training as a swordsman reinforced this concept. Azato's success as a swordsman proved that he was very mobile; a swordsman who is not mobile soon would be a dead swordsman. Azato is generally acknowledged to have developed his style to closely follow Matsumura's principles.

Master Azato was very astute and well aware of local and international political affairs. When Russia began building the Trans-Siberian Railroad, he accurately predicted that Japan and Russia would go to war. This was many years before the Russo-Japanese War of 1904. Master Azato was also an expert in Minari no Heiho (strategy of appearance) and an expert in "military intelligence" as it applied to Okinawa during this time period. He gathered considerable information about the various Okinawan samurai. This information not only included their names and addresses but also their strengths, weakness, favorite techniques, and a record of their combat success or failures.

Itosu on the other hand used his great strength to his advantage. Itosu believed that a karateka could develop his body until it was as hard as steel. If we examine Itosu's version of the Gojushiho Kata we can gain much insight to Itosu's technique and attitude. The Itosu version of this kata differs somewhat from other versions in the way the numerous nukite or "spear hand" thrusts are executed. Most of the nukite techniques appearing in this kata are executed with the open left hand being held near the elbow of the right arm. Itosu's method when executing this same technique is to chamber the left closed fist on the left hip. Clearly Itosu is grabbing his opponent, pulling him off balance and using his right spear hand to finish his opponent.

He depended on body hardening to protect him in case his blocks failed. Itosu's technique seems to be fairly simple. His record of success in combat is legendary. His many victories are proof that at least for him, his heiho or strategy was correct. There is no record of either Itosu or Azato ever being defeated.

On the left is technique from Matsumura's Gojushiho kata; on the right the same technique from Itosu's Gojushiho kata.

Itosu's technique reflects the confidence Itosu had in his great strength. On the other hand Matsumura's technique places him in a better position to continue the attack if needed.

Shuri Castle main gate 1853, during Matthew Perry's visit. Author's collection

110

Dedication of a monument to Anko Itosu Aug. 8, 1964
From L to R (1) Choshin Chibana, (2) Katsuya Miyahira, (3) Shugoro Nakazato, and (4)
Chozo Nakama…Chibana and Nakama had been students of Itosu
Sid Campbell's collection

AZATO AND ITOSU'S STUDENTS

According to Okinawan Karate Folklore, Azato had only two students, Funakoshi Gichin and Ogushiku (Oshiro) Chogo. Funakoshi went on to be instrumental in introducing Okinawan Karate-Do to Japan and eventually his students developed Shotokan, one of the world's most popular karate styles.

Unlike Azato, Itosu left many students to continue his teachings. His students developed most of the Shurite styles practiced today. The following are some of Itosu's students these students and their students are known as *Itosu-Ha:*

Kensu Yabu (1866-1937)
Chomo Hanashiro (1869-1944)
Kenyu Kudenken (1865-1940)
Chotoku Kyan (1870)-1945)
Choki Motobu (1870-1944)
Kanken Toyama (1888-1966)
Gichin Funakoshi (1870-1958)

Chorin Yamakawa (1898-?)
Moden Yabiku (1880-1941)
Chosin Chibana (1885-1969)
Anbun Takuda (1886-1945)
Choyo Oshiro (18889-1934)
Kenwa Mabuni (1889-1952)
Shimpan Shiroma (1889-1954)

"Anger begins with folly and ends with regret"

A lesson from a Chinese fortune cookie.

111

*On the left Anbun Takuda; below a gathering of Okinawan master meet in 1936 to replace the old traditional name of Karate (tode) meaning Chinese hand with karate meaning empty hands. Bottom row left to right: Chotoku Kyan, Kensu Yabu, Chomo Hanashiro; second row left to right; Shinpan Shiroma, unidentified, Choshin Chibana, Genwa Nakazone. Out of the eight masters **attending this meeting**, five were of Itosu-ha.*
Both photos are from the Author's collection.

ITOSU-HA

Anko Itosu had many students and a number of these students had a great impact on the spread and development of Okinawan Karate. Probably the following individuals are the Itosu-ha practitioners that had the greatest impact on the spread of Itosu's art through out the world: ***Gichin Funakoshi, Kanken Toyama, Kenwa Mabuni and Choshin Chibana.***

> *"True wealth does not depend on money; it depends on how you serve your fellow man."*
> A lesson from a Chinese fortune cookie.

Gichin Funakoshi was born into a Shuri *shizoku* family in 1868. Sickly as a young child young Funakoshi developed a strong friendship with the son of Anko Azato at a fairly young age Azato was one of Okinawa's most famous samurai of this time era. It was not long before young Funakoshi was accepted as a student of Master Azato. Through Azato he was introduced to Master Itosu who was a close friend of Anko Azato. Therefore, Funakoshi was actually a student of both Itosu and Azato.

Gichin Funakoshi became a school teacher and became one of the many Okinawan Karate Instructors who taught karate in the Okinawan public schools. Around 1920 Gichin Funakoshi moved to Tokyo, Japan and introduced karate to Japan. His art spread through the various Japanese Universities and his teachings became the style of Shotokan; which became the dominant style of karate taught and practice in Japan.

Gichin Funakoshi 1922
Photo credit: Author's collection

For many years before the knowledge about the origins of karate became generally known through out the world; to speak of karate was to speak of Shotokan. This was perhaps to first karate style that spread from Japan/Okinawa into the United States then to Europe and the rest of the world.

Gichin Funakoshi loyalty to his samurai heritage taught him to be a gentleman first and a karate master second. He was well schooled in both the "pen and the sword." It may very well be that without the activities of Gichin Funakoshi the art of karate may have become extinct. Sensei Funakoshi died in 1957.

Kanken Toyama (1888-1966) started his martial arts career by studying karate under Itarashiki. Itarashiki had been a student of Bushi Matsumura. He began training under Itosu in 1906. He also studied Nahate under Kanryo Higashionna in the early 1900's. Toyama also studied with Kensu Yabu, Kuwae Ryosei, plus Chinese white crane masters in Taiwan.

The Toyama family traced its lineage back to the Okinawan King, Sho Shin. In the 1930's Kanken changed his name from Oyadomari to Toyama. The Oyadomari family was among the founders of Okinawa Tomarite karate. They were famous samurai.

Kanken Toyama moved to Tokyo, Japan in 1932. Shortly after, he established the Shudokan. Kanken Toyama saw the art of Okinawan Karate change from Tode (Chinese hand) to Karate (empty hand). His Shudokan Karate is widely practiced in Japan and can be found in many countries through out the world.

Kenwa Mabuni (1889-1952) was a descendent of an old Okinawan samurai family. His ancestors were the Lords of Mabuni Village. He began his study of karate under Master Itosu in 1902. He studied under Itosu until Itosu's death in 1915.

After the death of Itosu he began studying under Kanryo Higashionna. Mabuni also studied sai jutsu under Tawata, and Bojutsu under Soeishi and white crane under Gokenki. In the 1930's he moved to Osaka Japan. He called his style "Shito Ryu" which became a major style in Japan and later spread all over the world.

Choshin Chibana (1885-1969) is often called the "Last Bushi of Shuri", Okinawa. He was a descendent of King Sho Shitsu, who was King of Okinawa in the mid 1600's.

Kenwa Mabuni seated in the middle. Gichen Funakoshi standing far left.
Photo credit: Author's collection

Choshin Chibana began studying under at the age of 15 years. He trained under Itosu until the old master died in 1916. Out of all of Itosu's students, it is Chibana's method that is the best representative of the original Itosu method. Choshin Chibana called his style Shorin Ryu; which can also be pronounced Kobayashi Ryu.

Choshin Chibana founder of Kobayashi Ryu
"The Last Bushi of Shuri"

Photo credit: Sid Campbell's collection

Choshin Chibana left a number of students among these are: Ankichi Arakaki (1899-1929, Chozo Nakama (1899-1981), Yuchoku Higa (1910-1994), Katsuya Miyahira (1914-2011), Shugoro Nakazato (1920-), (Seito Ishigawa 1924-), and Katsuyuki Shimabukuro (1928-).

There are perhaps two of Sensei Chibana's students that have played a great role in spreading the art of karate from Okinawa to the rest of the world. These are Katsuya Miyahira and Shugoro Nakazato.

Katsuya Miyahira has played an important role in spreading the Kobayashi Ryu style of Chibana into South America, and the Philippines. Miyahira's Shidokan style has hundreds of black belt students in these areas.

Shugoro Nakazato calls his version of Choshin Choshin's Shorin Ryu "Shorin Kan". Through out the world there are thousands of devotees to the Shorin Kan method.

Photo on the right :Sensei Miyahira teaching Jorge Brinkman kata. Credit Author's collection

On the left: 1968 Shugoro Nakazato standing Choshin Chibana sitting. Photo credit: Author's collection

Below L to R: Shugoro Nakazato and son Minoru. Photo credit: Charles Dean collection

Front Row Left to Right: Pat Haley, Doug Perry, Chris Estes, and Shawn Riley,
Back row L to R: Mike Arnold, Ronald Lindsey, Eddie Bethea, and Noel Smith
All of the above follow Matsumura-ha; Sensei's Haley, Perry, Estes, Riley, Bethea,
and Smith follow the Itosu-ha branch of Matsumura-ha while Mike Arnold received
much of his training in the Kyan-ha branch of Matsumura-ha and Ronald Lindsey
trains in the Matsumura Seito (Orthodox) branch of Matsumura-ha.
"All are different; yet all are the same"

Drawing by the author

116

KYAN-HA

In the 1960's in Sensei Fusei Kise's Seishin Kan Dojo in Koza, Okinawa there was very little art work decorating the dojo. The only picture I can remember was a small 3x5 inch photo of a skinny old man. I asked several of the Okinawan Blackbelt students about this photo. However, no one knew who this old man was or if he was still alive or anything about him. Finally I asked Sensei Kise about the photo and he told me that it was a photo of "Chumeigwa." It was a long time before I learned anything else about the man in the photo.

Chumeigwa means "small eyed Kyan" and it was the nick name of one of Okinawa's most famous Karate masters. His name was Chotoku Kyan.

This is a copy of the 3x5 inch photo that was on display in Sensei Kise's Dojo. Photo credit: Author's collection

Chotoku Kyan (1870-1945) was born in Shuri, Okinawa. His father, Chofu, was of the Samurai class and was in the service of the Okinawan King and insured that his son, Chotoku, received the type of education befitting the son of an Okinawan Bushi.

Chotoku Kyan was introduced to karate by studying under his father when he was about 12 years old. Chotoku preserved his father's teachings and also studied under the following Okinawan Masters and learned the following kata:

Sokon Matsumura
   Kata: Seisan, Naihanchi and Gojushiho
Yara Chatan
   Kata: Kusanku
Kohan Oyadomari
   Kata: Pai Sai
Maeda Pechin
   Kata: Wansu
Kosaku Matsumora
   Kata: Chinto
Tokumine Pechin
   Kata: Bo Kata "Tokumine no Kun"

This list of the sources for Chotoku Kyan's kata was given to me by Mike Arnold who trained in Houston Texas in a dojo founded by Mike Richardson. Mr. Richardson was a student of Zenryo Shimabukuro the founder of the Shorin Ryu Seibukan Dojo which is of the Chotoku Kyan lineage.

Chotoku Kyan's karate was a blend of Matsumura's Shurite and the Tomarite of Oyadomari and Matsumora. He was very small yet the Okinawan people regarded him as a strong powerful man. He fought in many contests and historical records state that he was never defeated. Kyan's strength was not based on muscular or physical strength. Kyan was an expert on leverage, timing and using natural forces; his strength was not the strength of youth but the strength of techniques that rises above the dependence on strong muscles. His was a rare art. Perhaps the passage found in the Holy Bible, Psalms 33:16, gives us and insight and a better understanding of Kyan's strength:

"No king is saved by the size of his army; no warrior escapes by his great strength."

Chotoku Kyan taught a number of people who went on to become great masters. The following are some of his students:

Ankichi Arakaki
Taro Shimabukuro
Shoshin Nagamine (Matsubayashi Ryu)
Joen Nakazato (Shorinji Ryu)
Zenryo Shimabukuro (Shorin Ryu Seibukan)
Tatsuo Shimabukuro (Isshin Ryu)
Eizo Shimabukuro (Shorin Ryu Shobayashi)

Photo of Chotoku Kyan and some of his students (1930's or early 1940's era).
Joen Nakazato on the far left and to his left is Chotoku Kyan
Photo credit: Author's collection

118

Out of the seven people that are generally acknowledged as the principle students of Chotoku Kyan all but two of them (Ankichi Arakaki and Taro Shimabukuro) went on to become famous Grandmaster and developed their own styles and spread their version of Chotoku Kyan's karate to thousands of people scattered across the world.

Shoshin Nagamine (1907-1997) studied under Ankichi Arakaki, Taro Shimabukuro, Chojin Kuba, Kodatsu Iha, and Choki Motobu as well as Chotoku Kyan. Nagamine Sensei founded Matsubayashi (Shorin) Ryu in 1947.

Sensei Nagamine was instrumental in the founding of the first Okinawan Karate Federation and he was elected as this organization's first Vice President in 1956. Shoshin Nagamine was a fine martial artist and a gentleman. He produced many students; he passed on the following 18 kata:

Shoshin Nagamine Photo credit: Author's collection

Fukyu Ichi, Ni; Pinan Sho Dan, Ni Dan, San Dan, Yon Dan and Go Dan; Naihanchi Sho Dan, Ni Dan, and San Dan; Ananku, Wakan, Rohai, Wansu, Pai Sai, Gojushiho, Chinto, and Kusanku. He also taught the use of the Bo, Nunchaku, Sai, Tonfa, and Kama.

Shoshin Nagamine Photo credit: Dev. Ogle Collection

Zenryo Shimabukuro (1904-1969) started studying under Chotoku Kyan in 1928 and studied under the old master until 1944. Zenryo Shimabukuro probably studied under Master Kyan longer than any of Kyan's other students.

Seibukan Dojo July 22, 1962
(1) Ben Swartz, (2) Mike Richardson, (3) Grandmaster Zenryo Shimabukuro, (4) Walt Daley
(5) Zempo Shimabukuro
Photo credit: Author's collection

Below: Mike Richardson receiving a promotion from Sensei Shimabukuro. Photo credit: Author's collection

Zenryo Shimabukuro played a major role in organizing and forming the Okinawan branch of the all Japanese Karatedo Federation, and the All Okinawan Karatedo Federation.

Zenryo Shimabukuro passed on Chotoku Kyan's kata to his student in their original form. He was succeeded by his son, Zempo.

It is generally agreed by students and historian knowledgeable in Chotoku Kyan's karate that he taught only four individuals his complete system. These individuals are ***Ankichi Arakaki, Taro Shimabukuro, Zenryo Shimabukuro, and Joen Nakazato;*** all are now deceased.

Joen Nakazato, (1922-2011), began his study under Chotoku Kyan in 1935. At this time Kyan was teaching karate at the Okinawan Prefectural Agricultural School. Nakazato enrolled in this school in 1933. Joen Nakazato studied karate under Chotoku Kyan until 1940 when Nakazato was drafted into the Japanese military.

Nakazato Sensei returned to Okinawa from World War II in 1947. He began teaching Chotoku Kyan's art in the court yard of his home in Chinen Village. In 2010 He was still living in his Chinen Village home and still teaching in his dojo next to his home.

Joen Nakazato student of Chotoku Kyan and founder of Shorinji Ryu Photo Credit: The Author's collection

Tatsuo Shimabukuro founder of Isshin Ryu Photo credit: Author's collection

Tatsuo Shimabukuro (1908-1975) was born in the tiny village of Kyan located in central Okinawa. He began his karate training from his uncle. In 1931 or 1932 he began training under Chotoku Kyan. He trained with Kyan for 4 years.

In 1936 he began studying Goju Ryu under Chojun Miyagi. In 1938 through 1939 he studied with Choki Motobu. He was a farmer and did not serve in the Japanese military during World War II.

He started teaching karate in Kyan Village Okinawa in 1947. He began calling his style "Chumeigwa" but in 1956 he changed the name to ***Isshin Ryu.***

Tatsuo Shimabukuro taught many students. He was a great exporter of Okinawa karate. He was a pioneer among Okinawan karate Masters by opening his classes to many American military servicemen (primarily Marine Corps personnel) in the early to mid 1950's.

Tatsou Shimabukuro founded the system called **Isshin Ryu Karatedo.** Isshin means one heart or one mind and is an old warrior principle of the single minded, whole-hearted attitude needed to learn a martial art. Grandmaster Shimabukuro's style started in the tiny village of Kyan; now Isshin Ryu is one of the world's most popular karate styles.

Top photo: Tatsuo Shimabukuro at his Central Dojo. Bottom Photo: Group photo
Tatsuo Shimabukuro front row center, on his left is his son Kichiro.
Photo credits: Paul Bystedt collection

"An inch of time buys an inch of gold.
An inch of gold can not buy an inch of time."
A lesson from a Chinese fortune cookie

Eizo Shimabukuro (born in 1925) is a brother of Tatsuo Shimabukuro and like his brother; Eizo Shimabukuro is one of Okinawa's greatest Karate Masters. Eizo Shimabukuro began his training in 1937 under Chotoku Kyan and trained with Kyan until 1943. In 1938 he started to train in Goju Ryu under Chojun Miyagi. In 1943 Eizo Shimabukuro moved to Osaka, Japan; there, he trained with Choki Motobu. He also trained under his brother Tatsuo Shimabukuro the founder of Isshin Ryu.

In 1948 Eizo Shimabukuro was back in Okinawa and opened his first Karate Dojo. In 1955 he continued his karate education by studying under Zenryo Shimabukuro. In 1955, Eizo Shimabukuro was promoted to 10 Dan (Ju Dan) by Kanken Toyama and appointed the Okinawa representative to the All Japan Karatedo Federation. In the 1960's he donned a white belt and became a student of Choshin Chibana and learned the kata of Anko Itosu.

Photo on the right: Sensei Shimabukuro in 1979 at the age of 61. Below: a group of students and Sensei Shimabukuro

I believe the American student on the top row second from the right is Sam Pearson. Both photos credit: John Murphy collection

The question of how effective was the fighting art of the Okinawan Bushi can be answered by the following story about Eizo Shimabukuro. This story is from an interview with Bill Hayes a number of years ago. Bill Hayes is one of Eizo Shimabukuro's senior students. The interview was for the "Maishin Shorinji Magazine" that I produced a few years ago. So let me start with the question I asked Mr. Hayes:

Question asked to Bill Hayes: Grandmaster Shimabukuro was and is famous for his toe kicks and other fighting skills. Are you familiar with the story of him defeating an American Boxer with several toe kicks to the inside of the boxer's thighs? I am sure you experienced these kicks…your thoughts on these kicks and his other skills.

Mr. Hayes's answer: "Grandmaster Shimabukuro is known for his "Honto waza" (his true and effective techniques), one of which is his famous toe kick. One of the better known stories about his use of the toe kick harkens back to the 1940's. Just after the end of World War II, Shimabukuro O'Sensei was held as a prisoner of war and was forced to work at the Tengan Warehouse. American occupying forces were very suspicious of all Okinawans (they did not know their character and mistakenly compared them to the defeated Japanese). These suspicions and misunderstandings led to frequent physical maltreatment of the Okinawans.

One day during a work break a boxing match was held between the Americans and the Okinawans. Shimabukuro's squad leader received a challenge from a 250 pound American named Brown. He and O'Sensei were about the same age (22 or 23) but O'Sensei weighed only about 120 pounds! They faced off at about 6 feet apart and made no moves for over a minute. Then Brown tried to take the initiative; in the process O'Sensei performed Taisabaki (dodging) and threw a toe kick that caught Brown in the thigh knocking him down. The fight was over in an instant and the Okinawan sang a song of praise for Okinawan karate.

After recovering, Brown complimented young Shimabukuro and showed his humility and helpfulness by making sure O'Sensei had a little gift of some sort. When the work day was over O'Sensei was allowed to return home."

Grandmaster Eizo Shimabukuro, small by western standards, is a little man made of steel. He has made his contribution to the preservation of Okinawan Karate and he continues to do so as he teaches daily in his dojo near Kin Village in Central Okinawan.

Masters such as Shimabukuro Sensei are rapidly disappearing from the island where they once were common place. If you have ever trained with one of these old Okinawan Masters; cherish the memory because they will soon all be gone.

"Who can doubt the effectiveness of the Okinawan Bushi's art?"

ENDNOTES, SOURCES AND EXPLANATIONS

Much of the information comes from General Okinawan Karate History and Folklore plus conversations with various Okinawan Karate Masters, and their American students. Some of these conversations and correspondence occurred over 30 years ago. Therefore, some errors may exist as I present my sources and explanations. Nevertheless, I will present these to the best of my ability.

Sokon (Bushi) Matsumura: General History

3-1   *Source: Source: Fusei Kise, Seizan Kinjo*

3-2   *Ibid*

3-3   *Source: Interviews with Okinawan Karate Masters conducted by Ernest Estrada in 1978.*

3-4   *Source: General Karate Folklore handed down to me from my Shorin Ryu Matsumura Seito* **teachers.**

3-5   *Ibid*

3-6   *Source: Bishop, Mark.* Okinawa Karate: Teachers, Styles, and Secret Techniques. *A: C Black, 1989. Pg 63.*

3-7   *Source: conversations with Rick Rose, Fusei Kise and Yuichi Kuda; Rick Rose was a student of Hohan Soken and Fusei Kise*

3-8   *Explanation: Wai Shi Xian is somewhat of a mystery.* The Bubishi *written by Patrick McCarthy   copyright 1990 on page 14 indicates that Wai Shi Xian was a master of the "Five Ancestor Fist" and may have been one of Kanryo Higashionna's teachers. Ernest Estrada in an interview with Katsuya Miyahira states that Wai Shi Xian was one of Bushi Matsumura's teachers. Alexander L. Co in his book,* Five-Ancestor Fist Kung Fu *published by Charles E. Tuttle Co. in 1996; states the founder of the "Five Ancestor Fist Style, Chya Giok Beng, was born in Fukein Province in 1853. In all probability Wai Shi Xian predates the style of the Five Ancestor Fist. Bushi Matsumura's training also predates the creation of this style. Wai Shi Xian remains a mystery.*

Matsumura's Kata

3-8   *Sources: conversations with Rick Rose and Fusei Kise*

3-9   *Source: Information told to me by Yuichi Kuda and told to Chuck Chandler by Takaya Yabiku. The main Hakutsuru Kata Matsumura learned in China was simply called over time it became known as Matsumura Hakutsuru, Matsumura Family Hakutsuru, or Machimuraya touti nu Hakutsuru (Matsumura Family's Chinese hand White Crane kata)..*

Matsumura the Man

4-11   *Source: Correspondence with Ernest Estrada mid-1980's and conversations with Fusei Kise.*

3-12   **Ibid**

Matsumura and His Wife

3-13   *Sources: conversation with my Okinawan Matsumura Seito teachers.*

3-14   **Ibid**

Okinawan Whip Kicks

General Sources for this section are conversations with Seizan Kinjo.

Matsumura and Kushigawa Uehara

Sources: Story of this version of the famous clash between Matsumura and Uehara was told to me by Seizan Kinjo.

Matsumura the Weapons Master

Ibid

Matsumura and Nomura Clash

This story was provided by Anthony Sandoval.

The Meiji Restoration

Most of the information for this section comes from "Okinawa, The History of an Island Nation by George Kerr; published by Charles Tuttle Company 1958.

3-15   *Source: Kerr, George. Okinawa: History of an Island People. Published by Charles Tuttle Co. 1958, pg. 352*
3-16   *Explanation: Shogun…. The Military Governor of Japan during the Feudal Era*
3-17   *Source: conversation with Yuichi Kuda.*
3-18   *Source: conversations with Fusei Kise and Yuichi Kuda*

Matsumura's Students

Explanation: The words hands used in this passage refer to Matsumura's style of karate. When Matsumura gave his 'hands" to his Grandson Nabe, he was indicating that Nabe Matsumura was his successor. Historians often ask an interesting question…Did Bushi Matsumura give a "Menkyo Kaiden" to anyone? No one really knows the answer to this question. The Menkyo Kaiden (a certificate of final teachings) is a Japanese tradition and a master usually gives such a document to his successor. Matsumura was schooled in the Chinese traditions; Japanese martial arts traditions were quite new or were not in wide usage in the Ryukyu Islands during this time. Therefore, it is quite possible that Matsumura did not issue a Menkyo Kaiden to anyone. The list of Matsumura's students comes from bits and pieces of information from numerous sources collected over 40 years.

Matsumura Bucho Ikku

This copy of the Matsumura Bucho Ikku is from "Uechi Ryu Karate-Do Master Text"
By Kanei Uechi and other Uechi Ryu Seniors

Matsumura-Ha

3-19   *Sources: conversations with Yuichi Kuda and Fusei Kise.*

Anko Itosu and His Friend Anko Azato

3-20   *Sources: Conversations with Yuichi Kuda*

The sources for the following "sub-topics" are general Okinawan Karate Folk lore, conversation with my Okinawan teachers plus conversations and correspondence with many Karate Instructors that I have conducted over many years.

Sub-topics:
Azato and Itosu's Students
Itosu-Ha
Kyan-Ha

Naihanchi Kata practice
Credit: Chuck Chandler collection

"A person's character is his destiny."

A lesson from a Chinese fortune cookie.

"Nai Ju Soto Go"

An old Samurai Adage that is occupies a place of honor at the front of Sensei Kuda's Dojo

**This adage is translated to read "inside soft, outside hard".
The adage has many meanings both physical and mental. One physical meaning is to be soft and flexible on the inside and strong and hard on the outside.
The adage also gives advice on how to construct a good sword….soft and flexible steel on the inside….hard steel on the outside.
One mental meaning gives the Sensei good advice in dealing with students; be kind but stern.**

From the Author's collection

CHAPTER 4

OKINAWA'S LAST SAMURAI

沖縄最後の武士

Okinawa's Last Samurai

Author's collection

Picture on the previous page is from the Author's collection.

"Okinawa's Last Samurai"...Grandmaster Hohan Soken
1889- 1982
Painting by Chuck Chandler
Author's collection

空手生徒の心得

一、常に礼儀正しくふるまり事.

二、稽古中は精神力のみを集中せよ.

三、空手をする時は肉体と精神を一つにする心精神体は常に調和すべきで去る。

四、師範と他道場の先輩の指導をよく聞き決してその指導を忘れるな。

五、聞く事見る事は向上するために重要な事である。

六、上達するために六真の空手の精神を得るより努力せよ。

七、稽古は基礎の積み重ねであり中断すると前進できない。

八、常に技術の向上に努める事向上

九、自慢自信過剰は練習を堕落させる。

十、過食過飲喫煙を控え九支るの悪習慣、

十一、空手稽古は限度が無い二つ二つ着実にこなし将来確実に少林寺門下に入門できる。

祖堅方範

Maxims for Karate Students

1. *Always act in a courteous manner.*
2. *During training, concentrate to the limits of your mental endurance. Give your all, mentally and physically, as training without concentration prevents advancement.*
3. *The physical and mental training of karate should be combined as one. The heart, mind and body should be in unison at all times.*
4. *Heed the advice of your teachers and of the more advanced students of other dojo. Listen and never forget their advice.*
5. *Listening and watching are key points to advancement.*
6. *In order to advance, one must strive to obtain the true spirit of karate.*
7. *Training is on a continuous basis and one learns a little at a time. Do not take breaks from training as it will result in a step backwards.*
8. *Always strive for advancement and when advanced, one must not brag or boast.*
9. *Self-praise and over-confidence is a sickness that corrupts training.*
10. *Refrain from over-eating, drinking, and smoking for these bad habits hinder the effectiveness of your training.*
11. *Karate training has no limits. Step by step, study by study, and one day in the future you will undoubtedly enter the Temple of Shaolin.*

Hohan Soken

Author's collection

The beginning of the Meiji Era (1868) in Japanese History sealed the fate of the warrior class-not only in Japan but also in Okinawa and the other Ryukyu Islands. Although the Meiji Era began in 1868, the breakdown of the old feudal system of Okinawa did not fully develop until the late 1870's. However, old ways die slowly and the Samurai class of Okinawa continued to practice their ancient self protection arts of Tode and Kobujutsu in secret until these disciplines were introduced and incorporated into the Okinawan Public School in 1903. The average Okinawan resident knew very little about these fighting arts until the arts were revealed to the general public through the school system.

Even after this public introduction, some of the old samurai class did not agree with the introduction of their ancient and cherished art to the common people of Okinawa. Famous old Okinawan Samurai family systems such as Matsumura, Kogushiku, Motobu, Nakaima, Ogushiku and others continue to teach their art in secret to a few select students for many years.

Almost any practitioner of Okinawan Karatedo knows that there are three main groups of Okinawan karate. These are Shurite, Tomarite and Nahate. However, few followers of Okinawan karate realize that this grouping is really not very old and only dates back to the 1920's or early 1930's. Prior to this there was only Okinawan karatejutsu; which after 1903 was divided into two groups (1) School Karate…that which was taught in the Okinawan Public Schools and (2) Village Karate….that which was taught only to a limited number of students and remained a secret or semi-secret art until well into the twentieth century and in some cases this secrecy was still in place until after World War II.

As the years have gone by, those Okinawan karateka of the Samurai Class have one by one passed away. There are none left; they all have died. In this writer's opinion, one of the last of the old masters and the last of the Okinawan Samurai died on December 2, 1982; his name was Hohan Soken. Those of us who knew him and trained with him have experienced something very rare.

In January 1983 I wrote an article titled *"The Last Samurai"* and this article was published in one of the leading martial arts magazine (I believe it was "Kick Illustrated" but I'm not sure) since that time I have continued to research Hohan Soken's life and the teachings Grandmaster Soken left to all of his students. The following is an update my 1983 article and offers more information to the readers. I am sure I will leave out much needed information. As with all writings of a historical nature this attempt will "ruffle feathers" for some and "smooth feathers" for others".

Ronald Lindsey
Bastrop, Texas….July 2009

HOHAN SOKEN'S EARLY LIFE

Hohan Soken was born into the Samurai Class of Okinawan Gentry on May 25, 1889. This was only 12 years after the King of Okinawa, Sho Tai, had been forced by the Japanese Military to abdicate his throne and to go into exile in Tokyo, Japan. Soken's mother was a granddaughter of Sokon "Bushi" Matsumura, one of Okinawa's most famous Samurai. The old Bushi had been a Body Guard to three generations of Okinawan Kings and was one of the 96 retainers the Okinawan King took with him into exile in Tokyo. [4-1]

Sometime later Bushi Matsumura had either escaped or was allowed to return to Okinawa. The oral traditions passed on to the practioners of Shorin Ryu Matsumura Seito Karatedo state the Matsumura escaped from Japan and returned to Okinawa.

Hohan Soken 78 years old:
Photo credit: Author's collection

Hohan Soken's uncle, Nabe Matsumura, was Soken's mother's brother. Nabe Matsumura had been a scribe for King Sho Tai. He was to have been one of King Sho Tai's retainers who would serve his king in exile. Oral traditions state that Bushi Matsumura used his influence to have his grandson Nabe removed from the list of retainers Sho Tai would take with him into exile. Nabe Matsumura, fearing that the Japanese might consider him as threat or an undesirable, would arrest him. He went into hiding on the island of Iejima just off the Motobu Peninsula. It is not known how long Nabe hid from the Japanese. [4-2]

Like most of the Okinawan Samurai families, the Matsumura family was left penniless after the Japanese take over of Okinawa in 1877. They became displaced samurai and were forced to work at what ever jobs they could find. The Matsumura family settled in the Nishihara village area and

Iejima seen from Nago Bay
Photo credit: Mike Robert's Color
Productions

became farmers. This was the life Hohan Soken was born into; a life of hard work in the fields with little chance for education or to change his fate. It is said that Soken's parents died when he was quite young.

Before he died, Bushi Matsumura gave his "Ti" or hands to his Grandson Nabe Matsumura; that is to say the old "Bushi" made Nabe his successor to his system of karate/kobujutsu. [4-3] Since the Okinawan families were very clan oriented, there were certain fighting techniques and knowledge reserved for family members that would not be taught to non family members. [4-4]

The reader needs to understand that in the minds of the Okinawan samurai of this day, the family fighting art was considered to be their "trade secret" and as such, for many this was their means to earn a living. Even though the Okinawan Samurai class had been abolished, most members of this class expected the Chinese to intervene on their behalf and run the Japanese out of Okinawa and restore King Sho Tai to his throne. This hope remained with the former samurai for several decades. Therefore the samurai families wished to keep their closely guarded fighting secrets within their family to secure employment when their king returned. [4-5]

Nabe Matsumura
1850's -1930's
Grandson of Bushi Matsumura

Information about this photo:

The following information comes from Rick Rose a long time student of Hohan Soken.

This photo of Nabe Matsumura is actually from a small photo similar too a "locket photo of Nabe Matsumura's face.

The body is from a photo of Hohan Soken. The small locket photo was all Hohan Soken could find of his old teacher when he returned to Okinawa in 1952. The composite photo was constructed after Soken's return.

Photo credit: Author's collection

When Nabe Matsumura accepted Hohan Soken as his student, in fact Hohan Soken was for many years his only student; he was carrying out the age old Okinawan Samurai tradition of teaching only family members the complete family martial art. Since Nabe Matsumura did not have any children he chose his sister's child, young Hohan Soken, to receive the "hands "of Matsumura. Soken was not only to learn the karate and kobujutsu of the Matsumura family but he would also be taught the other aspects of the art to include the history of his ancestors and the moralistic code of the Okinawa Bushi. In 1902 Hohan Soken began a journey along a path that he would follow for 80 years; this was same path that generations of Okinawan Bushi had taken for hundreds of years. This was the path of the Bushi and Hohan Soken would be one of the last Okinawans to walk this path. [4-6]

Before we go any farther with our story about Hohan Soken's training I would like to present the readers with some information I have collected over the years. Much of it is speculation but it comes from good sources. [4-7]

Very little information exists about Nabe Matsumura. He was a secretive man. We know that after the abolishment of the Okinawan warrior class in 1877; Nabe had reason to fear the Japanese and hid on the Island of Ie in the Northern area of Okinawa. When he came out of hiding he settled in the village of Nishihara. This was the village Bushi Matsumura chose to live in when he returned from the King's exile in Tokyo and he found himself unemployed.

Rickshaw in pre-1900 Japan. Photo Credit: Wikimedia Commons

136

Nabe Matsumura earned a living by farming, guarding the area crops at night and pulling a rickshaw in the near by cities. Oral traditions handed down to the practitioners of Shorin Ryu Matsumura Seito state that when Hohan Soken was old enough, he went to work in the fields for farmer named "Ko Ishigawa". The oral legends go on to say that Ko Ishigawa was a karate man of considerable skill. Young Soken would often accompany Ishigawa to Naha where they would sell what ever crops that were in season. When they returned to Nishihara, they would load their ox cart with fish to sell or preserve for food. During these trips Hohan Soken often took a hand held makiwara along to practice on. Also Ishigawa had a special technique used to kill the fish with a snap of his wrist and fingers.

According to Chuck Chandler and Takaiya Yabiku, a number of Hohan Soken's senior Okinawan students believe that Ko Ishigawa was actually Nabe Matsumura. Some speculate that Nabe Matsumura changed his name to avoid trouble with the Japanese.

Others state that the Okinawan people often changed their names. Men would often use their wives last names; so, the use of several names is not uncommon in Okinawa. It is said that when Soken's parents died Nabe Matsumura and his wife raised young Soken as their own child.

I asked Sensei Yuichi Kuda about Nabe Matsumura and he told me that Nabe was only his "baby san" name and that he did not know his other names or his birth or death dates.

Nakamoto Masahiro in his recent book titled "Kobudo Okinawa Traditional Martial Art" published by Bunbukan, 2006 refers to Nabe Matsumura as Nagahama Nabi no Tanmei, a cousin of Sokon Matsumura.

In Ernest Estrada's interview in the late 1970's with Grandmaster Hohan Soken states that Master Soken referred to his uncle Nabe Matsumura as a grandson of Bushi Matsumura. This agrees with the information I received in Okinawa during the 1960's.

Drawing from the Author's collection.

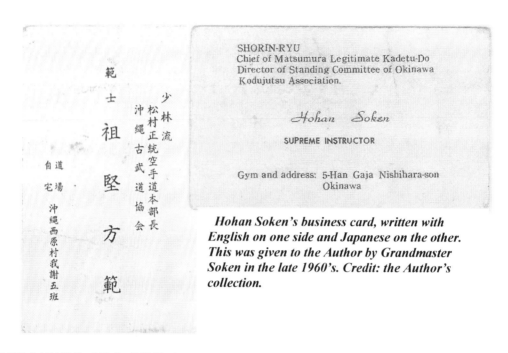

少林流
松村正統空手道本部長
沖縄古武道協会

範士　祖堅方範

自道場
宅場
沖縄西原村我謝五班

SHORIN-RYU
Chief of Matsumura Legitimate Kadetu-Do
Director of Standing Committee of Okinawa
Kodujutsu Association.

Hohan Soken

SUPREME INSTRUCTOR

Gym and address: 5-Han Gaja Nishihara-son
Okinawa

Hohan Soken's business card, written with English on one side and Japanese on the other. This was given to the Author by Grandmaster Soken in the late 1960's. Credit: the Author's collection.

THE TRAINING OF A BUSHI

The record of Hohan Soken's training under his uncle Nabe Matsumura has been fairly well documented. These records give us a valuable glimpse at how the Okinawan Bushi were trained.

All training was done in secret. Initially many long hours were devoted to proper walking Hohan Soken while remembering his training from the early days often said that he walked for 3 years before he was allowed to begin kata practice. Part of this type of training consisted of cutting banana leaves and placing them on the ground; young Soken was taught proper walking step by step until he could step on the banana leaves with such control that he would not mash or bruise the leaves.

Training also included toughening the hands by gripping, twisting and striking the "Matsu ki" or pine trees. The bark of the Ryukyu Pine tree was very rough and initially would scrape and cut the skin of young Soken; but the wounds were treated with Okinawan herbal remedies and the training continued. Training sessions were long and severe. Young Soken worked hard in the fields all day and at night he would practice "touti", the practice would last until early in the morning. Training also consisted of various exercises called "koteaite" (wrist hitting) these exercises consisted of two man drills designed to toughen the hands, arms, feet, legs and bodies of the practitioners. Kata were practiced over and over with approximately one year of training devoted to each kata. [4-7]

Readers need to understand that all martial arts have different levels of training that the students must travel through as they learn the art. The levels are: (1) Sho Den or basic level of techniques, (2) Chu Den or mid level of techniques, (3) Oku Den or hidden techniques, (4) Hi Den or secret techniques and (5) Kai Den or final teachings.

It should be pointed out that this terminology is of a Japanese origin. In many Japanese fighting system; often there is an official recognition ceremony marking the student's progress through these various levels. However, in Okinawa these terms are mainly used to loosely explain how a student progresses and there are no hard and fast rules that informs a student at what level he or she may be in at any given time.

GRANDMASTER SOKEN'S KATA

It well known that Hohan Soken learned the following kata from his uncle Nabe Matsumura; this is roughly the order in which the kata were generally taught by Hohan Soken (I left out the Rohai kata from this list, this will be discussed later):

1. Naihanchi Sho Dan, 2. Naihanchi Ni Dan, 3. Pinan Sho Dan, 4. Pinan Ni Dan, 5. Pai Sai (Dai), 6. Chinto, 7. Gojushiho, 8. Kusanku, and 9. Hakutsuru.

It is not generally known that Hohan Soken had been taught the Matsumura Sanchin kata, Shurite Seisan kata, Matsumura Kusanku, Shiho Kusanku and Kusanku Mai by his uncle Nabe Matsumura.

When describing his kata Soken would often say "study the **Naihanchi kata**, this is where you will find my secret". He learned only Naihanchi Sho Dan and Ni Dan from his uncle. When asked why he only learned the first two Naihanchi kata from his uncle, he replied that is all that his uncle knew. Soken, later in the 1950's, learned Naihanchi San Dan from his friend Chosin Chibana.

Hohan Soken and Mitsu Inoue Feb. 1957

This photo was taken about the same time that one of Soken's students died from practicing hard Sanchin. Photo Credit: Resources Unlimited

Soken was often asked why he was taught only two **Pinan kata** while all other Shorin styles had five Pinan kata. Soken's answer was that he learned only what his uncle taught him and that he believed his uncle had only two Pinan kata. Hohan Soken once actively taught both a **Sanchin kata** and **Seisan kata**; but he quit teaching them because some of his students were practicing these kata two hard. Soken believe that both of these kata as with all of his kata were to be practiced softly by experienced students.

In the late 1950's, one of his students died while practicing hard Sanchin kata. After this event he quit openly teaching the Matsumura Sanchin kata. A short time later he quit teaching Seisan kata.

From Soken's aunt (Bushi Matsumura's granddaughter and Hohan Soken's mother's sister) he was taught the Pai Sai (Sho) kata. This was one of Hohan Soken's favorite kata and the one he chose to demonstrate in 1972 when he visited the United States. It is not clear from whom Hohan Soken learned the kata Rohai Ge, Rohai Chu, and Rohai Jo. It may be that he also learned these from his uncle.

Above photo were filmed in 1972 by Gene Penninger on Super 8mm film. The above excerpts are of Hohan Soken doing Naihanchi Sho Dan; he is 83 years old at the time of this filming. In spite of his age and the condition of the film you can still see his power and skill.
Photo credit: George Alexander's collection.

The kata **Chinto** is not one of the older kata that Bushi Matsumura brought from China to Okinawa. Rather Chinto is believed to have come from the ship wrecked Chinese sailor called "Chinto" who drifted ashore on Okinawa. This kata apparently was developed by Matsumura from the techniques that he learned from Chinto. Some say that Matsumura's experience with Chinto occurred in the 1860's approximately 20 years after Matsumura

Hohan Soken performing the Chinto Kate. Photo credit: George Alexander's collection

had returned from his Shaolin Temple experience in China. Chinto kata became one of the methods used through out Matsumura-Ha to teach balance.

The **Rohai kata** prior to the 1870's had been associated with the karate taught around the city of Tomari. The old saying that "the Bushi of Tomari have one leg" refers to one the crane stance common to the Rohai kata. It is not clear how this group of three kata ended up in the style taught by Hohan Soken.

When I was practicing in Okinawa the Rohai kata were usually called Sensei Soken's kata. This led me to believe that Sensei Soken had brought these kata into the system.

In fact I did not learn the true name of these kata until several years after I had left Okinawa. This is my perception in regards to the Rohai kata.

Even though we don't really know how the Rohai kata made their way into Hohan Soken's system; we do know that they are deadly kata. The deadliness of the Rohai kata technique seems to increase as we move from the first kata, Rohai Ge, to the middle kata, Rohai Chu and finally the deadliest technique are seen in last kata, Rohai Jo. It is almost as if there is only one Rohai kata with three variations.

Photos to the left are of Hohan Soken demonstrating moves common to all of his Rohai Kata. Photo credit: George Alexander's collection.

Hohan Soken considered the kata **Gojushiho** to be the kata that lifted the student into another level of development. The Gojushiho kata as practiced in the style inherited from Sokon "Bushi" Matsumura by Nabe Matsumura and later by Hohan Soken introduces the students to methods of developing power that are from the Shaolin Hakutsuru or White Crane and these techniques are not easily found in the kata taught before Gojushiho. As one learns Gojushiho; he or she is entering into the "Oku Den" or hidden techniques.

To the right Hohan Soken demonstrates a throwing move from the Gojushiho kata. Photo credit: George Alexander's collection.

Hohan Soken often said that his Great-grandfather Bushi Matsumura had learned Shaolin Kenpo in China. Shaolin Kenpo included the Shaolin Five Animal Style (Tiger, Leopard, Snake, Dragon and White Crane). Soken said that the Pinan kata represents the Tiger, the Naihanchi kata represents the leopard, the Pai Sai kata

Moves from the Kusanku Kata. Photo credit: George Alexander's collection

represents the snake, the Kusanku kata represents the dragon and crane. Hakutsuru kata represents the white crane. The kata Gojushiho ties everything together ands represents all of the Shaolin animals especially the dragon. It seems as though the Gojushiho kata was considered more advance than the Kusanku kata however, it was usually taught before Kusanku.

Although the old "Machimura-ya (Matsumura family-Okinawan dialect)" system of touti had three **Kusanku kata** (Shiho Kusanku, Matsumura Kusanku and Kusanku Mai); Hohan Soken usually taught only the Kusanku Mai and most of his American students and many of his Okinawan students are not even aware of the other two Kusanku kata. [4-8]

Hohan Soken trained for ten years (1902 until 1912) before he began to learn what his uncle called "real karate". Until this time he had only been schooled on the basic principles. At the age of 23 years Soken was ready to learn the secrets of the Shaolin White Crane or Hakutsuru kata that Bushi Matsumura had brought back to Okinawa from China in 1845.

This rare kata was designed to improve balance develop "true strength" that did not require the use of great physical strength.

This strength called "Chi" enable karateka to advance beyond their natural ability and reportedly this was the secret that allowed Bushi Matsumura to be the "Bucho" or "Boss warrior" of Okinawa and successfully serve three generations of Okinawan Kings.

Hohan Soken at the age of 83 performing Matsumura Hakutsuru. Photo credit: Resources Unlimited

The Hakutsuru Kata actually fine tuned skills that had already been developed in other kata. Soken did much of this training such as tachi kata (stance training) plus sparring while standing on a small raft floating on a pond near the Shuri Castle. The purpose of this training was to improve balance. However, the key to Hakutusuru is kata training, and this was taught in secret.

Hohan Soken performing the Hakutsuru kata. Photo Credit: George Alexander's collection

Many of the Okinawan Samurai class sought out Bushi Matsumura in his day and Nabe Matsumura in his day and asked to be taught the Hakutsuru Kata. Oral traditions passed on the students of Shorin Ryu Matsumura Seito state that Itosu Anko and his student Gichen Funakoshi asked Nabe Matsumura to teach them the Hakutsuru Kata but Matsumura refused to teach them the Matsumura Hakutsuru Kata. The traditions go on to say that "Nabe no Tanme" preferred to keep his teaching among family members.

This led to an incident that is called **"the Fence Peeper"**; the following story is an oral tradition that is familiar to many students of Hohan Soken. According to the story, after his request to be taught the Matsumura Hakutsuru Kata had been denied, Gichen Funakoshi started to observe Nabe Matsumura practice the Kata through a hole in Nabe's back yard fence. After a short time Nabe caught Funakoshi observing his kata. This put a stop to these observations and other attempt to learn Nabe Matsumura's Kata.

GRANDMASTER HOHAN SOKEN SEEKS OTHER TEACHERS

It was traditional for the Okinawan karateka to seek more than one teacher. It must have been around the time of World War I that Soken asked an old man in living in Nishihara Village named Komesu Ushi no Tanme to teach him his Rokushaku Bo technique. Since Soken and Nabe Matsumura lived in Nishihara Village it is quite possible that his uncle knew this old man and asked him to teach his nephew.

Komesu Ushi was called "Tanme" or Ushi no Tanme; Nabe Matsumura was called Nabe no Tanme. The English equivalent of "Tanme" would be an "elder"; both terms refer to a wise old man. These are terms of respect and admiration; usually not official titles.

Ushi no Tanme had been taught the Bo or staff technique from Chikinjima (Tsuken Island….Japanese pronunciation: Tsukenjima) by Chikin Kraka. Chikinjima was an island located on the eastern edge of Nakagusku Bay. Chikin Kraka or Manataka Tsuken (Japanese name) was an Okinawan Samurai who became a farmer after the Meiji Restoration.

Chikin Kraka was a descendent of the famous Okinawan Bushi, Chikin Akatchu, from Chikin Island. No one knows when Chikin Kraka was born or when he died; but Hohan Soken spoke of meeting the old master and training under him. [4-9]

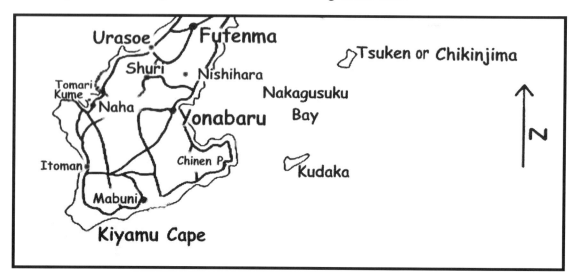

Map of Southern Okinawa showing Chikinjima Photo credit Author's collection

It should be noted that there are some minor disagreements as to source of many of Hohan Soken's weapons kata. There are those who claim that Bushi Matsumura did not use the weapons common to Okinawa. But history and good sense does not support this claim. How could he achieve his status as "Bucho" or Head Bushi with out being very knowledgeable of weapons that were common not only to Okinawa, but also of Japan and China?

Information given to American students of Shorin Ryu Matsumura Seito in the 1960's stated that Bushi Matsumura was an expert with the weapons of Okinawa and that Hohan Soken had learned most of his weapons technique from his uncle Nabe Matsumura.

There is also some dispute over the question "Did Soken develop the Chikin Bo kata from what he learned from Ushi Tanme or was Soken actually taught this kata. There are no good answers to this question.

In 1924 Sensei Soken became part of study group called "Kenkyu-Kai" this group was quit extensive and included prominent masters such as Kenwa Mabuni and the Chinese tea merchant and "White Crane" Fist master named Gokenki. [4-10]

Gokenki demonstrating one of his Kata with Kenwa Mabuni in the back ground. Photo credit: Author's collection

144

According to Takaya Yabiku, Hohan Soken would often go to Gokenki's teashop accompanied by a friend named Kana Kinjo or Kanashiro. Kinjo was from the Kin Village/Ishigawa area, he was from a samurai family who had become farmers after the Meiji Restoration. Soken and Kinjo learned some of Gokenki's kata and technique; they also taught Gokenki some of their kata.

There are those who say that Kana Kinjo studied with Nabe Matsumura. Kana Kinjo may have also been called Kang Kanashiro. Soken Sensei often spoke of his friend Kinjo Kana. Soken introduced Takaiya Yabiku to Kana Kinjo in 1969 and Sensei Yabiku trained with Kana Kinjo until Kinjo's death.

Takaya Yabiku said that Kana Kinjo left Okinawa in the late 1920's to live in Hong Kong, China. There, he learned a White Crane like art from a Chinese master named Nori. Kana Kinjo was apparently avoiding Japanese military service when he went to Hong Kong. It is believed he returned to Okinawa after World War II.

Kang Kinjo
Photo credit: A. J. Advincula

Kang Kanashiro also went to Hong Kong during the same time frame as Kana Kinjo. Kinjo and Kanashiro are the same name. Therefore, it is quite possible that these are the same individual. Kang Kinjo (Kanashiro) also taught A.J. Advincula, who was a student of Tatsou Shimabukuro.

During a meeting of the Kenkyu-Kai in 1924 Hohan Soken met an older Karate Sensei named Kamura or Kanamura (it is unclear as to who the old Sensei was). Sensei Kamura observed Soken performing his karate and was highly impressed and asked if Soken would become his primary student. Soken agreed to this and began training under Sensei Kamura. Later that same year Soken had a disagreement with Sensei Kamura which left Soken very upset; the results of which Soken decided to leave Okinawa. *(4-11)*

For many years there has been a persistent rumor among the practitioners of Shorin Ryu Matsumura Seito practitioners as to the real reason Hohan Soken left Okinawa. There are those who claim he left to avoid serving in the Japanese Military. Other say he got into trouble with the Japanese law and was a wanted man. Hohan Soken always claimed he left to seek his fortune.

Many believe Soken went directly from Okinawa to Argentina. He in fact worked for a while on a merchant ship and traveled to Taiwan on several occasions and also traveled to Vietnam. While in Taiwan he is said to have met with an Old Chinese White Crane master named "Oh ho So" or Sho. From this old gentleman Soken learned a number of White Crane kata. *(4-12)*

Hohan Soken is actually alleged to have traveled at lest one time to Taiwan several years before he left for Okinawan. Once he was supposed to have gone to Taiwan with his friend Chotoku Kyan; Kyan was said to have cancelled out because his wife got sick and Soken went alone. In Taiwan he is alleged to have trained with a Master So and learned some of his kata. [4-13]

When I was in Okinawa, from time to time I heard stories of an old man who name was "So" from whom Sensei Soken was alleged to have learned special techniques. It was said that Master Soken did not teach these techniques to anyone.

In the 1980's Greg Ohl, who studied in Okinawa under Sensei Kise and Grand master Soken during the late 1970's, told me about an interesting incident that happened while he was practicing in Grandmaster Soken's dojo. During this incident Sensei Soken demonstrated a block that the students had never seen. When questioned about the block; Sensei Soken said he had learned this from an old man whose technique was much different from his Shorin Ryu style and he had not taught this technique to his students.

L to R Hohan Soken, Greg Ohl, Fusei Kise
Greg Ohl's collection

Years later information from Takaya Yabiku identifies this mysterious old man as "Oh o So" from Taiwan. According to Sensei Yabiku, Grandmaster Soken had taught some of Master So's technique to various students. These techniques closely resembling the White Crane style of Fukein Province China.

Below So Hakutsuru Kata: Author's collection

MOVING TO ARGENTINA

In 1924 Hohan Soken moved to Argentina. He settled in the city of Linares, Argentina. Linares had a large Okinawan community and Soken found work in a laundry and later learned to be a photographer. He continued to practice karate and taught his art to four Okinawan men in Argentina. These were (1) Kana-san, (2) Hina-san, (3) Mitake Higa-san, (4) Mitsugi-san. All four of these men have been deceased since the 1980's. [4-14]

Hohan Soken returned to his home land in 1952. He found Okinawa greatly changed. Although World War II had ended in 1945 and the island was rebuilding; signs of the war's devastation were every where. Many of Soken's friends and relatives had simply vanished during the Battle for Okinawa. Soken tried to find his Uncle and teacher Nabe Matsumura; but, he had disappeared. Soken also found that Okinawa karate had changed greatly.

Shuri Castle in ruin after World War II
Photo Credit: Author's collection

Drawing from the
Author's collection

147

Ernest Estrada did an interview with Shinpo Matayoshi in the late 1970's. During the interview Matayoshi spoke of Hohan Soken and his old village methods. The following is an account of this interview which is about Hohan Soken. This account was sent to me in a letter during the mid 1980's from Ernest Estrada. The following is part of this letter describing Estrada's "rough draft or field notes" of the interview with Shinpo Matayoshi:

HOHAN SOKEN APPRED TO HAVE DEPTH IN THIS TECHNIQUE BUT HE DID NOT SHARE HIS KNOWLEDGE W/OUTSIDERS (??). HE TAUGHT VILLAGE KARATE & KOBUDO. VERY OLD METHODS. HE DIDN'T CHANGE MUCH CUZ HE LEFT OKINAWA W/ WHAT HE KNEW TO ARGENTINA? THEN HE CAME BACK W/THE SAME TECANIQUES OF HIS VILLAGE. HE DIDN'T CHANGE & THAT IS GOOD. HE PRESERVED HIS KOBUDO KNOWLEDGE (HE CALLED IT KOBUJUTSU & NOT KOBUDO). SOKEN SAID THAT KOBUJUTSU IS OLD METHODS & KOBUDO WAS NEW METHODS. SOKEN DID NOT TEACH THEORY BUT ACTION. MANY PEOPLE THOUGHT THAT THAT WAS ALL. HIS SECRETS, LIKE MIND, ARE BASED ON MOTION & KNOWLEDGE OF THE BODY. HE PASSED ON TO STUDENTS BUT THEY WILL NEVER REACH HIS LEVEL.
— ARAGAKI = TRAINS HARD – SOKEN'S SENIOR MOST STUDENT. STUDENT OF CHIBANA, too.

KUDA = TEACHES WEAPINS BUT NOT W/LOVE OF SOKEN. GOOD MAN.

AKISEI - (LAUGH) I KNOW HIM. COMMENTS — NONE.
KISEI "IMPROVISES" TOO MUCH. DIFFICULT TO SEE WHAT HE IS TRYING TO ACCOMPLISH.

It is clear that Matayoshi Sensei was convinced that the art that Grandmaster Soken brought back from Argentina in 1952 was the old style of Okinawan touti and kobujutsu.

The readers are reminded that prior to 1936, Okinawan karate was called Toude…meaning Chinese hand not empty hand. Many styles continued to use the term Toude until the 1950's or later.

"Conceited soldiers seldom win battles."

A lesson from a Chinese fortune cookie.

OKINAWAN TODE

When Hohan Soken left Okinawa in 1924 he left with a fighting art that he learned mainly from his uncle, Nabe Matsumura; but also from Gokenki, Ushi no Tanme and probably others. The statuses of the fighting arts of Okinawa in 1924 were as follows: *There were still many former Okinawa Samurai or Bushi who still practiced and taught the karate/kobujutsu of their samurai ancestors. These old warriors taught their art in secret or semi- secret. One of these old warriors was Nabe Matsumura. Now these old men really did not have dojos most taught in their backyards or in the surrounding woods or in any place that would offer secrecy. Their teachings were not organized to teach the masses. Class numbers were small; five students were considered a huge class. Many only taught family members. There were no styles names, no standardization of terms or standardization of techniques. Kata followed a given pattern but each individual was taught according to his age and physical abilities. There was no strict code of dojo etiquette (reshikki). There was no Shurite, no Tomarite, or Nahate….there was only Okinawa Karate and the "kara" in karate meant Chinese not empty. This was the "village karate or village kobujutsu" and this is what Hohan Soken left Okinawa with in 1924 and this is what he brought back in 1952. The teachers and practitioners of this art were or had been members of the "Obstinate Party" and most were anti Japanese in their political beliefs.* [4-15]

Shinpan Shiroma leading high school students in kata in front of Shuri Castle in 1937. This is an example of teaching student in School karate. Photo credit Author's collection

Hohan Soken about 79 years old. Photo credit: Robert
Teller collection.

In 1903 Anko Itosu began teaching karate in the Okinawan public schools. In order to do this, the old fighting art over a period of several years was watered down and made less lethal. Over time the karate taught in the school came to be called "school karate".

In order to teach many people at one time methods of teaching had to be altered. First of kata training had to broken down by the numbers for many students in mass formation; they were taught to perform their kata with each count being one move at a time. This allowed for more accuracy in kata movement and also caused the kata to be performed in a "jerky" manner with a bust of power with each move. In the village karate methods only a few students performed the kata at one time. When only a few students perform the kata together; more moves could be executed per count. This results in a kata performance that blends the kata more than the jerky method of the school karate kata performance. The jerky method allows for the strength contained in the kata to become more apparent. The smoother kata of the village method hides the power to the point that the power contained in the kata becomes difficult to see. (4-16)

Perhaps the greatest difference between village and school methods is the attitude toward the desired results of the training. The village method is a "jutsu" the object of this training is for protection; be it self protection or the protection of those whom you are guarding. The purpose is combat....character development plays a secondary role. On the other hand the school karate training placed character development first and the combat aspects of the art second.

Sensei Yuichi Kuda once told me that when Itosu's introduced Okinawa karate into the public school system of Okinawa. His action angered many of the old Okinawans of the former Bushi class. The old village method stressed secrecy in both kata and bunkai; while the school method practiced everything in the open. Itosu had to change the art to please the public education officials and to pacify the former members of the warrior class. This meant that over time the old fighting methods of the Okinawan Bushi were being maintained by the village karate/kobujutsu methods. School karate was changed; moving away from the fighting arts of the Okinawan Bushi.

Hohan Soken often said that studying his method of karate and kobujutsu was like going back in time to the days of when Bushi Matsumura was the King's bodyguard. To understand this statement let us take a look at the Bushi of this day. The idea of calling Okinawan Karate the weaponless art or calling Okinawans weaponless would have probably been insulting to them. They were rarely or never without a weapon. A peace of rope, a hachimaki (band of cloth wrapped around the head) an obi or belt could be used as a weapon.

All social classes of Okinawa wore a hair pin called a jiffa. These were thrust through the top knot of both men and women. For men the wearing of the jiffa was outlawed in 1892. Old women were still wearing jiffa in the 1950's. The 1954 era movie "The House of the August Moon" clearly shows Okinawan women wearing jiffa in their hair. Hohan Soken was still teaching his student to use and make jiffas in the late 1960's.

The wooden geta (wooden clogs used as shoes) were used as weapons. The techniques of using the geta as a weapon were once taught in the kata "Ichi Gina Pai Sai". This kata was once popular in the Koza Area. Hohan Soken taught some of his student a knife kata along with bunkai.

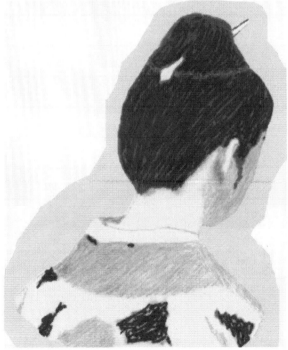

Okinawan Lady wearing a jiffa in her hair.
Drawing by the author
Author's collection

The wearing and use of the "Tessen" was common. These iron ribbed folding fans could serve as a weapon and in Japan several Ryu were developed to teach the use of this weapon.

Sensei Takaya Yabiku is a taxi drive in Naha, Okinawa. He was advised by Grandmaster Hohan to keep several sharpened wooden pencils on the dash board of his cab.

The old grandmaster also advised him to keep a pencil in his pocket. Sensei Yabiku took Grandmaster Soken's advice and put several sharpened wooden pencils on the dash board of his taxi cab.

A short time later a passenger in Sensei Yabiku's cab pulled a knife on Sensei and tried to rob him. Quickly grabbing a pencil off the dash board Yabiku stabbed the robber in the eye. The man fled the cab in pain. To Grandmaster Soken, the jiffa was not obsolete.

Choki Motobu 1871-1944
Picture Credit: Robert Teller Collection.

Nakamoto Masahiro in his book *"Okinawa Traditional Old Martial Arts…Kobudo"* states that the old "Ti" tradition of Bushi Matsumura was carried on by Choki Motobu.

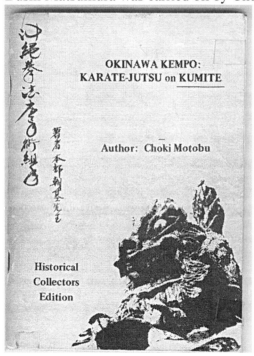

Through Choki Motobu's Book, *"Okinawa Kempo: Karatejutsu on Kumite"*. We can have a rare look at the techniques of old style Okinawan Karatejutsu. This book printed in the 1920's was one of the first books printed about Okinawan Karate; it represents the ancestor of modern karate.

Okinawa Kempo: Karate-Jutsu on Kumite by Choki Motobu. Credit: Bill Wiswell and the Ryukyu Enterprise.

152

Photos from Choki Motobu's book "Okinawa Kempo: Karate-Jutsu on Kumite"
Note: Motobu's technique, he holds his fist out in front similar to the old bare knuckle boxers of the late 1800's
Photo credit: Bill Wiswell, Ryukyu Enterprise

Hohan Soken's fighting posture closely resembles the techniques demonstrated in Choki Motobu's book and Soken's technique was exactly as he claimed; it was the old Matsumura method. Photo credit: Tom Hunicutt collection.

O'Sensei Soken's fighting posture allowed him to intercept his opponent's attack and execute a counter attack before his opponent's attack could reach him. His techniques were very efficient and effective. Many masters studied with him because of his strategies. Yuichi Kuda said that Grandmaster Soken's ideas and strategies were among the best in Okinawa.

These are the types of techniques that made the Okinawan fighting arts so effective. Hohan Soken, his ancestors, contemporaries and students practiced fighting techniques very similar to those recorded in Choki Motobu's rare book; this is the old style of Okinawan Karatejutsu, Tode, Ti or what ever else you wish to call it.

When standing away from his opponent (at a distance of about the height of his opponent); Sensei Soken would hold his lead hand low. This would enable him to stop his opponent's kick. In such a case the old master would hold his rear hand at his solar plexus; usually he held this hand open. Sensei Seizan Kinjo called this rear hand a "spare block". I have continue to use Sensei Kinjo's term for this technique.

The photo on the above left shows Sensei Soken in a fighting posture with his lead hand held low. Photo credit: Resources Unlimited. The photo on the upper right shows Sensei Soken intercepting a kick with a low scooping block. Note: the position of his left hand. Credit: Author's collection

Drawing of an Okinawan Bushi showing wearing a clock with large open sleeves. Credit Author's collection.

Sensei Soken held his spare block hand differently from most other master from other styles. Most masters held their "spare block" hand with the palm upward. Grandmaster Soken held his spare block pointing slightly upward with the palm facing to the side.

I asked Sensei Yuichi Kuda about the way Sensei Soken carried his spare block. Sensei Kuda stated that in the old days people wore cloaks or robs with large open sleeves. Sensei Kuda went on to say that some karate masters carried their spare block with the palm upward as if they were pulling the sleeve of the cloak on the lead arm back above the elbow to free the arm from the cloak and lessen the chance of their opponent grabbing the cloak sleeve during a fight.

Sensei Kuda continued by saying that when many of the old Bushi fought unarmed duels with other samurai they would often free their upper body from the cloak to keep the cloak from being grabbed by their opponent. There would be no reason to hold the palm of the spare block up if the cloak were removed from the upper body leaving the arms free from the cloak. Soken felt that his method gave him greater use of his hands. Sensei Kuda said that Soken's method was based on real fighting.

During a recent phone conversation with Gary Stanfield who studied in Okinawa under both Fusei Kise and Hohan Soken from abut 1965 thru 1967. We discussed some of the differences between Grandmasters Soken and Fusei Kise's methods of karate and kobujutsu. We both agreed that one of the major differences was that Sensei Kise's method was more aggressive and powerful. On the other hand Sensei Soken seemed to place a higher

Photo on the left is of Master Shugoro Nakazato portraying Bushi Matsumura in a play. This photo helps to explain Sensei Kuda's remarks about the Okinawan Bushi often fighting with their upper body exposed. Photo credit: Sid Campbell collection

Sensei Shian Toma, O'Sensei Hohan Soken, Sensei Fusei Kise, and Gary Stanfield; photo taken in the mid 1960's. Photo credit: Gary Stanfield collection

value on balance than did Sensei Kise. These differences were probably due to the differences in the ages of the two masters. In the late 1960's Sensei Kise was a little over 35 years of age and Grandmaster Soken was nearing 80 years of age. Nevertheless, differences did exist. One of the principle differences was in the value placed on speed and balance. O'Sensei Soken placed a higher value on balance over speed while Sensei Kise placed a higher value on speed. Sensei Soken's kata were not a catalog of strengthening exercises; rather they were a collection of fighting principles, techniques and ideas. For an example: the length and width of his stances (tachi kata) were based on common sense and the need for mobility. Sensei Soken's ideas on the length of stances can best be understood with the following adage:

"Let your kata stance be your every day stance; let your every day stance be your fighting stance."

The above two photo are of stances from the 1920's. They are from "Tode" or old style karate. The drawing on below left is from modern karate. This type of stance strengthens the legs, but may teach the practioners to become less mobile. Credits; the above left, Bill Wiswell and Ryukyu Enterprise. The other photos and drawing credit: the Author's collection

Remember:
The immobile army is a defeated army; the immobile samurai is a dead samurai.

Common sense from an old adage!

157

DEFENDING GRANDMASTER SOKEN'S HONOR

Since Hohan Soken's death in 1982; a few individuals from time to time have accused Grandmaster Soken of being a fake. Now, I believed this so called "talk" stems from a few Okinawan masters who are jealous of Hohan Soken's reputation and of Soken calling his style Shorin Ryu Matsumura Seito Karate/Kobudo. [4-17]

The following is presentation of photographs, and various bits of information about Hohan Soken as it relates to his reputation. I will let the readers judge for themselves as to the authenticity of Hohan Soken.

Let us begin this discussion by going back to Ernest Estrada's interview with Shinpo Matayoshi. I have enclosed a copy of part of a letter Mr. Estrada wrote to me describing this interview. Part of the Matayoshi interview discussed Hohan Soken. It is clear from Shinpo Matayoshi's remarks that he held Sensei Soken in very high regards as an authentic master of "old Okinawan village karate/kobujutsu".

The following story was told to me by Greg Ohl who witnessed the event. In the mid to late 1970's; Jyokei Kushi, a senior student of Grandmaster Shoshin Nagamine, died and a tournament was held to honor Sensei Kushi and to raise money for his widow.

When Mr. Ohl arrived at the tournament he observed a number of Okinawan masters and other karateka gathered around Nagamine Sensei. Grandmaster Nagamine was enjoying the respect and honor being shown to him by those gathered around him. After 15 minutes or so, Grandmaster Soken arrived at the tournament. Those gathered around Master Nagamine shifted over to Master Soken and just as the group had showed respect and honor to Master Nagamine; they did the same for Master Soken. A short while later Master Nagamine, always a gentleman, escorted Master Soken to a place of honor to watch the tournament.

In his book ***"Okinawa Traditional Old Martial Arts—Kobudo"***, Nakamoto Masahiro describes an interesting incident that happened in 1924 on Okinawan. This information was given to Nakamoto Sensei by the late ***Nakama Chozo***. It seems that at the Matsuyama Udun, a well known sai expert named Tokumura Seki (a student of Nakamoto Seicho) ridiculed Hohan Soken by asking him if he knew how to use a sai. Soken politely ignored Tokumura's remarks. Chotoku Kyan, who was also present, told Tokumura that this man (referring to Soken) is an expert with the sai. Soken then demonstrated his sai technique. Tokumura then ask Soken where he was from; Soken replied "I am from the country side". Tokumura then said "you are very good for someone from the country side".

In 1956 the all Okinawan Karate Federation was started, Hohan Soken was asked by Seitoku Higa to join this organization. Late in 1964 Hohan Soken received a Shihan grade from this organization. Up until this time Hohan Soken held no rank of any kind. He came from the era in time before martial arts ranks had been developed.

In 1958 Chosin Chibana wrote the following letter to Hohan Soken:

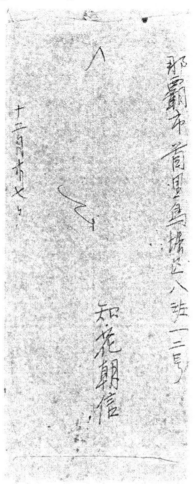

Above photo is the envelope of a letter Chosin Chibana wrote to Hohan Soken. The envelope is dated Dec. 28, 1958. The letter and envelop were given to Chuck Chandler by Takaya Yabiku and Chuck Chandler gave the letter to the Author. I do not know if this has been printed in any previous book or publication. Credit: Takaya Yabiku collection

Drawing on the left is by the Author

拝啓　前略　...（手紙本文）...

知花朝信

祖堅方範殿

十二日廿二日

一、会長の上に顧問を置く事
一、...
一、範士...

祖堅方範
　八段

比嘉佑直
上地完徳
　教士、八段

久志助恵

上原三郎

宮里武真

仲里周五郎

宮平勝吉

喜屋武真栄

宮城盛喜
　教士、

知花朝信

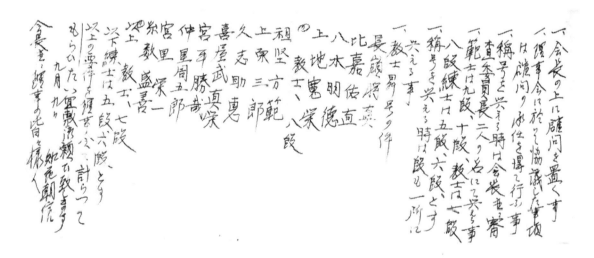

Letter written to Hohan Soken from Choshin Chibana; post marked Dec. 28, 1958
Letter given to Chuck Chandler by Takaya Yabiku
Credit: Takaya Yabiku collection

160

The following letter sent to Hohan Soken by Choshin Chibana on December 26, 1958 was translated from Japanese to English by the ladies of the Okinawan Tomo no Kai of Austin, Texas:

Dear Sir,

I just want to drop you a note. I hope this letter finds you in good health. Things are well with me.

As we have spoken of previously, I would like to invite you to my house on January 2ⁿᵈ at 7 pm. Yuchoku, Miyahira, Nakazato, and others will be here, so I humbly request the honor of your presence as well.

To: Hohan Soken
December 26, 1958
From: Choshin Chibana

Second part appears to be an attachment of activities carried out on September 9 by the All Okinawa Karate-do Rengo Kai:

To all the members and the committee:

1. *The authority of the committee supersedes that of the president.*
1. *The decisions made during director meetings must be approved by the Committee.*
1. *Individual titles must be approved and given by both the President and the Judge.*
1. *Masters are 9 Dan and 10 Dan*
   Shihan (Instructors) are 7 and 10 Dan
   Assistant Instructors are 5 and 6 Dan
1. *Title and rank must be awarded together*
1. *Instructor's names and ranks:*
   8 Dan... Shoshin Nagamine
   Yuchoku Higa
   Meitoku Yagi
   Kanei Uechi

   7 Dan...Hohan Soken
   Saburo Uehara
   Jyoei Kushi
   Shinei Kyan
   Katsuya Miyahira
   Shugoro Nakazato
   Eiichi Miyazato
   Seiki Itokazu

Please consider the above points during the Director meetings.

September 9
From: Choshin Chibana
To: The Members and the Committee

It is clear that the above letter from Choshin Chibana to Hohan Soken offers proof that Grandmaster Chibana and the other members of the "All Okinawa Karate-do Rengo Kai" considered Hohan Soken to be a legitimate karateka.

Cathy Cohen, wife of Ken Cohen, demonstrating Pai Sai Sho kata at a tournament held in the 1960's at Kadena Air Force Base, Okinawa. In the back ground are Mr. Tamaya, Hohan Soken, Seizan Kinjo, and Fusei Kise. Photo credit: Author's collection.

Ken Cohen, who was a student of Sensei Fusei Kise and Grandmaster Soken in the 1960's told me story about Master Soken attending a "Bo Festival" held near Ishigawa (near the narrowest part of Okinawa) during the 1960's. Master Soken attended the event with several of his American students. Upon arrival, they found the activity in full swing with various practitioners practicing their Bo kata and so forth.

When Grandmaster Soken got out of the car; all of the festival participants sat down to watch the old master. Sensei Soken demonstrated his Chikin no Bo kata. A short time later he got back in the car and his students drove him back home. It was clear to Ken Cohen that the people at this activity held Hohan Soken in very high esteem.

Steve Warren, who studied in Okinawa during the 1970's, tells an interesting story about Master Soken and a leather kicking bag. Sensei Kise had a karate class on Kadena Air Force Base on Okinawa. The class was held at the base USO Club. One of their training equipment was leather kicking bag that was getting some age on it but was still serviceable.

Once when Sensei Soken was visiting the USO class he examined the kicking bag and asked Sensei Kise if he could strike the bag with his spear hand (nukite). Sensei Kise answered yes. The old master got into his kamae and struck the bag with his finger tips.

Thrusting deep into the bag, Grandmaster Soken penetrated the leather bag with his nukite attack. He was about 83 years old when this happened.

Sensei Yuichi Kuda once told me a story about Master Soken that will give the reader a glimpse of the old master's personality and serve as a testimony of the respect the Okinawan martial artists gave to the old master. It seems that some time in the late 1960's. Master Soken was asked to demonstrate the effectiveness of Okinawan kobujutsu against some "kendoka" (practitioners of kendo) using either bokens or bamboo shina. The demonstration was to be held at a Kendo tournament which was being held in Okinawa.

During the demonstration, Grandmaster Soken fought against men much less than half his age. He time and time again successfully dodged, blocked and countered all of the attacks being "aimed" at him by the kendoka. He defeated all of those who challenged him. After the event Master Soken was honored with a certificate acknowledging his expertise with Okinawa's traditional weapons.

Upon arriving back home Sensei Soken rolled up the certificate and with a laugh said something like "what is this" and placed the certificate in a small space behind a picture hanging over his front door.

The following are a number of photos showing Grandmaster Soken as a member of several organizations, or attending various functions with other Okinawan Masters.

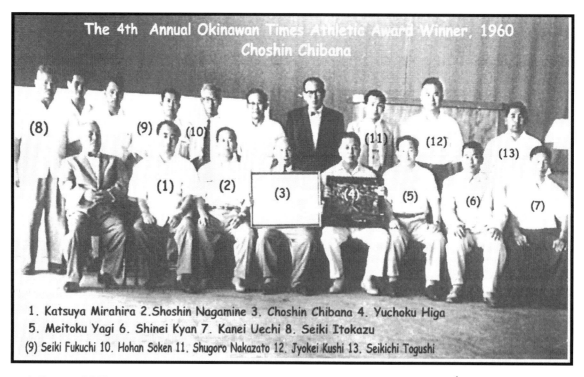

The 4th Annual Okinawan Times Athletic Award Winner, 1960
Choshin Chibana

1. Katsuya Mirahira 2. Shoshin Nagamine 3. Choshin Chibana 4. Yuchoku Higa
5. Meitoku Yagi 6. Shinei Kyan 7. Kanei Uechi 8. Seiki Itokazu
(9) Seiki Fukuchi 10. Hohan Soken 11. Shugoro Nakazato 12. Jyokei Kushi 13. Seikichi Togushi

A Group of Okinawan Karate Masters honoring Chosin Chibana the winner of 4th Annual Okinawan Times Athletic Award in 1960. Hohan Soken is on row two, fifth from the left. The next photo is of the 1st meeting of Okinawa's Kobudo Association. Credit both photo: Author's collection

First Meeting of the Okinawan Kobudo Kyokai (Association) June 17, 1961

1. Santos Kina 2. Shigeru Nakamura 3. Shinei Kyan 4. Shosei Kina 5. Seitoku Higa 6. Hohan Soken 7. Seiyu Nakazone 8. Chozo Nakama 9. Sabaro Kochinda 10. Tatsuo Shimabukuro 11. Zenryo Shimabukuro 12. Yoshitome Kajo 13. Shinyu Isa 14. Masami Chinen 15. Konzo Nakandakari

全沖縄空手古武道連合会 演武と試合大会記念
1967. 6. 11.

Zen Okinawa Karate Kobudo Rengo Kai June 11, 1967

[1] Seikichi Uehara   [6] Hohan Soken   [11] Katsuya Mirahira   [16] Seikichi Odo
[2] Seiki Itokazu   [7] Shigeru Nakamura   [12] Meitoku Yagi   [17] Konzo Nakandakari
[3] Shinken Taira   [8] Tatsuo Shimabukuro [13] Zenryo Shimabukuro [18] Frank Hargrove
[4] Seitoku Higa   [9] Shugoro Nakazato   [14] Seiyu Oyata
[5] Shosei Kina   [10] Chozo Nakama   [15] Fusei Kise

In both of the above photo Hohan Soken is seated in a place of honor. Photo credit: Author's collection

165

In 1972 Kanei Uechi and Uechi Ryu Seniors wrote a book about Okinawa Karate and Kobudo. This book titled "Uechi Ryu Karate-Do Master Text" is 934 pages and covers a vast amount of information about Okinawan Karate/Kobudo in general and Uechi Ryu Karatedo in particular. Included in this book is information on 24 of the Masters or Grandmasters alive on Okinawa when this book was written. Hohan Soken is one of the 24 interviewed; below is the first page of a two page article on Sensei Soken from this book. It is clear the Grandmaster Uechi and Uechi Ryu Seniors considered Hohan Soken to be a legitimate Okinawan karate master.

少林流松村正統沖縄古武道協会

祖 堅 方 範 氏

会　　　長　　祖堅方範（範士）
本　　　籍　　沖縄県西原村字我謝104番地
現 住 所　　　同　　上
生年月日　　明治24年5月25日
職　　業　　農　業

武　　歴

　明治37年、13歳の頃、沖縄の呼名でナビータンメー（日本名不明—当時は唐名＝中国名、日本名、沖縄名があって、一般に唐名と日本名は使われていなかった）のもとに入門し、その後、30歳すぎまでナビータンメーを唯一の師として空手の修業に専念する。

　祖堅氏の流派は「武士松村」こと松村宗棍師の正統の流派であり、松村氏より現在の祖堅氏までは三代の道統が継承されている。祖堅氏は師ナビータンメーが古武道にはそれほど通じていなかったので、西原の伊保の浜に住んでいた米須ウシータンメーに古武道の伝授を仰ぎ、その後自ら創意工夫しながら研究を続けた。

　武術の種類が変るごとに師匠も変るのが当時の武術界だったが、自ら師の立場に立つ現在、祖堅氏は多くの師に就いて身に修めた全ての古武術を統括する形で、総合的に伝授を施し、後進が師を求めて転々と道場を変えることのないように配慮している。この配慮の背景には師弟関係の節度を強く保持したいという祖堅氏の志向がみられる。限られた時間で、限られたエネルギーで、限られた可能性のもとで、多くの師に就くということは、今述べた限定的・人間的

789

166

Okinawa karate master attend a tournament at Kadena AFB. 1960's. This group of masters are members of the All Okinawan Kobudo Kyokai. From left to right back row: Konzo Nakandakari, Seikichi Uehara, Seitoku Higa, Hohan Soken, Shian Toma, and Fusei Kise First row: Tom Hunnicutt, Seizan Kinjo, Eji Shima. Photo credit: Tom Hunnicutt collection

Drawing by Albert Lucio…Author's collection

SOKEN'S STUDENTS

Hohan Soken produced many students both Okinawan and American as well as other nationalities. It will be impossible to name each one; I will do my best to mention most of them.

To start off with; I will mention the big five of Hohan Soken's students. These individuals probably studied longer with the old master than any of his Okinawan students. They are picture below at the 1972 opening of Sensei Yuichi Kuda's dojo.

Photo taken at the 1972 Opening of Sensei Kuda's Kobu Kan Dojo
First row left to right: Seiki Arakaki, Yuichi Kuda, Hohan Soken, and Mitsou Inoue
Second row: Hiroshi Kikumura, Jushin Kohama, Kosei Nishihira, Eiji Shima, Hideo Nakazato
Soken's big five refers (these men are those who perhaps trained exclusively at Soken's dojo) Seiki
Arakaki, Mitsou Enoue, Jushin Kohama, Kosei Nishihira, and
Hideo Nakazato. Out of the big five, Arakaki, and Nishihira are deceased. Others in this picture that
are deceased are: Yuichi Kuda, and Hohan Soken.
Photo credit: George Alexander's collection

168

Seated from left to right Mitsou Inoue, Hohan Soken, Seiki Arakaki
Standing left to right Kosei Nishihira, Hideo Nakazato, Jushin Kohama,
unidentified. This photo was taken at the opening of Inoue Sensei's dojo.
It is interesting to note that kanji on the board between Mitsou Inuoe and
Hohan Soken states the following: "Shorin Ryu Karate/Kobujutsu Dojo."
Photo credit: Chuck Chandler collection.

Unofficial partial list of Grandmaster Soken's Okinawan and American students:

Seiki Arakaki, Roy Suenaka, David Mauk, Fred Sypher, Jimmy Coffman, Ken Cohen Jushin Kohama, Seizan Kinjo, Chotoku Makabe, Mitsou Enoue, Kosei Nishihira Fusei Kise, Takaya Yabiku, Hideo Nakazato, Yuichi Kuda , Nishimae Jinji , Zaha, Masamitsu Oshiro, Akamine, Nita, Gordon Hansen, Ed Thompson, Vincent Wiegand Tom Belamy, David Shelton, Ronald Lindsey, Brandon Pender, Ed Gingras, Charles Garrett, Ted Lange, Rick Rose, Gary Stanfield and Roy Osborn.

I have been unable to locate any official list of Hohan Soken's students, either Americans, Okinawans or any others. I apologize to anyone that I have excluded from this list.

Takaya Yabiku was for many years acting secretary to Master Hohan Soken. Sensei Yabiku has black belt ranks in Uechi Ryu, Goju Ryu and is a master of Shorin Ryu Matsumura Seito and Koshin-Ryu under Grandmaster Irimaji Seiji.

Left: Takaya Yabiku and above Masamitsu Oshiro both were long time students of O'Sensei Soken. Author's collection

FUSEI KISE'S DOJO

Sensei Mitsou Enoue once described Fusei Kise as one of the best trained karateka on Okinawa. Born in 1935 Sensei Kise grew up in hard times; his parents died early in his life and he also lived through World War II and the Battle of Okinawa. Fusei Kise is a survivor.

I wish to present to the reader with information about Fusei Kise along with numerous photos from many sources.

Sensei Kise's Dojo was located down a narrow alley in old Koza, in an area unofficially called **"The Bush."** Sensei Kise operated for some 10 years a small austere karate dojo call the **Seishin Kan** (pure heart building). It was here that numerous young Okinawans and a few American learn old, hard Okinawan Karate from a small 5'2", 130 pound man made of iron called Fusei Kise.

Mitsou Enoue as of 2000 the oldest surviving student of Grandmaster Hohan Soken. Photo credit: Author's collection

170

The building contained little art work and few photos. The floor of the dojo was covered with pock marks from sai being stuck in the floor. The dojo had a kick bag, a makiwara and a few other training devises. Rather than being the exception Sensei Kise's Seishin Kan was a typical Okinawan dojo of the 1960's.

Photo taken by Seizan Kinjo 1960's of the Author and his wife Kathy in front of Sensei Kise's Dojo
Photo credit: Author's collection
Below: Sensei Kise's Dojo, Bogu Sparring on Rank Test Day During the 1960's.
Photo credit: Mike Gavin

Sensei Kise taught Shorinji Ryu Karate until late 1967. At that time he began teaching Shorin Ryu Matsumura Seito. However, many Americans studying with Sensei Kise prior to mid 1967 were not aware of the style's name. Many Americans who actually learned Shorinji Ryu from Sensei Kise thought they had learned Shorin Ryu Matsumura Seito. This led to much confusion.

Sensei Kise often referred to Shorin Ryu Matsumura Seito Karate/Kobudo as "straight karate" meaning that the style traced itself directly back through Matsumura family members to Bushi Matsumura. Shorinji on the other hand traced back to Chotoku Kyan and then back to Bushi Matsumura. However, both methods are considered Matsumura-ha (Matsumura lineage). [4-18]

Rank Testing at the old Koza Dojo 1966. Seated at the table L to R Shigeru Nakamura, Seiyu Oyata, Shian Toma. Photo credit: Mike Gavin

Fusei Kise Nana (7) Dan
Certificate Okinawan Kenpo,
1 Jan. 1965
Credit: Author's collection

"To know and to act are one."
A lesson from a Chinese fortune cookie.

Kadena AFB Karate Club 1966

(3)

(1)

(2)

1. Hohan Soken   2. Fusei Kise   3. Roy Osborn

Above Photo of the Kadena AFB Karate Club. Photo credit: Roy Osborne collection
Below photo is of Sensei Tamaya, Hohan Soken and Fusei Kise in Sensei Kise new dojo built in the
1970's Photo credit: Author's collection

Group Photo late 1970's in Sensei Kise's new dojo. Seated from L to R Fusei Kise S. Tamaya, Yuichi Kuda and Chotoku Makabe. Photo credit: Author's collection

SHISA LIONS

Sensei Kise once told me a some what funning story about his youth. We were standing together in the alley near his dojo and an older Okinawan man and woman walked by. Sensei Kise and the Okinawan couple spoke to each other. I could tell by the tone of the conversation that this was a pleasant chat between old friends.

Shisa... Author's collection

After the couple left I asked Sensei Kise about the conversation and Sensei said they talked about when he was a boy in the Koza area. He would sometimes climb on the roofs of his neighbors' houses and break off the Shisa with his toe kicks. The old couple was reminding how wild Sensei Kise had been as a youth and seemed to be congratulating him for his success as a karate master.

The Shisa Lions, sometimes called Shisa Dogs or "Fu Dogs" are from Okinawan Mythology. These guardian creatures actually are of Chinese origin and may actually be based on a Chinese breed of dogs called "the Lion Dog". These were house dogs that barked when ever any thing or anyone came near the house and gained the reputation as guardian dogs.

From left to right….Shisa on a roof of an Okinawan house…..Credit: Wikimedia Commons Chinese Lion Dog….Credit: Chinese Creed and Customs by V. R. Burckhardt published in China 1953 by Book World Co.

Sensei Kise grew up tough and learned to survive in the dangerous Bars and Red Light area of Koza just out side of Kadena Air Base. Teaching karate became one of the ways he lifted himself out and away from a possible life of crime. Sensei Kise became one of the first Okinawan Karate masters to teach karate on a US Military Post in Okinawa.

A TALE OF FIVE SWORDS

In 1969, I had acquired two Vietnamese swords while on a TDY (temporary duty) mission to South Vietnam. When I returned to Okinawa, I showed these swords to Sensei Seizan Kinjo. Sensei Kinjo really like the Vietnamese sword and he wanted to trade me an old Chinese "Seven Star Sword" for the two Vietnamese swords. I agreed to the trade and I soon owned an antique Chinese sword with a broken handle. Nevertheless the Chinese sword was very old (I estimated that it was over 100 years old) and the Vietnamese swords appeared to be about 25 to 50 years old. So I was proud of my trade.

During the early 1980's Sensei Fusei Kise was visiting my home. I showed him several swords from my collection of Japanese swords. I also showed him the Chinese sword. He said that the Chinese sword was his. I offered to give him back the sword; but he declined the offer. I gave him two Japanese Samurai swords and everything ended well. Thus we have the tale of "Five Swords".

The Seven Star Chinese Sword from the story "A Tale of Five Swords."

Credit: Author's collection.

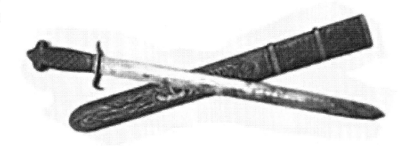

175

KICK TRAINING

From time to time Sensei Kise held a training session called "Kick Training"; this would consist of having his class perform about 8 to 10 different types of kicks with each black belt in class counting a cadence of ten repetitions for each kick. In other words if the were 20 black belts present and 10 different kick were practiced with 10 repetitions for each kick; than that particular training session would consist of 2000 kicks. Often there were upwards of 30 black belts present.

Such training developed strong and dangerous kicks. Sensei Kise's kicks were deadly. His feet were hardened to such an extent that they resembled hooves rather than feet. Often at "sake" or drinking parties these "feet" presented a problem.

Sensei Kise in the 1960's like many Okinawans was fond of strong alcoholic drink. His brand of choice in those days was *Johnny Walker Red* or *Jim Beam* and he would often over indulge to the extent that some of his students would have to put him to bed. Now the problem was that Sensei's senses and reflex actions were so highly developed that he might kick anyone who picked him up to put him to bed. The thought of getting kicked by those "hooves" presented a real problem. Finally,

Sensei Kise's deadly toe kick aimed at his opponent's liver. Photo credit: Author's collection

participants at these "sake" parties began bundling up Sensei Kise's feet in soft pillows before they picked him up. Even with the use of the pillows to soften his kicks; Sensei's kicks were still dangerous.

TESTING HIS TECHNIQUE

Fusei Kise like so many of the Okinawan karate masters of the past sought to test his technique in actual fighting. Often during the 1960's Sensei Kise would go to bars in the Gate 2/BC Street areas of Koza just east of Kadena AFB for the sole purpose of getting into a fight with US Servicemen who frequented these areas.

These affairs never lasted long; they would consist of the US service man attacking Kise suddenly with a kick or a punch. Sensei Kise answered with a quick dodging maneuver and counter with a Naihanchi Kata punch to the chin of the attacker and the event would be over.

176

From time to time Okinawan men would come to Sensei's dojo and call him out to settle a disagreement with combat. Americans training at the dojo remember and comment on such events with the following typical statement. "This Okinawan man came up to the Dojo and talked to Sensei Kise; Sensei then asked every one to leave the dojo and come back in 15 or 20 minutes. We all left and when we came back, the man who was talking with Sensei was laying unconscious in the ally in front of the dojo. When we finished class he was gone.

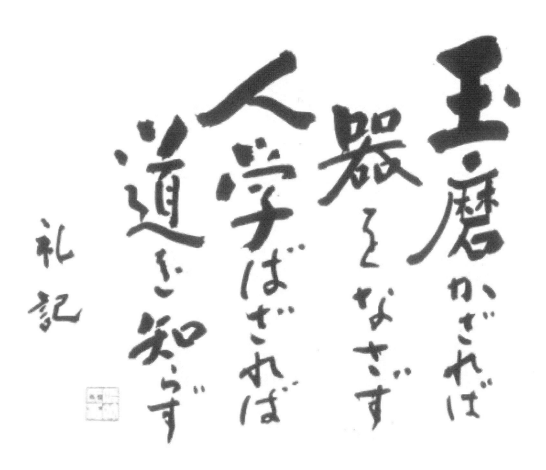

"An uncut gem does not sparkle; learn not, know not.
No one can be strong without hard practice and can not realize the real karate
without learning"

A gift from Sensei Fusei Kise.

Author's collection

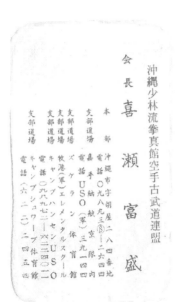

沖縄少林流拳真館空手古武道連盟

会長 喜瀬富盛

Okinawa Shorin-ryu Kenshinkan Karate
Kobudo Federation

Fusei Kise
CHAIRMAN 3/18/9893 22644

Main Dojo : 284, Goya Okinawa City   TEL 09893 2 2644
Branch Dojo: K. A. B. U S O   TEL 39144
    "   Sukuran Stillwel Fields House TEL 63-5270
    "   Machinato Elementary School
    "   Camp Hansen USO   TEL 098972-6224011
    "   Camp Shwab Stadium   TEL 631 - 4347

***Fusei Kise's Business Card given to the Author in
1980. Credit Author's collection***

***Photo L to R - Shian Toma, Seikichi
Odo and Fusei Kise. Photo credit: Roy
Jerry Hobbs collection. Below left
Shian Toma and Fusei Kise.... Below
right Fusei Kise 1985. Both photo
credits: Author's collection.***

178

YUICHI KUDA'S DOJO

Sensei Yuichi Kuda could well have been known as the "Gentleman from Machianato,
Okinawa." He was demanding yet kind, and he enjoyed teaching Karate/Kobujutsu. His style "Shorin Ryu Matsumura Kenpo" was a blend of the Okinawan Kenpo he learned from Grandmaster Shigeru Nakamura and Master Seiyu Oyata and Shorin Ryu Matsumura Seito Karate/Kobudo which he learned from Grandmaster Hohan Soken. Sensei Kuda also learn, as a child in Sakuga Village, the kobujutsu methods of this village; which included the fighting methods of his ancestors.

Sakuga Village was located on the Chinen Peninsula of Southern Okinawa. The village was totally destroyed during World War II and was never rebuilt.

The Kuda family was the hereditary Chieftains of Sakuga. Originally the family name was Chinen but after some good deed, performed for the Okinawan King; one of Sensei Kuda's ancestors was granted permission to change his name to Kuda meaning "rice field." The following photos are of Sensei Kuda and his dojo.

Top and left photos of Yuichi Kuda 1985 La Grange, Texas. Photo credit: Author's collection

少林流松村正統空手道
支部
浦添　師範　久田　友一
　　　　　　島　英治

Let to right Sensei Yuichi Kuda, Grandmaster Hohan Soken, and Sensei Eji Shima at the opening of Sensei Kuda's dojo in 1972. Kanji reads Shorin Ryu Matsumura Seito Karatedo Shihan Yuichi Kuda and Shihan Eji Shima. Photo credit: Yuichi Kuda collection.

Credit: "Little Pictures of Japan" Published by The Booklouse for Little Children."

Edited by Olive Miller Pictures by Katharine Sturges

少林流興武館空手古武術道場

Entrance to Sensei Kuda's Dojo; sign reads: Shorin Ryu Kobukan Karate/Kobujutsu Dojo. Photo Credit: Ernest Estrada. Below A young Yuichi Kuda stands in his dojo 1972 Photo credit: Author's collection

Below: Sensei Kuda's Kobukan Dojo Photo credit: Ernest Estrada's collection

181

Jan. 1, 1968 New Years Party at Seiyu Oyata's Kenpu Kan Dojo Seated L to R Shigeru Nakamura, Founder of Okinawa Kenpo Karatedo, Seiyu Oyata, Yuichi Kuda. Both Oyata Sensei and Kuda Sensei were excellent Sanshin players. Photo is a gift from Sensei Kuda.
Photo credit: Yuichi Kuda's collection

Below: Okinawan Sanchin made by Yuichi Kuda.
A gift from Sensei Kuda to the Author in 1985.
Photo Credit: Author's collection

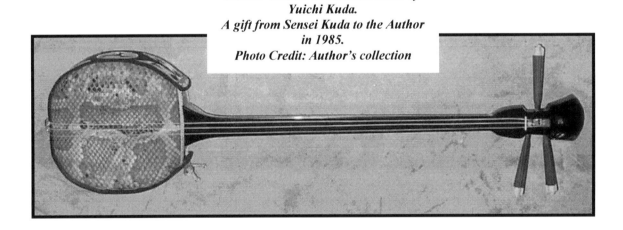

"Patience is gold"
A lesson from a Chinese fortune cookie

全沖縄少林流空手古武道連盟

範士 久田友一

浦添市字牧港一三九番地
電話〇九八八一七七一二六四九

ALL OKINAWA SHORINRYU
KARATE & KOBUDO ASSOCIATION

Yuichi Kuda

Chief Judge

Address 139 Makiminato Urasoe City
TEL. 0988—77— 2 6 4 9

*Sensei Kuda's business cards given to the Author
in September 1984. Credit: Author's collection*

*Below is a letter from Yuichi Kuda to the Author
stating who is qualified to teach his style. Letter
was written in the mid to late 1980's. Credit:
Author's collection.*

Letter written by Eric Wehmeyer
for Sensei Kuda and signed by
Sensei

Dear Ron,

I'm writing this letter for Sensei Kuda in regard to who has sufficient training of the Kata Sensei teaches. Also, who may travel and teach the Kata. Names are as follows: Ron Lindsey, Charles Tatum, Toshi Gillespie; these people may teach Kata nation wide. Greg Ohl may not. except with in the State of Minn. That is to say Mr. Ohl's Kata is good. however not sufficient to teach nation wide. Ken Penland may not teach nation wide, however California, Oregon, Washington, Nevada ect. the surrounding States. is okay.

Yuichi Kuda

久田友一

Sensei Soken during his time was considered the top weapons master on the Okinawa. Although Master Soken considered both karate and kobujutsu to be the same art; he often referred to his art (both armed and unarmed) as "*kobujutsu*" or old war art.

Sensei Soken's strategy when using the Okinawan weapons was based on several simple ideas or principles. The following is my interpretation of these principles:

1. Weapons are classified as: those that can grab or hold an object and those that can not; weapons that can cut and those that can not.

2. For weapons that can not grab use quick deflection and counters. For those that can grab use this asset by grabbing your opponent's weapon or weapon hand and deny him the use of his weapon.

3. For weapons that cut use light weapons and inflict injury on your opponent with quick cuts or stabs. For weapons that can't cut use big moves to block or strike your opponent. [4-19]

Sensei Soken anchored his Bo on his hip as did his friend Shigeru Nakamura and other Okinawan masters of this age group.

Sensei Soken's Bo technique is to be found in the Chikin no Bo kata of Chikinjima. The technique of this kata uses the Bo with big,

Sensei Soken showing his hip anchor point when using the Bo. Photo credit: Author's collection

and wide circular sweeping moves similar the cutting methods used by the Japanese samurai swordsmen.

Soken preferred a light pair of kama with an oval shaped cross section of the handle. His kama kata are difficult to perform with heavy kama.

Grandmaster Soken's' Bo Technique; Credit Author's collection

Soken Sensei often used an unusual method of holding the kama. He often held the kama high up on the handle near the blade. Soken had grown up at a time when the Okinawan farmers used the kama not only in their work but also to defend themselves. He knew the method the Okinawans used to fasten the blade to the handle was weak and the blade might pull out of the handle when cutting through a hard object like an arm bone. By gripping the handle near the blade he reinforced the method use to attach the blade to the handle. [4-20]

Hohan Soken at the age of 59 years; photo taken in the court yard of his home in Argentina in 1948. Note: The unusual method of hold the kama. Photo credit: Resources Unlimited

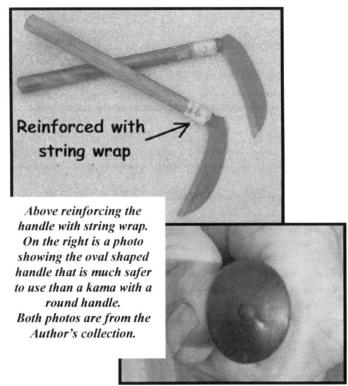

Reinforced with string wrap

Above reinforcing the handle with string wrap. On the right is a photo showing the oval shaped handle that is much safer to use than a kama with a round handle.
Both photos are from the Author's collection.

!966 Shilling Community Center Kadena AFB Okinawa, Sensei Soken performing Kusarigama Kata. Photo credit: Mike Gavin collection

Fusei Kise and Hohan Soken demonstrate fighting techniques with Bo and Sai at Torii Station in 1968. Standing second from the left is Tom Belamy and on the far right is Tom Honnicutt. Photo credit: Tom Hunnicutt collection

186

Most of the Okinawan masters who practiced with Tonfa had them made by local craftsmen during the 1950's and 1960's. Grandmaster Soken, Sensei Kise and others had their tonfa made by an old man in the central part of Okinawa. I do not remember his name but he made excellent tonfa. When he became too old to continue his trade his son took over the tonfa making business.

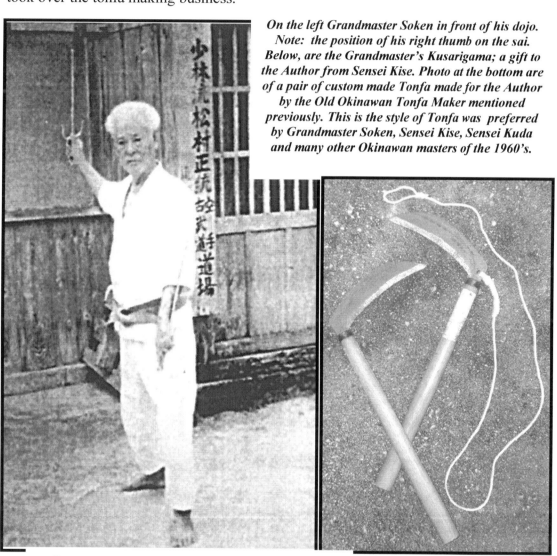

On the left Grandmaster Soken in front of his dojo. Note: the position of his right thumb on the sai. Below, are the Grandmaster's Kusarigama; a gift to the Author from Sensei Kise. Photo at the bottom are of a pair of custom made Tonfa made for the Author by the Old Okinawan Tonfa Maker mentioned previously. This is the style of Tonfa was preferred by Grandmaster Soken, Sensei Kise, Sensei Kuda and many other Okinawan masters of the 1960's.

Above photo credit: Resources Unlimited; above right and below Photo credit: the Author's collection

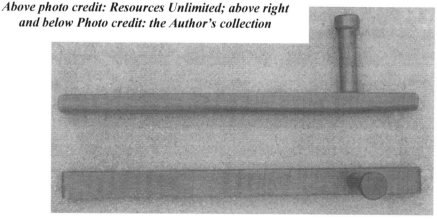

187

Death Poem

I have taught you all I know.
There is no more I can teach you.
I am a candle whose light has traveled far.
You are my candle to whom I have passed on my light.
It is you who will light the path for others.

Today I see around me the lights of Shaolin,
the flame of tomorrow.
My task is done, soon my flame will end.
Teach the true spirit of Karatedo and one
day you may enter the Temple of Shaolin.

O'Sensei Hohan Soken
May 25, 1889 – December 2, 1982

Grandmaster Hohan Soken a few years
before his death. Photo Credit: Author's
collection

END NOTES, SOURCES AND EXPLANATIONS

Most of the information found in this chapter comes from conversations with my Okinawan Shorin Ryu teachers. I have also tried to be more specific by identifying some sources with foot notes or by indicating the source in my text.

Hohan Soken's Early Life

4-1   Sources; oral traditions handed down to me Okinawan Shorin Ryu Matsumura Seito Teachers.
4-2   Ibid
4-3   Ibid
4-4   Ibid
4-5   Ibid
4-6   Ibid

The Training of a Bushi

4-7   Sources: Ernest Estrada's interviews with Hohan Soken conducted in the late 1970's and conversations from Yuichi Kuda, Fusei Kise and Seizan Kinjo.

Soken's Kata

Generally speaking the sources for the information presented in this section are from informal conversations with my Okinawan Karate Sensei.

4-8   In 1984, I demonstrate in front of Fusei Kise and Yuichi Kuda in the Kusanku kata I learned from Sensei Soken in 1970. Both Sensei Kise and Sensei Kuda told me that this was the Kusanku Mai Kata that came from Bushi Matsumura's wife. The kata I am calling Shiho Kusanku was called only Kusanku; the kata closely resembles the Shiho Kusanku Kata. Therefore, I call the kata Shiho Kusanku just to keep it separated from the other Kusanku Kata.
4-9   Source: conversations with Fusei Kise.
4-10   Tape recorded interview with Hohan Soken by an Okinawan Newspaper conducted in the late 1970's. I believe the newspaper was the Okinawan Time. Mrs. Steve Lapham translated the recording from Japanese to English.
4-11   Ibid
4-12   Source: Chuck Chandler's conversations with Takaya Yabiku late 1990's.
4-13   Ibid
4-14   Source: Late 1970's tape recorded interview between Grandmaster Soken and the Okinawan Times Newspaper.

Okinawan Tode

4-15   Sources: Ernest Estrada's interviews with Hohan Soken and Shinpo Matayoshi, conversations with Bill Hayes, Anthony Sandoval, Fusei Kise, Yuichi Kuda and my own experience and observations.
4-16   The terms village karate (old methods) and school karate (newer methods) were widely used by my Okinawan teachers.

Defending Grandmaster Soken's Honor

Generally the sources for this sub-chapter are found in the text. The information presented in this section was collected by the author starting about 40 years ago

4-17   Explanation: my goal in writing this subchapter was to present facts confirming the authenticity of Grandmaster Hohan Soken.

Grandmaster Soken's Students

Information presented in this sub-chapter comes from my experience and conversations with my Shorin Ryu Matsumura Seito teachers.

Sensei Kise's Dojo

Sources for this sub-chapter are mentioned in the text or they come from my experience.

4-18   Source: conversations with Sensei Kise

Sensei Kuda's Dojo

Sources for this sub-chapter are my experiences

Grandmaster Soken's Kobujutsu

4-19   Source: conversations with Yuchi Kuda
4-20   Ibid

Rain Coats made of grass were once common through out Japan, China and Okinawa.
Credit: "Chinese Creeds and Customs" by V. R. Burkhardt

PART 2

MY WALK WITH MATSUMURA

Computer generated drawing by the Author.
Author's collection

"Ju Ze Sei Go"

Softness over comes Hardness

An old Okinawan Bushi adage that influences the Okinawan Fighting Arts.

This old saying is at the front of Sensei Kise's Dojo

Credit the Author's collection

When Oriental Martial Arts were introduced into the Western World; all practitioners of these arts followed traditional learning methods. Therefore, in the beginning, all were traditionalist; however, over time, many sought ways to change or improve on the traditional approach to martial arts.

Today the pure traditionalist is very rare, modern methods are common place but few still use only traditional methods. In Okinawa and for those of us who claim to follow the traditional training methods of Okinawa Karate-Do or Karate-Jutsu; traditional training is based on learning and having complete faith in the traditional Kata. There are those who claim that Kata are obsolete; that Kata is not necessary and that and that some old masters, such as the late Grand Master Hohan Soken' did not rely on Kata as their principle teaching method. People who make such claims are foolish. Rather than scorn these individuals, they should be pitied. Each time the Karateka practices the old kata, they are taking a lesson from the kata's founder. Hohan Soken often said, "Practice your kata and you will teach yourself." Through the kata you will progress beyond your physical ability.

Okinawa has many traditional styles of Karate-Do. These styles are called "Ryu." Translated, literally Ryu means a river . . . a school where knowledge flows like water from teacher to student. If the Ryu is an old method that has not been "polluted" with sport (tournament) tactics, then the kata will provide the instruction and the guidance to truly learn Karate.

Most modern "Ryu" cannot truly be classified as Ko Ryu or Old Style. Prior to the turn of the 20th Century, all Karate in Okinawa was called Karate-Jutsu, the term; Karate-Do was not used until the 1930's and in some instances not until after World War II. When Karate was introduced into the Okinawa School Physical Education Programs in 1903 much of the old methods were lost. The karate "Ryu" soon fell into two categories: School Karate and Village Karate. It is the Kata of the old village styles that truly have value. In these formal exercises we find the strategy and techniques that enabled the Okinawa Samurai to persevere and prosper in a dangerous world.

The skills taught in the old Kata are two fold:

1. Strategic ... the thoughts; principles and concepts unique to a certain Kata, and to the Ryu or style.

2. Tactical ... the actual methods of carrying out these strategic concepts and principles.

These skills are taught through various strategies or "heiho jutsu". Heiho jutsu actually means… (hei)…or soldier's, (ho)..law, and (jutsu)…art. Together these terms would translate to "a soldier's law art. A more practical interpretation would be "rules for staying alive in combat". For the purpose of simplification….heiho jutsu and strategy will be used interchangeably. These strategies discussed in this section are as applicable today as they were during ancient times. They are for war be it army against army or combat between individuals.

The old fighting arts of Okinawa and China contain many combat strategies. Yet in my opinion we can "render" all of this down to four main strategies; these are as follows:

1. *Kokoro no Heiho ... the strategy of "mental attitude" or "heart."*

2. *Minari no Heiho ... the strategy of appearance.*
3. *Maai no Heiho ... distancing or the strategy and study of the combat distance.*

4. *Chushin no Heiho ...the strategy and study of the combat center.*

I learned Okinawan Karate and heiho jutsu from six Okinawan Sensei they are:

Seizan Kinjo... Shorin Ryu Matsumura Seito Karate/Kobujutsu
Hohan Soken...Shorin Ryu Matsumura Seito Karate/Kobujutsu
Fusei Kise... Shorin Ryu Matsumura Seito Karate/Kobujutsu
Yuchi Kuda... Shorin Ryu Matsumura Seito Karate/Kobujutsu
Seiyu Shinjo...Uechi Ryu Karatedo
Sekichi Odo... Okinawan Kenpo Karatedo

Through the discussion of the above four main strategies and numerous sub strategies, I hope to tell the reader about my teachers. I will explain how they affected me and how I try to emulate them through my practice and teachings. I also will show how these strategies played major roles in famous battles that shaped history.

The Japanese names and a great deal of the information concerning "Heihojutsu used in this discussion come from Fredrick J. Lovret's book, "the Way and the Power....Secrets of Japanese Strategy"; published by Paladin Press. My Okinawan teachers did not have names for a lot of their ideas and strategies; I have used Mr. Lovret's names for the strategies or heiho and my own experiences to discuss the use of these various points.

For the most part my teachers were simple men, they did not posses great formal educations; yet their knowledge of strategy, the human anatomy, the physical sciences of balance, power, economy of movement and human behavior were simply amazing. They counted among their friends military generals, international politicians and leaders as well as the owners of brothels, bars and members of the Yakuza. Some were gentlemen others were rouges but all were masters.

 The Golden Rule...*"Do unto others as you would have them do unto you"* is a Biblical Guide for mankind. If the human race would follow this guide line there would be no wars, no conflicts no arguments and no need for heiho jutsu; there would only be peace. However, the Bible says that "there will always be war and rumors of war"; therefore, there will always be a need for warriors and for the self protection arts. I invite you, the reader, to join me on "My Walk with Matsumura".

CHAPTER 5
KOKORO NO HEIHO
(THE STRATEGY OF MENTAL ATTITUDE)

Computer generated drawing by the Author.
Author's collection

Kokoro no Heiho

"The strategy of mental attitude"
Credit: Author's collection

The most important of all strategies is that of Mental Attitude or heart. The strategy of Mental Attitude is called ***Kokoro no Heiho.*** If the aspiring martial artist does not have the perseverance to attend class and learn, then those individuals will never become martial artists and this story could end with this point. However, a small percentage of these budding martial artists will stick around and train; so, it is for this reason we must continue our discussion.

Kokoro is a huge subject; it covers all aspects of life and no attempt to write on this subject will do Kokoro justice. Nevertheless, I am going to try. I will discuss this subject with six sub-topics (1). Heiho, which is built into each subtopic, (2) Wisdom, (3) Nintai or perseverance, (4) Loyalty, (5) Integrity and (6) Giri or obligation

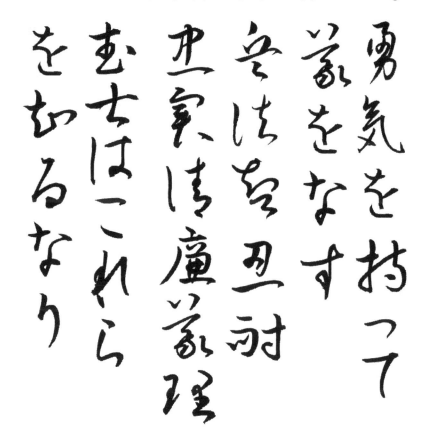

Have the courage to do what is right.
Heiho, Wisdom, Nintai, Loyalty, Integrity, Giri.
The Bushi knows these things.

WISDOM

*"The individualist without strategy who takes opponents lightly will inevitably
become the captive of others."*
Sun Tzu, Ancient Chinese Military Strategist

TAKING ADVANTAGE OF ANCIENT WISDOMS

I once had a Chinese Acupuncturist tell me that the European or western people are
people of metal and the Oriental or eastern people are people of wood. I guess this may
be true of modern European or western people. But, I believe we (the eastern and
western people) were once the same….we all were people of nature.

The Oriental people have maintained a culture based on natural methods long after the
western culture had more or less given up on the original natural methods in favor of
more scientific approach for answers that influence their lives. Now it seems that the
Oriental people may be moving away from the old natural methods while western
people may be re-discovering the natural approach that they once discarded.

Western cultural has long viewed events and have made decisions based on a straight or
linear fashion. They deal with things that are right or wrong; black or white. By doing
so the western culture is often in conflict with the eastern culture. The Eastern people
put great stock in controlling their emotions. They are a people who place great value in
their history. To the eastern people things or events are rarely black or white; rather
they are more likely to see things in shades of grey and more likely to be vague about
events rather than "clear cut".

I remember with a certain fondness of how some of my Okinawan teachers would deal
with the American karateka who asked simple questions such as "How are my
kata".….the Okinawan masters almost painfully would dodge the issue as long as they
could; but the master would finally answer with a statement that would usually be
something like this "Oh Kata good but needs a little more work". Hearing this the
American karateka would be left with the impression that he was doing great and he
only need a little more work….The truth was that the American karateka asking the
questions was terrible but the Okinawan Sensei, always a gentleman could not tell him
that….his answer reflects the vagueness of the eastern people.

"Okinawan fishing boat"

Drawing by the author

198

To examine the attitude and thinking of Eastern people and to relate these thoughts and ideas to the eastern fighting arts; we must understand "balance". This term is the very essence of the Eastern Culture ands all aspects associated with this culture to include the fighting arts.

Taji the symbol of Yin and Yang

This balance is called "*Yin and Yang*" and is best express by the "*Taiji*". This ancient symbol has expanded beyond its original intention of representing the shaded and sunny side of a mountain with the two colors of black and white coiling around each other and each sharing by being a part of each other (which is represented by the smaller black and white circles). This is the Oriental concept of the balance of the universe and is the essence of the oriental culture. This concept has been around for over 2000 years.

The Yin and Yang concept are often associated with traditional oriental medicine and Kyusho Jutsu (a striking art based on hitting vital acupuncture points). However, this discussion is not about kyusho jutsu. The following gives some idea as the properties or correspondences of Yin and Yang: According to Oriental beliefs all things belong to the greater cosmos, and yin or yang is neither good nor bad. Every thing in the universe corresponds to this theory. These correspondences are as numerous as there are items or things; each with its own tag of yin or yang. The following is a listing of a few of these so called correspondences: [5-1]

Yin	Yang
Earth	Heavan
Night	Day
Moon	Sun
Low	High
Heaviness	Lightness
Falling Tendency	Rising Tendency
Movement Inward	Movement Outward
Relatively Stationary	Movement
Caution	Reckless
Shyness	Boldness
Softness	Hardness
Relaxation	Stiffness

There is another similar Oriental concept that has been around for over 400 years. This is the concept of the *Five Elements.* Like the Yin and Yang concept, this is a far reaching system that classifies living things, functions, activities and qualities. [5-2]

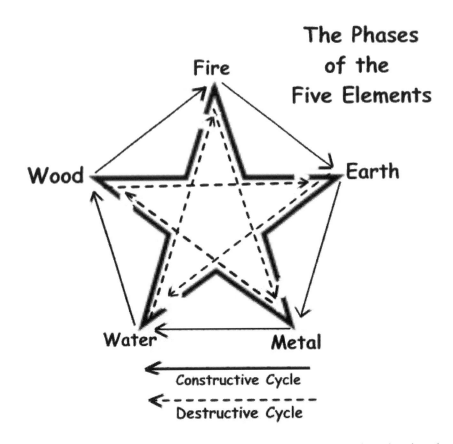

The Phases of the Five Elements

Constructive Cycle
Destructive Cycle

Unlike the classification of Yin and Yang which is interpreted as having been more or less granted by nature (although man kind is constantly debating as to whether or not certain things are yin or yang) the Five Element Classification is always in a phase of growing, shrinkage or other types of change. These changes are usually man made.

The Five Elements are (1) Fire, (2) Earth, (3) Metal, (4) Water, and (5) Wood. Each of these elements have both yin and yang properties and to briefly explain this concept we must arrange them in a five star shape.

To understand the previous star shaped drawing, you need to become aware that the theory of the Five Elements contains two cycles; *(1) The Constructive Cycle (illustrated with the solid arrows connecting the points of the star) and (2) The Destructive Cycle (illustrated with broken line arrows on the inside of the star).*

CONSTRUCTIVE CYCLE

If we start at the top of the star with the element (1) Fire, and move along clockwise, the solid arrow leads to earth. The burning of a fire leaves ashes. Ashes are a mineral substance that forms soil or (Earth). (2) Moving from Earth clockwise the arrow leads to Metal. The mining of the Earth creates metal. (3) From Metal, the arrow moves to Water. Water can be produced from the condensation of moisture on the surface of metal. (4) Moving from water, the arrow moves to Wood. Trees grow and thrive with ample amounts of water. (5) Moving from wood, the solid arrow leads to Fire. Fire uses wood to burn. As you can see, in this cycle, each element is enhanced if not create by the previous element, thus the name "Constructive Cycle".

DESTRUCTIVE CYCLE

Looking at the inside of our drawing, we see a series if dashed lines with arrows (destructive cycle line) points at one end. These lines and arrows form the Destructive Cycle. Starting with (1) Fire and moving down, the Destructive Cycle Line points to metal. This is the first part of the Destructive Cycle. Fire can destroy metal by melting it. (2) Next we move up the Destructive Cycle Line from metal to wood. The sharp metal ax can chop down the strongest of trees. (3) Following the Destructive Line from wood across to earth. We find that earth is weakened or destroyed by plants taking nutrients such as minerals from soil. (4) Moving from earth the Destructive Line points downward to water, we know that earthen dams are used to restrict the flow of water. (5) Moving from water, the Destructive Line points upward to fire. Water is widely used to extinguish or control fires. This completes the cycle. In the Destructive Cycle we find that each element is controlled or destroyed by another element.

Ancient Oriental warriors and military strategist were familiar with the Concept of the Yin and Yang and with the Concept of the Five Element or similar concepts. The Yin and Yang serve as to be a guide for the martial artist's ideas and concept on power and balance; while the Phases of the Five Elements form a basis for fighting strategies or heiho jutsu.

HEIHO JUTSU BASED ON THE FIVE ELEMENTS

The Phases of the Five Element have been used to develop many fighting strategies. Let us examine several adages that are based on these ideas:

(1). When your opponent crouches kick his leg. This is an old Okinawan fighting strategy from the Kojo or Kogushiku family style. In this case the crouched position of your opponent would be an Earth posture. Since wood destroys the earth, you attack your opponent with wood technique such as a low side kick. The kick would be representative of the roots of a tree. In this case wood destroys earth.

Kojo Technique
Author's
collection

2). Another old adage that is attributed to Bushi Matsumura advises one to wait for your opponent to fall apart mentally. In a heated situation that has not broken out into a physical confrontation, but; yet conditions are such that you can not walk away from the situation. Assume a bigger than normal stance...an earth position. This may force your opponent to commit or to quite the scene altogether. Your opponent's non committal represents a water posture. Since water takes the shape of any container it is placed in, water is formless. If you can force him to commit, you then can adjust your position to defeat him. Earth then destroys water.

3) A fiery attacker comes at you, determined to do you great harm. You switch into the water mode and blend with his technique. Poke your finger into his eye as this target presents itself. In this case water destroys fire.

Fire is defeated by water, classic example of staying calm and let your opponent defeat himself.
Author's collection

Below, blending according to your opponent's attack is a water technique...Author's collection

The classic encounter of the famous Boston strongman John L. Sullivan fighting Gentleman Jim Corbett is perhaps the most famous example of a person fighting in wood mode and defeating a more powerful person who was using the earth mode.

In 1892 the mighty John L. Sullivan, lost a boxing match to, a classic scientific boxer, Jim Corbett. Sullivan with his mighty power lacked the mobility of Corbett. Sullivan's style was earth. Corbett on the other hand with his jabs and classic boxing techniques fought in the wood style. Sullivan's power techniques proved useless against Corbett's mobility.

In the late 1960's I had the opportunity to spar many times with the famous Seiyu Shinjo's oldest son Kiyohide Shinjo. Master Shinjo's Uechi Ryu Dojo was located in Kadena village, Okinawa. I was a good boxer and I fought the younger Shinjo with common boxing techniques. Shinjo answered back with lighting front kicks with the outer edge of his feet. His legs were longer than my arm reach. Therefore, he could kick me before I could punch him. His favorite targets for his kicks were my thighs and lower body. I fought with wood tactics. He beat me with metal techniques. An axe can chop a tree down; therefore, metal defeats wood.

To use the Five Element theory one must realize that water and earth are more defensive and are of a yin tendency while wood and fire are more of an offensive nature therefore would correspond to more of a yang tendency. Metal is a tool to be used by all other elements.

The reader must also be aware of a third cycle which is often referred to as the ***Reverse Cycle***. This is a reversal of the destructive cycle. An example of which would be water destroying fire but a small amount of water will not put out a large fire.

Kiyohide Shinjo 1970 era Photo credit:
"Uechi Ryu Karate-Do Master Text" by Kanei Uechi and
other Uechi Ryu Seniors.

"Nothing is one hundred per cent certain.
Every advantage has its disadvantage; for every plus there is a minus....this is yin and yang." *A quote from the college of common sense.*

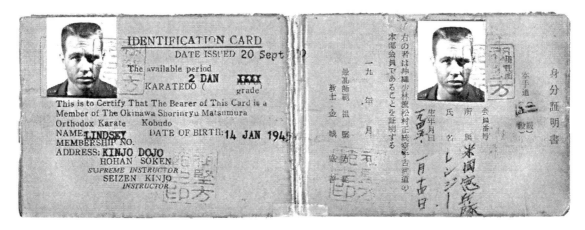

Ronald Lindsey's Membership Card to the Okinawan Shorinryu Matsumura Orthodox
(Seito) Karatedo Association. Credit: Author's collection

In one of the versions of Bushi Matsumura's "Bucho Ikko": Matsumura writes about ***"the boldness of the tiger and the fleetness of the bird"***. The Shaolin Five Animal System is made up of the tiger, leopard, snake, dragon and crane. If we examine these five animals we will find that the tiger and the crane are the opposite of each other as far as techniques are concerned. In my opinion, both the tiger and crane have their own uniqueness of form. While the other animals share much of the tiger's form and some of the crane's form; from a technique point of view, the leopard, snake and dragon are specialist in individual techniques. They are not noted for their individual style or form.

The leopard is very similar to the tiger in technique but the leopard can climb trees which influences its special techniques. The snake is a specialist in striking. The snake develops a sixth sense of knowing at what distance to strike. The dragon with its strong legs and tail is a specialist in sweeping the feet and legs of its opponents.

The tiger is the first animal studied. The tiger's technique is large and powerful, the tiger's attitude is one of boldness; this is the style of youth. The crane's technique is small and mobile. This is the technique of older or people with less strength. The crane is a weak animal, yet he can defeat all of the other animals. The strength of the crane is mobility. This is the model for many Okinawan Shorin Ryu systems. [5-3]

"The flying crane defeats all of its enemies; the immobile bushi defeats only himself."
Credit: Author's collection

THE BUSHI'S WISDOM

Sokon "Bushi" Matsumura in his letter to Ryosei Kuwae, written in the 1880's, offers sound advice and guidelines as to the proper attitude. This letter called **"Matsumura Bucho Ikko"** contains valuable on information and advice on motivation, wisdom, intelligence and knowledge. The advice is as valuable today as it was in the days of Bushi Matsumura and Ryosei Kuwae.

This version of "Matsumura's Bucho Ikko" is from John Sells's book "Unante the Secrets of Karate (Second Addition)"; I am quoting Sell's version and I am going to comment about my opinions concerning the meaning of Sell's version of Matsumura's writings. I will add my comments in italicized wording following Matsumura's remarks.

MATSUMURA BUCHO IKKO

"To Kuwae Ryusei:

These are my teachings that you must understand and make your own. You must firmly resolve to study deeply if you wish to understand the truth of the Martial Arts.
This resolve is very important. Fundamentally, the literary arts (Bun) and the martial arts (Bu) are the same. Each has three elements.

Sokon Matsumura
Photo credit: Chuck Chandler

As far as art is concerned there are Shishu no Gaku, Kunko no Gaku, and Jussha no Gaku. Shishu no Gaku is the act of the creative writing and reading; in other words, the study of literature. Kunko no Gaku means to study the past to gain an understanding of ethics by relating past events to our way of life. Both Shishu no Gaku and Kunko no Gaku are incomplete until supplemented by Jussha no Gaku, the study of the moral aspects of Confucius.

Have a tranquil heart and you can prevail over a village, a country or the world. The study of Jusshu no Gaku is the supreme study over both Shishu no Gaku and Kunko no Gaku. They are then the three elements necessary for the study of arts.

It is my opinion that the above passage refers to, or is influenced by an old Okinawan and Chinese adages that probably are older than the "Matsumura Bucho Ikko". One of adages is often called the "First Okinawan Golden Rule"; the rule states that those who are scholarly and have great knowledge of their specific fields often have a lack of common sense. It is generally understood that one should gain common sense and practical knowledge though experience and longevity of life.

"Through experience wisdom is nurtured"
A lesson from a Chinese fortune cookie.

205

Okinawa's First Golden Saying

"Those who are scholarly and have great knowledge of their specific fields often lack common sense.
To go to the next level of their education, you must not only become scholarly and intelligent,
But you must also become wise with various experiences in good sense."
Information and quote comes from:
"Ryukyu Hiden Karate"
By Takaya Yabiku
Published by:
Resources Unlimited
125 So. Main St.
Summerville, S.C. 294883

Calligraphy by Shifu Hwang

Intelligence is an inherited trait; it is the potential or ability to learn. By its self, intelligence does not give you knowledge or wisdom. Yet even a person of average intelligence is capable of gaining much knowledge and can become very wise.

Knowledge is the accumulation of many facts that are usually gained through a formal education. A person with great knowledge has the potential of becoming very wise. Yet, knowledge alone does not create wisdom.

Wisdom comes from learning many things; the most important of which is learning from the mistakes of the past and using the knowledge gained to prevent people from making the same mistakes again. Wisdom does not require the collection of knowledge gained through formal education. Yet a formal education is desirable and will contribute greatly to the creation of wisdom. Wisdom is gained through experience and experience is a by product of time. The Okinawan term "Tanme" which is an honorable term granted by the Okinawan Culture to certain old men who were considered wise. The use of this term indicates the value this and other cultures place on age and wisdom.

If we consider Budo, there are three precepts. They are Kukushi no Bugei, Meimoko no Bugei, and Budo no Bugei. Kukushi no Bugei is nothing more than a technical knowledge of Bugei. Like a woman, it is superficial and has no depth. Meimoko no Bugei refers to a person who has physical understanding of Bugei. He can be a powerful and violent person who can even harm his own family.

Budo no Bugei is what I admire. With this you can let the enemy destroy himself, just wait with calm heart and the enemy will defeat himself. People who practice Budo no Bugei are loyal to their friends, to their parents and to their country. They

will do nothing that is considered unnatural or contrary to nature. We have the seven virtues of bu and they are:

1. **Bu prohibits violence**
2. **Bu keeps discipline as in soldiers**
3. **Bu keeps control among the population**
4. **Bu spreads virtues**
5. **Bu gives one a peaceful heart**
6. **Bu helps keep the peace between people**
7. **Bu makes people of a nation prosperous**

Our forefathers handed these seven virtues down to us. Just as Jussha no Gaku is supreme in the arts, so Budo is supreme in the martial arts. Mon-Bu (art and martial arts) have the same common elements. We do not need Kukushi no Bugei or Meimoko no Bugei; they are not necessary. We do need Budo no Bugei...this is the most important thing.

I leave these words to my wise and beloved student Kuwae
Matsumura Sokon"

The Matsumura Bucho Ikko gives us three examples of what a warrior's mental attitude should and should not be. In this writing, Matsumura's three Precepts of Budo offers a description of three types of people who are involved in the study of the fighting arts **(Kukushi no Bugei, Meimoko no Bugei and Budo no Bugei.)**.

The first type **Kukushi no Bugei** *is what we see most often. They talk about training but in fact avoid serious training. There is an old saying that* **"Many people want to know ... but few want to learn."** *True learning requires hard work; few people are willing to put forth the effort to truly learn. It is easier to just talk about it. This old saying is referring to the Kukushi no Bugei. These individuals are also called* **"Kushi Bushi"** *(mouth warriors).They will be the first to leave during kata practice. Many of the modern day martial arts fads cater to these types of individuals...* **study with us you don't have to learn kata;** *this is the slogan for many of the Kushi Bushi.*

Bushi Matsumura's great grandson, Hohan Soken, often described two types of karate students. **"One is dedicated and motivated and wishes to truly learn. The other is an individual who only wants to say he is learning karate. There are more of the latter, they only wish to say that they know karate, they are not willing to learn ... these are worthless individuals."**

It is the **Meimoko no Bugei** *that is truly dangerous. One of the little hidden truths about traditional Okinawan training is that this method has a tendency to filter out undesirable students. The potential* **Kushi Bushi and Meimoko no Bugei** *find this type training too difficult and usually quit before the have learned any thing of value and as a result present little or no threat to society.* **But, every once in awhile some one manages to train long enough to learn to hurt some one.** *A person with real karate*

207

skills with out the moral training that teaches restraint; can be a danger to society. All Karate Sensei should guard against producing the Meimoko no Bugei.

*Matsumura goes on to describe the dedicated student. The **"Budo no Bugei"** is an individual who even though he or she may be a teacher, will continue to learn ... to seek out other masters and engage in self study ... and continue to improve.*

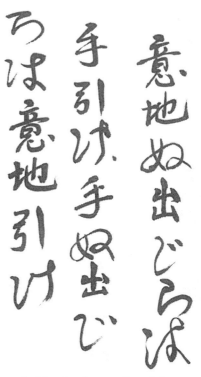

Okinawan Second Golden Saying:
"Hold back and do not use violence when you get angry. When you are about to use violence, control your anger."
Information and quote comes from:
"Ryukyu Hiden Karate"
By Takaya Yabiku
Published by:
Resources Unlimited
125 S. Main St.
Summerville, SC. 294883

Calligraphy by Shifu Hwang

The Budo no Bugei is a person who is quiet and well prepared. The Budo no Bugei has a strong will and is not self centered. This type of person devotes all one's spirit to a technique with no thought of ego or results'. It is interesting to note that Matsumura places a high value on being well educated. Matsumura also puts great value in the study of history. He emphasizes that Bun (knowledge) is very important and that Bu (warrior's art) and Bun (knowledge) are the same. In other words, you can't have one without the other. Matsumura would say that:

"The pen is not mightier than the sword; and the sword is not mightier than the pen…they are the same. The pen is nothing with out the sword and the sword is nothing without the pen."

The reader must understand that Bushi Matsumura wrote this letter to his student Kuwae on or about 1880. This was before the modern concepts of Karatedo or Budo were developed. Therefore, when he uses the term "Budo" he is not writing about "Budo" meaning" war way"; but rather during his time, the term "Do" probably meant a "method". I do not believe the term" Justsu" or "Do" were in great usage at this time in history. I believed that the most often used term in the days of Bushi Matsumura was simply "Ti".

"It is wise not to awaken a sleeping tiger.
Careful with ones words, cautious with one's action."
Lessons from two Chinese fortune cookies.

WISE AND HISTORICAL USE OF KOKORO NO HEIHO

The proper attitude does not encourage a person to become a pacifist; rather the proper attitude will give the student the incentive to train and learn deadly techniques. **"Speak softly but carry a big stick,"** could well be the motto of the well trained strategist.

There are many sub strategies that are essential and cannot be mastered without the proper attitude. Among these are Haragei no Heiho, Shibumi no Heiho, Obiyakashi no Heiho, Sente no Heiho, Sutemi no Heiho, Hishige no Heiho, Keikaku no Heiho, and Henka no Heiho.

HARAGEI AND SHIBUMI NO HEIHO

The first two of these strategies, Haragei and Shibumi are very closely related and one supports the other.

We can describe Haragei no Heiho as a "sixth sense," a gut feeling or an

The price of freedom is eternal vigilance.
If you want peace, prepare for war.

Drawing by the author....Author's collection

intuition that one acquires after many years of traditional training. To acquire this skill, the mind must be taught to be alert and vigilant. The body must be taught to relax.

Fear releases adrenaline which causes a person to temporary become very strong and capable of performing great physical feats that would not be possible under normal conditions. Yet bravery does not release this hormone. Bravery without caution is bad. Fear with panic is bad. Both fear and bravery are natural emotions that have been both an asset and a liability to the warrior since the dawn of time.

One aspect of Haragei no Heiho that deals with combat and with life in general is how the individual deals with fear and with bravery. First of all, no one is fearless. The term is not possible because a truly fearless person would die before reaching adulthood. The fear of injury or of death is a major key to the longevity of life. Is Bravery the opposite of fear; or are they the same emotion?

Credit: Author's collection

"Be not proud when victorious...never give up."
A lesson from a Chinese fortune cookie.

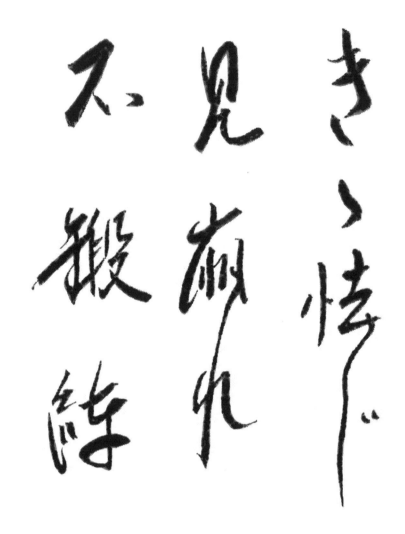

Kikioji Mikuzure Futanren
A Historic Samurai Maxim

Kikioji…being afraid before fighting because of the enemy's reputation.
Mikuzure…being afraid because the enemy looks fierce and strong.
Futanren…being afraid because of inadequate training.

Any one of these is enough to loose the contest for the samurai.
This maxim applies to all martial arts and combat in general and
can be used as a basis for developing strategy.

A gift from Sensei Fusei Kise….Author's collection

Shibumi no Heiho is the strategy of moving gracefully and naturally in a relaxed manner. Moves and techniques become automatic and are executed in a flowing manner. Shibumi is very difficult to achieve, especially for individuals who posses great physical strength. This strength becomes a crutch that will inhibit the development of Shibumi. True technique and real strength does not require strong muscles; all that is required is the mastery of Shibumi.

Shibumi no Heiho is the art of a calm confident warrior. Often such a person is in a leadership position. All people in leadership position are plagued with what I call "Haunting Questions of Leadership." I have written a short little poem that I believe best describes these questions and gives sound advice on how to answer such questions:

"Haunting Questions of Leadership....what will others think?....will my decision affect my career?....will it cost me money?...will I fail?....do I have the skills for the job?....there are as many of these questions as there are leaves on a tree.

Yet the answers are few and they are simple: Put your trust in God... always protect the innocent...tell the truth.....and do what you think is right.
Remember, it is the person you see in the mirror that you need to satisfy."

In the famous encounter between Bushi Matsumura and Nomura, the wise old warrior, Matsumura, demonstrates his skill in Heiho Jutsu. The uncanny ability of the old master to always be in the correct place, always make the correct moves, and always use the correct strategies is no accident; nor is it magic. This ability is only the product of training...many years of correct training and experience. This skill developed by the old master is called ***Haragei no Heiho***. Haragei is a mental process that makes the warrior aware that something such as an attack is going to happen. Shibumi no Heiho is the physical ability that then enables the warrior to react correctly to the threat that was perceived through Haragei. Shibumi is the quick efficient moves that separate the master from the novice.

An old Higo Province Japanese Sword Tsuba from the 1500's.

Credit: Author's collection

211

A sub strategy that contributes greatly to Haragei and Shibumi is ***Shidai no Heiho***; which deals with selecting your own terrain or selecting your position in relation to your opponent. You must observe your opponent as much as possible. Look for things such as which arm is larger. This may determine if he is right handed or left handed, look at his walking...does he favor any leg...does he move smoothly? All of this information will help you to choose your position. At the same time your observation must analyze the ground around you. Avoid any terrain, which will weaken you. The old masters learned to avoid the attack and control their opponents by positioning themselves to where they could touch their opponent, but the opponent could not touch them.

Most people before they attack are going to do something to telegraph their intentions. They may clinch their fist, or they may tighten their facial muscles. Some will simple change the expression of their body language. Such actions are classic examples of what contributes to the development of Haragei. The wise strategist develops his mind to be alert and see signs will enable him to correctly counter the attacker's every move with smooth and efficient blocks and counters that are the essence of Shibumi; and, like Haragei, Shibumi is developed over a long period of time through correct practice.

Combat can be classified as either ***Goho*** or ***Juho***. Goho is power vs. power with the strongest winning. Goho is the fighting method of beginners. Those who understand only Goho are effective only if they are stronger than their opponent.

During the American Civil War the North lost the battles of Fredericksburg and Chancellorsville because the Union commander used Goho to try and overwhelm the Confederates who were strongly entrenched. Union forces repeatedly advanced across a large open area into the withering musket fire of the entrenched Confederates.

A short time later at the Battle of Gettysburg, the Confederate Commander, Robert E. Lee, repeated the mistake the Union made at Fredericksburg and Chancellorsville. At Gettysburg, Lee's forces boldly charged time after time at the Union forces strongly employed among the heights southeast of Gettysburg. The Confederate Army was shattered. These battles serve to remind us that Goho is often a failed concept.

Juho follows the old adage that "Softness overcomes Hardness." B. H. Liddel Hart, the famous 20th Century Military Strategist, would describe Juho as the "Indirect" method; he would describe Goho as the "Direct" method. Those who are schooled in Juho do not seek a direct confrontation that will pit power against power. This strategist seeks the indirect approach and will bypass his opponent's power by looping around to gain access to his enemy's vitals. ***Goho is for the novice; Juho is the master's art.***

During the Battle of Gettysburg, one of General Lee's subordinates, General James Longstreet urged Lee to loop around the Union's left flank to avoid the Union strength and attack the rear echelon units of the Union Army. The envelopment or flanking move suggested by Longstreet is a classic example of Juho. This move would have enabled Lee's forces to get behind the Union strength and destroy the Union Army's vital areas. General Lee, like the Union Commander at Fredericksburg and Chancellorsville was not

capable of switching from Goho to Juho ... General Lee's Kokoro or mental attitude was faulty and the battle was lost.

"It is wise to develop great physical strength; but it is unwise to depend on it."

Dependency on Goho is a mistake; Juho or softness will overcome hardness. The relaxation techniques taught in proper kata training will provide the guidance that will enable the karateka to master these concepts.

"Softness over comes hardness"

The late Grandmaster Hohan Soken quit teaching the kata Sanchin and Seisan because his students were performing them too hard. Master Soken believed it would take at least 10 years of training before a student would learn too relax properly. Remember the strength of Goho is temporary it starts to fade at the age of 35 years or so; yet, the wisdom and technique of Juho will last a life time.

OBIYAKASHI NO HEIHO

This is the strategy of "Saber Rattling." In the strategy of Obiyakashi, one puts up a front or a bluff in hopes that this is enough to avoid a fight. However, there is a down side to the strategy of Obiyakashi that belongs in this discussion of Kokoro no Heiho.

Once the saber rattling is done, once the bluff is made; you may have to back up these actions with force. *"Ki Kara saru mo ichiryu...Even monkeys fall out of trees"*...this is an old samurai adage that serves to remind us that even an expert can be defeated by a novice. The strategist must always consider all opponents as dangerous regardless of their skills. Do not allow yourself the luxury of being over confident. "Don't bite off more than you can chew," and don't bluff unless you can back it up.

"Remember, the confidence of amateurs is the envy of professionals".

SENTE, SUTEMI, AND HISHIGI NO HEIHO

Sente is the strategy of initiating the action; many times this involves hitting first. The martial artist must develop a strong mind that will enable him to strike first... *"He who hesitates is lost."* In most altercations, the one who strikes first wins. Wise Sente is striking when the element of surprise is on your side.

During the initial phase of the Battle of Gettysburg, during the American Civil War; the Confederate General, Richard Ewell, was ordered to take the heights just southeast of the town. These heights during this early phase of the battle were unoccupied by the Union forces; Ewell hesitated and decided to take the heights on the following day. While he waited the Union forces occupied the high ground and commanded the position of strength throughout the entire battle. General Ewell failed to carry out the strategy of Sente and the Battle of Gettysburg was lost.

Sente is a bold move and requires strong mental powers. ***Sutemi and Hishige*** are two strategies that must always accompany Sente. Sutemi is the strategy of sacrificing. When you decide to hit first, you risk the danger of being hit as you come near your opponent. You must be willing to take a hit in order to deliver a hit; this is what makes Sente a risky situation. Sutemi also requires a strong mental attitude and considerable training.

In the traditional Karate dojo of Okinawa, students are trained to take hits. The correct teachings of Naihanchi and Sanchin Kata require the Sensei to pound the bodies of his students while they are performing theses kata... this pounding teaches the mind and body to absorb these strikes. When and if the real situation arises, these traditional students will not fear being hit. Therefore, Sente then becomes a very valuable weapon in their arsenal.

Hishige is the other strategy that must accompany Sente. Hishige is the strategy of total combat. You must be prepared to crush and finish your adversary before you commit to the strategy of Sente. Hishige can also be called the "Killer Instinct." This strategy is not for the squeamish; the mastery of Hishige requires a strong mental attitude.

One of the problems associated with modern tournament karate is that it is simply a game of "slap tag." In most instances, a "point" scored is not powerful enough to disable the opponent. The object is only to score a point ... Hishige is not considered ... this can develop bad habits. In the old arts, Hishige was an important strategy that was taught through various kata and kumite training.

Sente, Sutemi and Hishige are very important concepts and history is full of battles and wars that were lost because one or all of the participants failed to employ these three strategies as one.

The Japanese surprise attack on Pearl Harbor, Hawaii on December 7, 1941 was a brilliant example of Sente. In one swift blow, the Japanese Navy crippled the American Pacific Fleet and left the entire west coast of the United States open for attack. The Japanese naval task force commander, Admiral Nagumo's use of Sente was successful; but he failed to use Sutemi and Hishige. Nagumo's fear of America's undamaged aircraft carriers caused him not to employ Sutemi; he was not willing to accept the risk of being hit when he used the strategy of Sente. Instead he backed off and retired, leaving the battle half won. He was in a position to completely crush the American Forces in Hawaii, but he failed to use Sente, Sutemi and Hishige together. Japan may have achieved an early victory if Nagumo's strategy in this instance would have been correct.

In real combat, once you've knocked your opponent down, you simply cannot let him regain his feet; you must crush your opponent to obtain total victory. Remember real combat is a matter of life and death. The famous 1930's era movie actor, W. C. Fields, says it best:

"Never give a sucker an even break."

KEIKAKU NO HEIHO

Keikaku is the strategy of planning. Real martial artist, warriors, soldiers and strategists spend their entire lives planning and preparing for something they hope never happens... combat. No kata, no amount of training, planning or preparation can completely prepare a person for combat. Real combat is a horrible experience. Training and preparation, however insufficient are the only way one can prepare for this experience.

A boxer trains for months before a fight; armies are constantly training. The martial artist trains for a lifetime; the principle vehicle used in martial arts training is the kata. The kata gives one the tools for engaging in individual combat. The kata also teaches strategy and to a certain degree, prepares both the mind and body for combat. However, kata alone simply will not get the job done. The karateka must adopt additional training methods to gain confidence in the use of his hands, feet and other body parts to carry out the techniques taught in the kata.

A strong kokoro is absolutely mandatory for the karateka to develop the training methods that will convert his body into an arsenal of weapons. Modern karate is inadequate in providing this type of training; we must turn to the past; to the training methods of Ko Ryu (old style) Karate-Jutsu to understand and develop our weapons.

The traditional dojo of Okinawa and China contain specialized equipment designed to harden and strengthen the hands, fingers, feet, toes and other parts of the body to such an extent that they can become weapons. To accomplish this task, most traditional dojo will have the following equipment:

1. Makiwara punching or kicking post. Name actually means straw bundle. It is used to condition hands, knuckles, and arm joints to hit objects hard with no fear of pain.

On using the Makiwara
"Go slow start off punching it 10 times with each hand 3 times a week...add two times each week at the end of a year you are punch it over 100 times. Then reduce it at same rate until you are punching it 50 times. Then build back up to 100 times. Follow this method for year after year for the best results."
Sensei Seiyu Shinjo

Go slow and train only under the supervision of a qualified instructor.

Developing the toe kick
Author's collection

2. Toe kicking Makiwara... used to condition the foot and toes. The toe kick once developed, is a devastating weapon.

In Okinawa old automobile tires are often used as "toe kicking makiwara". Training the toes as a weapon is an important technique of authentic Okinawan karate.

3. Chikaraishi or "Power stones." These are used to develop the wrists, hands, fingers, and shoulders.

4. Kanshu - The fingers are thrust into buckets of dried beans, corn, sand or gravel to strengthen the hands and fingers into weapons.

"Fingers are more effective as weapons than are the fists."
Seizan Kinjo

5. Tetsu Bo - Iron Staff (Bo) A heavy iron bar is used in twirling patterns; this exercise greatly strengthens the wrist, forearms and shoulders.

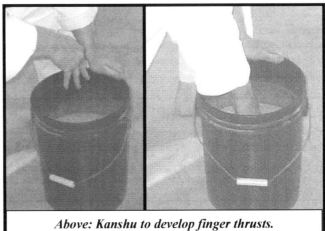

Above: Kanshu to develop finger thrusts.
Below: twirling the Tetsu Bo.
Photo credits: Author's collection.

216

6. Kame-heavy ceramic jars are used to strengthen the fingers and hands.

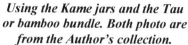

Using the Kame jars and the Tau or bamboo bundle. Both photo are from the Author's collection.

7. Tau - "Bamboo Bundle" Bamboo sticks are tied together and used to strengthen the fingers, developing the Nukite or "Spear hand." The Spear hand is thrust into the Bamboo

8. Large Stones or Iron Balls (Tetsu Tama) are used in various exercises to strengthen the upper body.

Using a large round stone to strengthen the upper body

9. Koteaite or Kotecti-ti – this is arm, leg and body toughening; this should be practiced in every traditional dojo.

Koteaite training techniques that are used in tradition Karate Dojo through out the world.

From the Author's collection

217

It is logical for the average person to assume that with all of this preparation for violence, the martial artist would become a violent person. However, just the opposite is true. It is very rare for any traditional martial artist to be involved in violent activities.

All civilizations and all of the world's cultures from the past to the present follow some type of moralistic code. This code may be the teaching of Buddha, the morals associated with Shintoism, God's Ten Commandments or any of a number of moralistic principles that guide civilization. The precepts such as Matsumura's "Seven Virtues of Bu" or Sakugawa's "Five Precepts'" inspire modern martial artist throughout the world. Those religious moral codes, along with moralistic precepts from great masters teach the martial artist to be a nonviolent person.

Correct performance of kata involves the cultivation of a mental state called "Mushin or a state of mind without thought. Mushin is a trance-like mental state; the kata performer is able to go from move to move without any thought. Perfection of the kata is their only concern. This type of performance requires the mind and body to coordinate and concentrate to a high degree of perfection. This state of mind releases tension; it offers solitude from the problems of life. Mushin is that part of Kokoro no Heiho that assists the martial artist to learn to be violent without having to resort to violence.

"In ancient times skillful warriors first made themselves invincible, and then watched for vulnerability in their opponents".

Sun Tzu, Ancient Chinese Military Strategist

HENKA NO HEIHO

Henka no Heiho is the strategy of change, this is an important strategy that influences all facets of combat. The term "Kawari" or Kawari no Heiho also means change and could be used here instead of Henka no Heiho.

Matsumura stresses the importance of Henka it relates to mental attitude when he states in his "Bucho Ikko*".... "You must deal with your own mind well and wait for others to fall apart mentally. Win the battle by the calmness of your mind and steal the mind of your opponent ... adopt to change".* In a conflict there are two or more mental attitudes involved ... your attitude and the attitude of your opponent or opponents. If you can change your opponent's mind, you can defeat him; you may be able to defeat him without violence. Many attacks are often thwarted by putting your hand inside your coat or pocket. The would-be-attacker thinks you are armed; he changes his mind and does not attack.

In 1314 at the very start of the Battle of Bannockburn; Robert the Bruce (soon to be the King of Scotland) rode out in front of the Scottish Army toward the larger and more powerful English force gathering some 400 yards away. Henry de Bohun, the leader of the English forces, seeing Bruce out in front, rode out to meet him. Robert the Bruce was clad in light armor and carried his famous battle axe; de Bohun was heavily armored and carried a lance. As the two came together; Bruce suddenly rose up in his stirrups and brought the battle axe down ... splitting de Bohun's head, killing him instantly. The English army was stunned ... their attitude had been aggressive and strong ... in a twinkling of an eye; Bruce had caused a change in their attitude. He had stolen their minds. Before the English could regain their composure; the Scotts attacked and routed the English. [5-4]

Henka requires a keen and alert mind; you must not be negligent in thought or in action. Recently a student of mine was attacked by five thugs; one of these was a 270 pound ex-football player. The big guy attacked first; however, my student's techniques were good, he broke the attacker's nose and cracked some ribs. The strong fighting spirit of my student put fear in the heart of the other four would be attackers and changed their attitude. If all five would have attacked together, victory would have probably been easy; however, my student was given the opportunity to change their minds and victory was his.

Shosotsu no Heiho is a strategy that contributes greatly to Henka. Shosotsu is controlling your opponents mind by ordering them about. Even the meanest and most dangerous of humans once was a child who took orders from their mothers. If you take advantage of this fact, you may be able to order your opponent around as an officer directs orders to his troops. This is a somewhat risky strategy, but it can work under certain circumstances. Law enforcement officers are taught this strategy. The order "Police... everybody put their hands up" is an example of Shosotsu. School teachers use this strategy when they demand their students to ***"Stop that"***.

When confronted by a group of would be attackers, you suddenly hit the one closest to you and order the others to "take this man to the hospital ... he is hurt," this may change their minds and end the fight. Shosotsu does not work against a well-trained and organized group, so use this strategy wisely. Henka becomes a major supporting strategy not only of Kokoro, but also of Minari, Maai and Chushin. The strategy of change is very important and will be discussed in detail as each of our main strategies are explored in depth.

A principle in common sense:
"The wise warrior does not cling to fixed methods or techniques. Never be so involved with a strategy or technique that you can not change if the strategy or technique begins to fail. Change according to events. The flexibility of the mind is your most powerful weapon."

Tembo style Tsuba from the late 1500's
Author's collection

心乃至柔之器
隨勢而動
智者不戰而勝

"You most powerful weapon is the flexibility of your mind;
change according to events.
The wise warrior wins without fighting."

Drawing by the Author….Calligraphy by Shifu Hwang…. Poem by the Author
Credit: the Author's collection

220

NINTAI....PERSEVERANCE

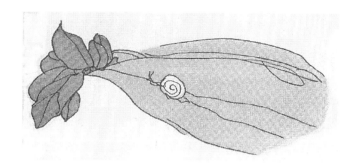

"Nintai"
"Climb as he must, the little snail does all he can;
but it will take him a long time to reach the top of Yonaha Dake.
The Bujin starts learning Bujutsu as a child;
but it will take a long time before he will be called Bushi.
Nintai makes everything possible."
Poem by Chikin Akagawa....Author's collection

Picture credit: "Little Pictures of Japan" published by The Book House for Children'
Pictures by Katharine Sturges
Note: Yonaha Dake (Mt. Yonaha) is the highest mountain on Okinawa.

"Nintai"

You can learn a martial art if you are young and strong, you can learn a martial art if your are old and weak, you can learn a martial art if you are handicapped; just about anyone can learn a martial art. There is one exception, you can not learn a martial art if you do not have *"Nintai"*. Nintai or perseverance is perhaps the most important concept used in the fighting arts and yet is probably one of the least known.

Nin.....means endure or stealth....Tai.... means to endure or to bear; when put together Nintai means perseverance or endurance. As with many Japanese terms, Nintai also carries with it a feeling that English or most other languages can not describe. In the case of Nintai, the feeling is of enduring through difficult or adverse conditions. In the case of the martial artist, this means endurance through tough training sessions conducted over many years.

For the martial artist the term "kibishii"or severe is used to describe traditional training. *Note: severe does not mean cruel.* The kibishi training is a mark of pride among martial artist who have endured through this type of training.

Martial arts training is not suppose to be "fun". There is an object to severe training. As the kaji (sword smith) uses fire to shape, strengthen, and temper steel into a sword. The karate sensei use severe training to shape, strengthen, and temper the body and mind of the karateka. The strong bodies created in the dojo will not stay strong for ever; all too soon age causes the strength of youth to erode away. However, the mental toughness created by kibishii training will stay with the karateka until the day he or she dies.

Matsumura in his "Bucho Ikko" states that budo strengthens the nation. Wellington stated that the activities conducted on the playing fields of Eaton created the victory at Waterloo. As any veteran can tell you those young men and women who have endured through severe athletic training during their school days will perform better in military service than those who have not experience tough athletic training. Nintai is a far reaching concept; the mental toughness associated through Nintai can help the individual through tough times.

This is Nintai

"Maishin Shorinji"
The difficult path to reach the Shaolin Temple;
an example of Nintai. Picture Credit: Paul Bystedt collection

"Meeting adversity well is the source of your strength".
A lesson in Nintai from a Chinese fortune cookie.
"Fight them until hell freezes over; then fight them on the ice."
A lesson in Nintai from Dutch Meyers
Football coach, Texas Christian University 1930's

222

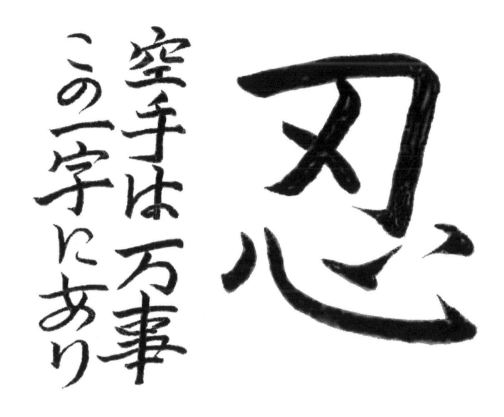

空手は万事
この一字にあり

忍

"Nin, once you understand this term; it is all you need to know about karate."

A gift from Sensei Kuda

This important concept must be fully understood and followed before anyone can learn a martial art.

Nin as it used in this calligraphy refers to something that is secret, difficult and can be learned only through hard work and determination.

Sensei Kuda indicated that this old adage was very important and should occupy a place of honor in a karate dojo.

From the Author's collection.

"Carry out one's original intentions."

A polite way of saying never quit.
An excellent example of Nintai….a gift from Fusei Kise.

Credit: The Author's collection

224

LOYALTY

If you look up loyalty in an English dictionary you will find only one word: loyalty meaning: quality, state, or instance of being loyal; faithful adherence, etc. If you look up a Japanese equivalent you will find more than one word for loyalty; the term I am using here is chugi or cyu-gi.

The term "Ryu" as in Shorin Ryu or Goju Ryu is generally assumed to mean a "style," school or method. But actually the term which is of Japanese origin, means a flow or a stream. A more practical definition would be a stream were knowledge flows down the stream from one person to another in the same fashion as leaves falling into a river and then floating down stream with the current.

Prior to World War II the term Ryu was not widely used on Okinawa. Rather than use "Ryu", the Okinawan were more likely to use the term "Do". For a few years after 1956 when Hohan Soken started calling his method of karate Shorin Ryu, some of his students were more likely to call his method "Shorin Do" rather than Shorin Ryu. However, now the term Ryu is widely accepted on Okinawa; however, the Okinawan Ryu is not the same as the Japanese Ryu.

In Japan, members of a Ryu are taught to conform to the principles of the Ryu. Everyone is cut from the same cookie cutter. On the other hand in Okinawa there is a long tradition that follows the concept of ***"Suhari"***. Suhari is actually an old Japanese principle that today (in my opinion) is more closely followed in Okinawa than on mainland Japan.

Suhari insures that the Okinawan fighting arts remain a viable and effective method. On the other hand the Japanese Ryu have evolved as an art that may be more concerned with all members of the Ryu looking alike rather than have an effective fighting method.

Loyalty as this term is used here pertains to the instructor and teacher relationship and is a two way street. The students are loyal to the teacher by respecting this person and learning their lesson well. The instructor is loyal to his student by teaching them to the best of his or her ability. The teacher must never stop learning and should be an example for all to follow.

From the Author's collection

225

Suhari

Su… indicates that a beginner must correctly copy all karate techniques from his instructor.

Ha… means that after a number of years of training, when the karateka has attained a high degree black belt, he is allowed to develop new techniques provided they are improvements. This applies to all movements except basic techniques.

Ri… is the highest form; it means that after an even longer period of training than for Ha, the Karateka must be able to perform all forms of karate automatically, not stopping to think about his moves.

Suhari an old samurai adage; the calligraphy is a
gift from Sensei Fusei Kise.
Credit the Author's collection.

LESSONS FROM THE TENGU

The legendary mountain goblins of Japan are called the *"Tengu"*. The Tengu have long received the credit or sometimes the blame for improbable events that occurred in Japan. For an example if an average sword smith forges a sword of great quality this would be a rare occurrence. Events such as this are just not likely to happen. To explain this; the sword smith may give the credit for his good fortune to the Tengu. [5-5]

So it is with the karate sensei. Time and experience may give the sensei the insight on principals that greatly improve his skills and knowledge. Unable to explain the exact origin of his new skill or techniques; the sensei would just claim the *"Tengu taught me"*.

This situation happened to me a few years ago. I was teaching a seminar at a karate camp in Morgantown, West Virginia. One of the participants in the camp and in my class was a very good karateka named Mike Farrell. I forget exactly what I was teaching but what ever it was, Mr. Farrell asked me who had taught me the technique that I was teaching. My answer was the "Tengu taught me". This particular group of techniques was one that I had learn over the years from numerous sources including my own experiences and to tell the truth I did not remember exactly how I had obtained these techniques.

I could tell from the expression on Mr. Farrell's face that he was not familiar with the term Tengu and he was trying to remember some Okinawan master by that name. After having a good laugh about this situation, I told Mr. Farrell about the Tengu and how this mythical character took a lot of credit and blame for mysterious things occurring in Japan.

The Tengu do exist and they do assist the sensei in continuing his or her martial arts education. These Tengu are more often called students. Your students are your greatest teachers. Karateka will never reach their full potential as martial artists until they start to teach. When you teach your students, they will ask you many questions. If you do not know the answer, your loyalty to your students will compel you to seek answers. This process occurs as long as you teach.

Antique Tengu Mask a gift from
Charles Tatum...Author's collection

227

THE LEGACY OF BOOM

Hohan Soken while teaching fighting techniques that would consist of having someone attack him with a variety of techniques (kicks, punches, grabs etc.); he would block or evade these attacks and then he would counter with a punch, kick, or finger strike. As Sensei Soken executed his block or counter he often would say "boom". All of his senior students that I studied with would also say "boom" in the same fashion as Sensei Soken. I now finding myself doing the same thing and I have notice some of my senior students are saying "boom" as they demonstrate blocks and counters; thus we have:

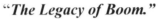

"The Legacy of Boom."

Sensei Hohan Soken demonstrating a block and counter. You can almost hear him say boom. Photo credit: Resources Unlimited

One mistake that many karate senseis routinely make is refusing to learn from some one other than their main teacher. This is the wrong attitude, you should learn from any one who will share information with you. Even if you are older and out rank a person you can still learn from them. Too often our egos prevent this from happening.

Too often a karate sensei refuses to change their teaching methods from those used by their teacher. Often this is misguided loyalty. If your goal is to teach a certain technique to your students and the teaching methods of your teachers are inadequate to accomplish your goal...alter your teaching methods. Remember ***"Suhari"*** and keep your art viable and usable. This is the traditional Okinawan method and the correct use of loyalty.

武術を学ぶ全の
ての者道塲門を
くぐるべし
鏡に映る我にこそ
真の評言を得る
日々の鍛錬なさ
ずして少林寺
の体得無し

"To learn Bujutsu you must walk through the dojo door.
Your most important critic is the person you see in the mirror.
Practice daily and step by step you will reach the Temple of Shaolin."

The above calligraphy is by Chikin Akagawa:
Author's collection

Southern Japanese Port…Credit: Paul Bystedt collection

INTEGRITY

In the late 1960's all Americans studying Shorin Ryu Matsumura Seito Karate in Okinawa were given a handout that described some of the history of the style along with other information of interest. A couple of paragraphs were about the student and instructor relationship. This short passage offered the following poem for advice:

Grandmaster Hohan Soken nearly 80 years old standing in front of his dojo
in Nishihara, Okinawa. Photo Credit: Author's collection

The Sensei's Wish
"All karateka are my sons; in order to have good sons all must try to do their utmost to walk a straight line and to continually try their best to practice the Sensei's teachings."
Quote taken from a hand out receive by the Author in late 1960's from Sensei Fuse Kise.

Too often instructors think that they must be the toughest guy in class. This is not important; the students are in your class to learn not to be "roughed up". Stern, hard training will create some bumps and bruises. But the Sensei should never be cruel. Do not ask your students to do any task that you have never done. Be thorough and keep your class safe.

Encourage your students to perform at the best of their abilities. But the instructor must realize that a student must grow into their technique. I remember studying Okinawan

Kenpo under Sekichi Odo and often I was having trouble performing a technique correctly since some of the Okinawan Kenpo techniques were different from Shorin Ryu techniques that I had previously learned. Sensei Odo seeing my difficulty would simply say "don't try too hard ...take it easy". Following Sensei Odo's advice I found that soon I could work my way through the difficult technique and learning became easier.

My friend, Jim Louge, once said to me that we (meaning the American service men and the Okinawans who studied in Okinawa during the 1950's through the 1960's and into the early 1970's) were some of the last people to learn the old Okinawan fighting arts.

During this era students had the last opportunity to train with Okinawan masters born in the 1880's through the early 1900's. These old masters were born and grew up at a time when many older Okinawans who had been samurai were still alive and the ways of the samurai were still remembered in Okinawa. These old men never knew sport karate or any other similar martial art; they only knew the old methods.

Grandmaster Seki Toma applying a Tuite technique on Jerry Hobbs. Photo credit: Roy Jerry Hobbs collection

There were many U. S. Military Servicemen who studied under these masters. It was the U.S Servicemen who initially brought the Okinawan Arts out of Okinawa to the United States and eventually to the rest of the world. These Servicemen have true and authentic lineages and teach authentic arts. Their lineages results from hard work and being in Okinawa during a very special time that no longer exists.

Over the last few years there have been numerous attempts by some younger karateka to create lineages similar to the lineages of these servicemen. I do not blame these young karateka for wanting to have sound lineages. But they should create such a lineages through hard work not through skullduggery. I would like to cover several examples where false or suspicious lineages that have been created.

The first that comes to mind is a thirty year old young man who has good kata and technique but then claims on the internet that he does not do karate, he only knows "ti". I spoke to this person on the phone and asked him what is "ti". He started to answer with the "text book definition" when I stopped him and stated that I knew the definition of Ti, but what is it; how does ti differ from karate, he had no answer. I also asked him how he knew what ti is when the Okinawan teachers I knew could not separate ti from karate. I checked with numerous other Okinawan stylists who studied in Okinawa during the 1960's. No one I spoke to could separate ti from karate. Yet this 30 year old man was proudly advertising on the internet that he practiced "ti"!

Another man states on the internet that he learned karate from the son of an American Marine Corps Colonel who was stationed on Okinawa during the late 1930's through the 1940's. The karateka making this claim seemed to be totally unaware that World War II occurred from the end of 1941 until the fall of 1945 and the United States had no Marines or any other members of the United State Armed Forces on Okinawa until the late spring of 1945. As stated on the internet this situation was not possible.

One other karateka claims that his father was stationed in Japan and that his father enrolled him in a jiujutsu class at the age of five years. That in itself is a ridicules statement.

A short time later his father was reassigned back to the United States and left his young son in Japan under the care of his jiujutsu teacher. The story goes on to state that this five year old boy lived in Japan for 17 years! During this time an Okinawan man, who was a member of the jiujutsu dojo taught him Okinawan karate. My question to this man making these claims was "how long did your father serve in the military prison at Ft. Leavenworth, Kansas?" If you are serving in the United States Military, you simply can not abandon your dependents in a foreign country or anywhere else. This story is completely false.

There is no need for serious karateka to engage in such falsehoods. Put the energy wasted on such activity into solid practice of a good style of bujutsu. Make your own lineage. My advice to young students is that you need to find a competent instructor and work hard and learn all you can. Realize that karate and other fighting arts are learned only through hard work. Remember the principle of "Suhari". When you gain sufficient knowledge and wisdom open a dojo and teach. Treat you students as if they are your children and teach them well.

"Sensei: remember you are a source of wisdom and strength for your family and your students. Do not ask anyone to do what you can't do or have never done; lead by example -- Lead from the front, not from the rear! --Responsibility is the burden of leadership."

In the above quote I hear the voices and see the faces of many people I once knew.

"You can't teach what you ain't never learned no more than you can come back from where you ain't never been".

S.M. Meeks, Equipment and Facility Manager
Texas A&M University Athletic Department
Late 1950's through early 1970's

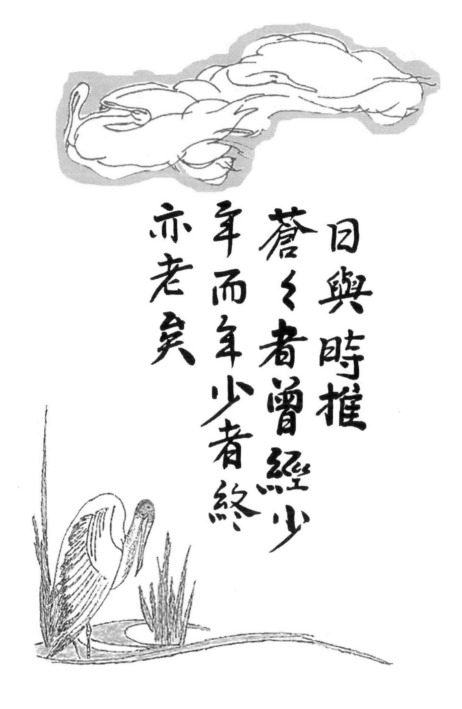

日與時推
蒼々者曾經少
年而年少者終
亦老矣

"It is just a matter of time.
What is old was once new; what is new will soon be old.
The old, the new;
it is just a matter of time."

Drawings from "Little Pictures of Japan" by Olive B. Millar and Katherine Sturges,
Published by The Book House for Children…calligraphy by Shifu Hwang
Poem is by the Author…Credit: Author's collection

GIRI...OBLIGATION

"Any man who does not provide for and protect his and his own is worse than the infidel."

Holy Bible: First Timothy 5-8

Giri is one of those Japanese terms that have a definition and a feeling. We can put the definition for Giri to "pen and paper" rather easily; but, to do so really does not define the term. I can best describe giri as a principle rather than a simple word meaning "obligation". Giri could be the most important principle or term in all of the language of Bujutsu. The lack of giri can do what the laws and armies of powerful nations have failed to do...and that is to stop the teaching and learning of the true martial arts.

My friend, Bob Herten, once told me an interesting story that strikes at the very heart of giri as far as Okinawan karate is concerned. A few years ago Bob and several of his students went to Okinawa to visit with some of the older Okinawan Karate Sensei.

They visited with a number of sensei and each of these old masters pleaded with Bob and his students not too let their old art of karate die out. It was clear to Bob Herten and his students that these Okinawan gentlemen were afraid that the younger Okinawan karateka were going to forsake their age old art and replace it with modern sport karate. The old men were afraid that the young Okinawan karateka were failing in their sense of giri. Could it be that sport karate is going to do what powerful nations have failed to do....and that is to stop the teaching of authentic Okinawan bujutsu?

The students of the real fighting arts must realize that they are studying an art that is designed for protection of yourself and others. As such the student must learn dangerous or even deadly techniques. Therefore, society needs to have assurance that this dangerous art is not misused. In order to accomplish this need; there are numerous moral lessons that are incorporated into the teachings of a competent karate sensei. Perhaps the most famous moralistic lesson available is the Dojo Kun. Most karate dojo or schools have a set of moral inspirations that are displayed in a place of honor for students and visitors to see. Many of these dojo kun are based on Tode Sakugawa's Five Precepts. These precepts are as follows:

FIVE PRECEPTS OF TODE SAKUGAWA
Strive for good moral character
Keep an honest and sincere way
Cultivate perseverance or a will for striving
Develop a respectful attitude
Restrain aggression through spiritual attainment

All members of the human species have a general obligation to their cultures and their societies. We have an obligation to be productive and not to burden our society. We have an obligation to procreate and continue our species. Mothers have the obligation to love and care for their children. Men are responsible to provide for and to protect their families. Men are also responsible for the education of their children. Men also need to understand that the greatest gift they can give their children is to love the children's mother.

WHO WILL CARRY ON THE WAY?

"Death is lighter than a feather; but giri (obligation) is heavier than a mountain."
An old Samurai adage…the actual reason many practice the fighting arts.
Credit: the Author's collection.

235

THE SECRET OF GIRI

I once expressed concern to Sensei Yuichi Kuda that my kata were drifting some what away from what I had learned in Okinawa. Sensei said that we all should try our best to keep our kata correct; but, it would be impossible to do this with complete accuracy. He said over time my karate would become my own and that this was inevitable.

Sensei Kuda went on to say that when Bushi Matsumura died his karate style died also, when Hohan Soken died his style also died; and so it is with each sensei. Your karate becomes your own. This is the natural course of action and it can not be changed and yet only by trying to emulate the sensei's art can the student grow into his or her own art.

"Do not fail to carry out your obligation!"

Ornate antique Oriental screen that stands in Charlie Dean's Dojo.
Photo credit Charlie Dean

Matsumura Attuidi Hakutsuru Kata
Seminar Bastrop, Tx.
Front Row L to R: Sherman Leake, Dan Gomez, Steve Warren, Ray Keller,
Ron Lindsey, Charles Tarum, Mike Farrell
Back Row L to R: Rick Langenstein, Steve Kaluza, Mark Wilson, John Ross, Tom Rahlfs,
Lara Rahlfs, Ron Locke, Jeff Maughan, Charles Dean

Above: Hakutsuru Seminar Bastrop, Tx. 2004…Below: Summer camp La Grange, Tx. 1985…. Photo credit: Author's collection

Shorin Ryu Matsumura Seito Karate/Kobujutsu Seminar Hatfield England 1990's
Photo Credit: Author's collection

Seminar Bastrop Texas 2000, Photo credit Author's collection

Dear Mr. RonId Levis   25. 12. 1990.

I received your letter. Thank you very much. I am happy to
hear that you and your family are well. I, too, have been busy
devoting my efforts to the Matsusokan organization committee. It
is with great pleasure that I address this first letter to you.

After the death of Master Hohan Soken, the Matsumura Seito
Karate-Do was approaching dissolution without an organization committee. An organization was formed with the new designation--
Matsusokan--in order to continue what Master Hohan Soken began in the
1950s. This organization has grown with the cooperation of Tony
Sandoval of America and Ted Lange of Australia. I appreciate the
fact that you will be joining us. I, also, appreciate the fact that
you have been devoting yourself to teaching others Master Hohan
Soken's Karate-Do. I would like to convey my appreciation as a
representative of the disciples of the late Master Soken.

I am looking forward to hearing from you again. I am enclosing
a photograph of myself. I would appreciate receiving your picture.

Sincerely yours,

MATSUSOKAN KARATE-DO KYOKAI

屋比久孝也
Takaya Yabiku

*Letter from Takaya Yabiku to the author, Ronald Lewis Lindsey, thanking him for teaching the late
Grandmaster Hohan Soken's art; Author's collection.*

*Drawing by Jerry Richards, Vision Graphics
Author's collection*

239

Dear Mr. Lindsey

Thank you very much for coming right in the busy of your day.

Visitor from Okinawa, and everyone of them were very happy to see OKINAWA SHORIN-RYU KARATE that you performing. I take your support as a great honor, also thank you for you made me proud that you told the story about SESOKO ROKUSHAKU-BO. I'm sure prefecture Okinawa government happy to hear that you are teaching OKINAWA KARATE in the state of the Texas. I'd like to stop by your place before I go to Japan on Dec. this year.

Everything went well with your support, and you are a credit to our Okinawa Tomonokai.

We wish you increasing good health and May you succeed.

We are deeply grateful to you for your kindness Please let us know if you need us to do something for you.

Again thank you for your contrebution and help.

On behalf of the Okinawa Tomonokai

Very truly yours

Shigeko Sesoko Burnie

A letter from the Okinawan Tomo no Kai of Austin, Texas

240

師の三尺後ろに付
きその影さえも決
して踏むべからず

"Walk three feet behind the Sensei's
shadow and do not ever step on it".

Poem taken from a handout given to students of
Fusei Kise in the 1960's.
Drawing by the Author
Author's collection

SOURCES, ENDNOTES AND EXPLANATIONS
CHAPTER 5

The source for most of the information presented in this chapter is my own experience. However, the sources for specific points of information are foot noted.

Wisdom

5-1   Source: "Acupuncture, A Comprehensive Text" Shanghai College of Traditional Medicine Translated by John O'Conner and Dan Bensky; published by Eastland Press Chicago Il.

5-2   Sources: "Encyclopedia of Dim Mak" by Erle Montaigue; published by Paladin Press "Advanced Pressure Point Fighting of Ryukyu Kempo" by George Dillman; published by George Dillman International

5-3   Source: Conversations with Sensei Yuichi Kuda and Fusei Kise

5-4   Source: The story about the "Battle of Bannock Burn" was found in an Atlanta Cutlery catalog .

Nintai

Sources are given in the text or come from my experience.

Loyalty
Most Sources are from the poem "Suhari" and from my own experience.

5-5

Source: Conversation with Sensei Yuichi Kuda

Integrity

Sources for this sub-chapter are given in the text or come from numerous conversation with American karateka.

Giri...Obligation

Some sources are presented in the text; others are from my experiences

"Encourage me and I will not forget you."

A lesson from a Chinese fortune cookie.

CHAPTER 6
MINARI NO HEIHO
(THE STRATEGY OF APPEARANCE)

Minari no Heiho

Picture on the previous page is a gift from Ronnie Locke.

Author's collection

The most difficult and important aspect of minari is learning to see yourself as others see you. Once you have accomplished this, you then change your appearance to have others see you as you wish to be seen. This strategy is as old as the human race. It is basic animal instinct for survival. It is the reason dogs "bristle up" and snarl; they wish to have their opponents see them as being larger and more vicious than they really are.

Women are truly experts on minari. The fashion and cosmetic industries play a key role in assisting women in their mastery of this strategy.

Armies of old sought to take advantage of this strategy by wearing brightly colored uniforms, which seemed to increase their numbers and impressed a less spectacular peasant army with their "superiority". Modern weapons and tactics have caused the modern armies to trade their brightly colored uniforms for camouflage.

The study of minari is very complicated; it takes a lifetime of learning to understand and master this aspect of the martial arts. Certainly such a study is beyond the scope of this book. Nevertheless, a martial artist must realize the need to think strategically and we must realize how important Minari no Heiho was to the martial artist of old and how important it is for the modern martial artist to have a "working knowledge" of this strategy.

LEARNING ABOUT YOUR ENEMIES

The old master of Okinawan Tode, Anko Azato is said to have maintained extensive records on the Okinawan Bushi. He learned their strength, weakness and various habits and other types of information about the Samurai of Okinawa. To Master Azato this group of people represented potential enemies, He learned everything he could about his potential adversaries. [6-1]

It is not possible to do this today because the number of potential enemies is too great. However, it is possible to learn about people in general. One way to accomplish this is to know the body and its points of balance and power; we can also learn the body's vital points and areas to strike. Such knowledge is of great benefit in a self defense situation.

"So, it is said that if you know others and yourself; you will win a hundred battles.
If you know others but know not yourself; you will win only one half of your battles.
If you know neither others nor yourself; you will lose all of your battles."

Sun Tsu, Ancient Chinese Military Strategist

"Naha Market scene 1880's"
Photo credit: Author's collection

 On page 248 is an Atemi (Hitting) Chart that was handed out to practitioners who were studying Okinawa Shorin Ryu Matsumura Seito Karate/Kobudo during the 1960's. It is interesting to note that the Okinawan Masters that I studied under in the late 1960's did not teach a hitting art based on Traditional Chinese Medicine with the Acupuncture points and so forth. Rather the method used by my Okinawan Instructors was based on simplicity. The old (U.S. Military) adage K.I.S.S. (Keep It Simple Stupid) could have been the motto used by my Okinawan Karate/Kobudo Masters.

We will start our study of Minari with the old chart that was run off on a mimeograph machine at one of the U.S. Military Bases in central Okinawan. This chart allegedly was based on Grandmaster Hohan Soken's teachings. As it appears here, the chart has under gone very few corrections and is a copy of the chart given to me by Seizan Kinjo in 1969.

The chart is simple but accurate and is a very effect tool in teaching atemi waza. Following the chart there will be an introduction to one of Sensei Soken's methods of striking vital points.

The study of Minari will continue with an explanation of Tachi Kata and Kamae in general. We will look at various stances, power and balance points; we will also examine how the karateka can become more powerful with out becoming physically stronger. We will also examine the natural weapons of the human body. The object of our discussion of Minari is to teach the reader that he or she can be powerful without having great physical strength and that they can use this knowledge and power to protect themselves and others.

One of our goals to be gained by studying this chapter is not to merely look at your opponent but learn to truly see you opponent. To look at your opponent is different than really seeing your opponent; this is what separates the novice from the master. This allows the reader and karateka in general to see the strengths and weaknesses in others and correct our "appearance" in order to correct our mistakes. This is one of the most important reasons we follow the traditional path to learning Bujutsu. Only through the mastery of *Minari no Heiho* can we accomplish this goal.

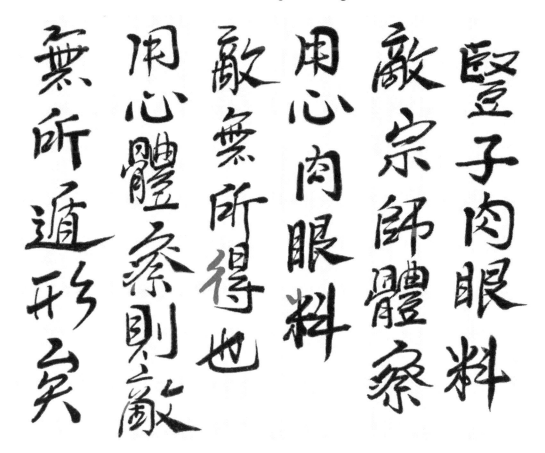

"The novice looks at his opponents.
The master learns to truly see his opponents.
Learn to look at nothing but see everything."

Poem is by the Author.
Calligraphy is Classic Chinese by Shifu Hwang.
Author's collection

"Correct kata training is the key to mastering Minari no Heiho."

Kuda Kise

KARATE INSTRUCTIONS

TRAINING

ILLUSTRATED VITALS OF HUMAN BODY

AND

APPELLATION

Original copy of Hitting chart
recieved in the 1960's
in Okinawa

First page

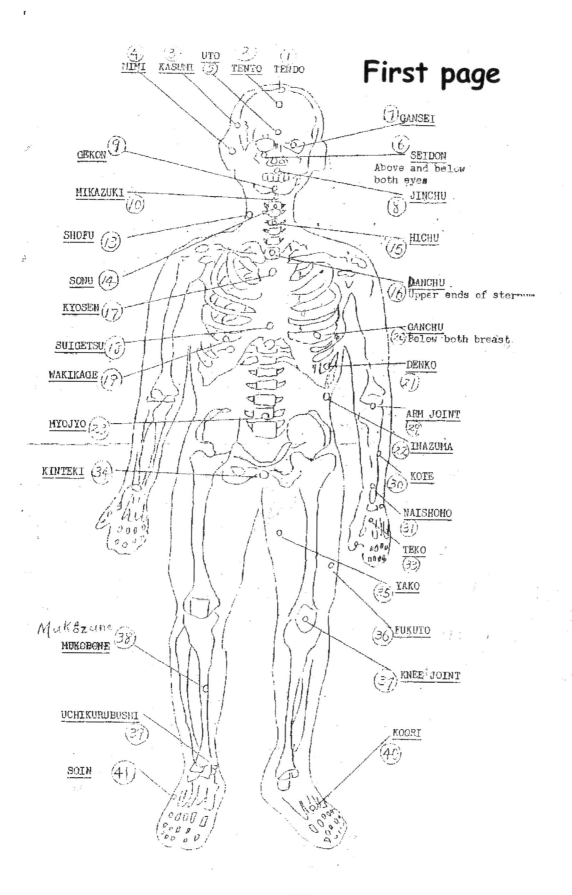

MIMI ④ KASUMI ③ UTO ⑤ TENTO ② TENDO ①

⑦ GANSEI

⑥ SEIDON
Above and below
both eyes

GEKON ⑨

MIKAZUKI ⑩

JINCHU ⑧

SHOFU ⑬

HICHU ⑮

SONU ⑭

DANCHU ⑯
Upper ends of sternum

KYOSEN ⑰

GANCHU ⑳
Below both breast.

SUIGETSU ⑱

DENKO ㉑

WAKIKAGE ⑲

ARM JOINT ㉙

MYOJYO ㉓

INAZUMA ㉒

KINTEKI ㉞

KOTE ㉚

NAISHOHO ㉛

TEKO ㉜

YAKO ㉟

MuKǒzune
MUKOBONE ㊳

FUKUTO ㊱

KNEE JOINT ㊲

UCHIKURUBUSHI ㊴

KOORI ㊵

SOIN ㊶

249

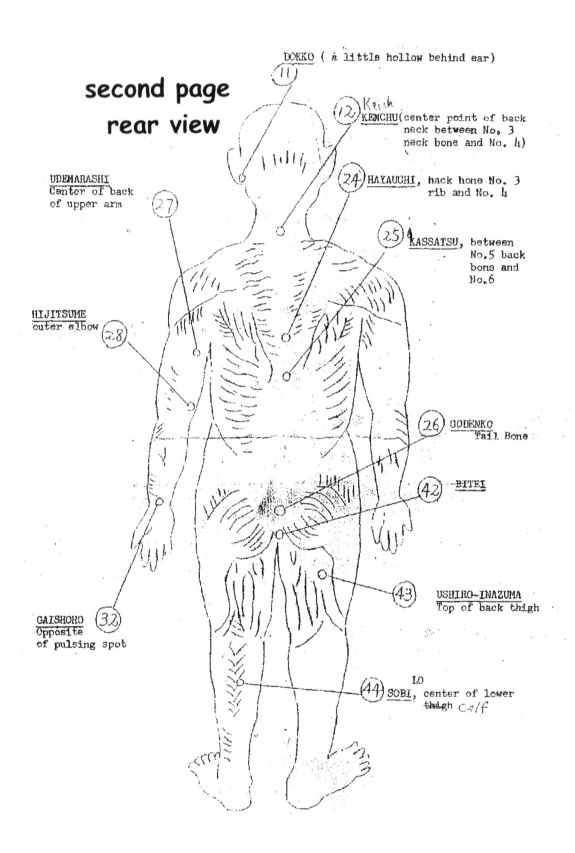

**second page
rear view**

DOKKO (a little hollow behind ear)

⑪

⑫ Keich
KENCHU(center point of back
neck between No. 3
neck bone and No. 4)

UDENARASHI
Center of back
of upper arm

㉗

㉔ HAYAUCHI, back bone No. 3
rib and No. 4

㉕ KASSATSU, between
No.5 back
bone and
No.6

HIJITSUME
outer elbow
㉘

㉖ GODENKO
Tail Bone

㊷ BITEI

㊸

USHIRO-INAZUMA
Top of back thigh

GAISHOHO ㉜
Opposite
of pulsing spot

LO
㊹ SOBI, center of lower
~~thigh~~ calf

1.	TENDO	Fatal	Causing severe shock to cerebrum and irritate brain nerves, and the sense and motor organs are to be lost
2.	TENTO	Fatal	Concussion of brain and severe stimulation of brain nerves
3.	KASUMI	"	Severe stimulation of brain nerves, and sense and motor organs are to be lost
4.	MIMI, Ear		
5.	MIKEN, Brow	Fatal	Rupture of sense and motor organs because of stimulation of brain nerves caused by the severe shock of cerebrum
6.	SEIDON.	Fainting	Because of nervous disorder with the irritated cerebrum
7.	GANSEI	"	Because of severe pain and facial nerve stimulation and of loss of eyesight
8.	JINCHU	Fatal	Because of loss of both organs of sense and motor caused by the stimulation of brain nerves
9.	GEKON	"	Because of loss of both organs of sense and motor caused by the stimulation of brain nerves
10.	MIKAZUKI	Fainting	Because of nervous disorder caused by the concussion
11.	DOKKO		
12.	KEICHU	Fatal	Because of loss of both organs of sense and motor caused by the stimulation of brain nerves
13.	SHOFU	"	Because of severe change of blood circulation cause by the stimulation of carotid arterry and pneumogastric nerve, and of loss of sense and motor organs
14.	SONU	"	Because of loss of motor organ caused by the severe change of blood circulation caused by the irritated artery below collar bone and nerve under tongue
15.	HICHU	"	Because of stoppage of breathing caused by the suppressed windpipe
16.	DANCHU	Fainting	Because of causing troubles to respiratory organs by stimulation lung artery running above the heart bronc.
17.	KYOSEN	"	Because of loss of motor functions caused by the nervous disorder by sever change of blood circulation by the sever shock of liver, stomack and heart
18.	SUIGETSU	Fatal	Severe contusion to liver and stomack. The severe shock is to effect the whole internal organs and to irritate the various nerves and to cause loss of their functions
19.	WAKIKAGE	"	Severe contusion to the lung and stimulation to the artery nerves. Causing stoppage of long mechanism and breath and blood circulation
20.	GANCHU	"	Stop the lung mechanism and stop breath and blood circulation
21.	DENKO	"	In case of right Denko, stimulation to the lung by the severe shock of the liver and nervous organs of both organs are to be lost In case of left, stimulation to the lung and heart by the severe shock of the stomack, and nervous organs are to be lost.

251

22.	INAZUMA	Front side face of upper abdomen between No. 11 rib and No. 12 Fatal. attack by ken, tettui and dagger
23.	MIOJYO, navel	One inch below the navel, fatal. attack by ken and kick.
24.	HAYAUCHI	Back between No. 3 rib and No. 4. Fatal. attack by ken and elbow
25.	KASSATSU	Between No. 5 and No. 6 of the back bone. Fatal. attack by ken, tettui and elbow
26.	GODENKO	The lowest end of the back bone (tail bone) Fatal. attack by ken and kick
27.	UDENARASHI	Center portion of back side of upper arm. attack by tettui and dagger
28.	HIKITSUME	Outer side of elbow, attack by tettui and dagger
29.	ARM JOINT *emp!*	Attack by tettui and dagger, or twist
30.	KOTE	Attack by tettui; dagger and elbow or on both flanks
31.	NAISHOHO, pulsing spot *L-8*	attack by ken, isshiken, tettui and dagger *(L-8)*
32.	GAISHOHO *Inside wrist, little finger side of wrist H-6*	Opposite side of the pulsing spot, attack by ken, *H-6* isshiken, tettui and dagger
33.	TEKO, Joint thumb and 1st finger, attack by ken, isshiken, tettui and dagger	

Vital Points of Kadan (Lower Row)
and Spots to be attacked

34.	KINTEKI, Testicles, fatal. Attack by ken, clasp, kick by knee-pan	
35.	YAKO	Front inner side of upper portion of thigh attack by ken and kick (so called front-groin)
36.	FUKUTO	Front outer side of lower portion of thigh attack by ken and kick
37.	KNEE JOINT	Attack by kick and tread and bend
38.	MUKOBONE	Shin bone. Front central side of the shin. attack by ken and kick
39.	UCHIKUROBUSHI	Anklebone. Attack by tettui and dagger
40.	KOORI	Instep of the feet. Attack by tread and crush
41.	SOIN	Rather outer side of the back of the feet. Attack by tread and crush
42.	BITEI	The lowest ends of the tail bone. Attack and kick by knee-pan
43.	USHIRO-INAZUMA	Top of the back of the thigh. Attack by ken and kick
44.	SOBI	Center of the back of the lower thigh. Attack by kick

REMARKS: Fatal spots out of the 44 vital points are as follows:

JYODEN (Upper Row)	Fatal spots	7	
CHUDAN (Middle Row)	" "	12	
KADAN (Lower Row)	" "	1	total 20 spots

4

A LESSON IN ATEMI WAZA FROM GRANDMASTER SOKEN

A hitting chart is an essential tool in learning the art of atemi. One of the essential skills in fighting is to be able to find and strike vital "spots" while going full speed in the heat of hand to hand combat. This art is often called **Atemi Waza.** One of the tools Hohan Soken used to teach the art of hitting vital targets while going full speed was an old adage…"*punch over - kick under*". To execute you simply punch over or kick under three points of the body; in doing so you are going to hit something that will hurt your opponent. The following illustration will help the reader to under stand this principle:

Punch over kick under

Points to punch over or kick under
  (1) Right shoulder
  (2) Base of neck
  (3) Left shoulder

Examples

(1) (2) (3)

Examples

Block your opponents punch;
counter with a strike over the
base of his neck,
hitting his temple area.

Block your opponent's punch;
kick under his right
shoulder for a counter.

This is a basic concept that was taught to beginning students and was practiced by both the novice and the expert. When the karateka practices this method and becomes skillful in the use of the "punch over kick under" concept; he or she will discover that the simplicity of this method is very practical. If your technique of *atemi waza* is complicated it will not work.

"KISS…Keep it simple stupid"
A timeless adage from the U.S. Army.

THE BUSHI'S SECRET

DEVELOPING KI:
THIS IS THE KEY TO BALANCE AND POWER

Everyone would like to be strong and powerful; yet most of us are not fortunate enough to have been born with great physical strength. Yet, in the minds of the Okinawan karateka, a person can be strong and not posses great physical strength. Even a 10 lb.baby can produce enough power to kill or injure a sumo wrestler under the right conditions. If the baby is dropped on to the head of the wrestler from a four story building; the wrestler will be killed or seriously injured. [6-2]

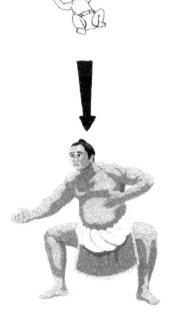

Now, no one is recommending that we experiment with this theory by dropping babies on people's heads. Rather I am trying to make a point: by using natural forces (such as gravity, body mechanics, and momentum) even weak, small or average people can obtain the necessary force to defeat strong powerful people. This force is call "Ki or Chi" and we obtain this force through the mastery of "Minari no Heiho".

"Tachi Kata" is an important ingredient in our discussion of Minari no Heiho. For practical purposes in this discussion. I am referring to "Tachi Kata" as the study of body positions from the waist downward. *Kamae,* on the other hand, is the same study of the rest of the body including spiritual or mental attitude. [6-3]

If there is a secret to the Okinawan Bushi's art of Karate/kobujutsu it is hard work; I should say hard boring work and one of the most tedious and boring of all tasks the traditional sensei will ask his or her students to learn is tachi kata. Too often this type of training is not done or is incomplete. This is sad because this training is so essential.

Hohan Soken practiced learning the various stances or "Dachi" and then learning to move or walk in these stances for three years before he learned anything else. Just as a building is only as strong as its foundation; the karateka is only as strong as his Tachi Kata. [6-4]

I will be discussing this aspect of training as it relates to the knowledge and skills I have learned from Sensei Seizan Kinjo, Hohan Soken, Fusei Kise and Yuichi Kuda. Other styles and Okinawan teachers may have similar or different theories. This does not mean anyone is wrong or right; it means that they are different. Remember the principle of "Suhari" and remember for every advantage there is a disadvantage….this is Yin and Yang.

THE TACHI KATA OF SHORIN RYU MATSUMURA SEITO

In the 1960' many if not most of the Okinawan teachers did not use names for different stances or techniques. Most of the terms, such as the names of tachi kata stances, I learned from Yuichi Kuda in 1984 or from other sources in the United States.

I wish to introduce to the reader to one of the training methods taught to me by Sensei Seizan Kinjo. I will use this concept to discuss power and balance as it relates to the various stances or tachi practiced in Shorin Ryu Matsumura Seito Karate /Kobujutsu.

A LESSON FROM SEIZAN KINJO

We will begin our study of "Tachi Kata" with a brief mention of several of the most important "points of balance" that governs your ability to be strong and effective in hand to hand combat.

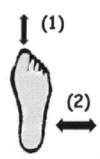

These points or principles deals with the foot or feet, and the method of contact your foot or feet have with the surface on which you are standing. Along the long axis of the foot (1) you have good balance and resistance to a push or pull from the front or back. Against a force being applied at a 90-degree angle to or from the ankle; balance

Balance Points of the foot: Credit Author's collection

is easily lost (2). This principle holds true regardless of your stance or foot position. It is a foundation principle of balance.

Standing on the ball of the foot or heel results in less balance than when standing on the entire sole of the foot.

When standing on one foot, you have

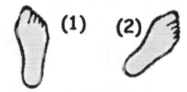

When standing on one foot that is pointed straight forward (1), you have less balance than standing on one foot that is pointed outward (2).

less balance when standing on a foot pointed straight forward (1) than when standing on a foot pointed outward at a 45 degree angle (2). When standing on either one or two feet you have greater balance when standing on the balls of the feet rather than when standing on the heels.

These seemingly simple rules or principles of balance need to be understood before the karateka can fully appreciate the study of Tachi Kata and the principles of power and balance that influences your strengths and weakness in combat.

Another teaching point I learned from Seizan Kinjo was the concept of locating balance and power points of the various stances. Sensei Kinjo would place two staffs or Bo on the outside edge of your feet. Wherever the Bo's would intersect forming an "X"; this would be the point of your balance and power. Again this principle holds true regardless of the stance or posture. Any force pushing or pulling the body toward the "X" will cause a loss of balance. Your power potentially is greater moving toward the "X" than away from the "X". Balance is greater against a force pushing or pulling the body away from the "X".

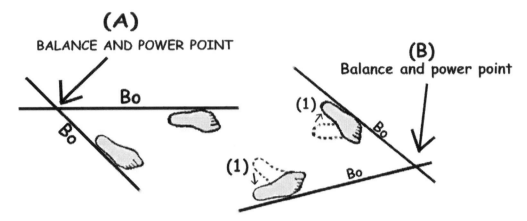

When the Bo or staffs are place along the out side of each foot, where they intersect is the balance and power point of the foot alinement. By changing the alinement of the feet, in this case pivoting on the balls of the feet (1) and moving the heels outward; we have projected our power and balance forward. By moving our power forward we can add power to an offensive technique such as a punch. However, we weaken our defensive position by putting our balance in front. Again Yin and Yang come into play.

THE DACHI OR STANCES

In my opinion the karateka should not consider the stance by name but rather consider the name as it relates to function; with the stance being a tool which is used to carry out a function. In order to do this it is necessary that we know the properties of each of our so called stances so we can select the correct one to use according to the situation.

Therefore, I have grouped certain stances together according to the distance the feet of each stance are apart. It is important that we become familiar with the terms Tachi Nagasa (stance length and Tachi Haba (stance width). These terms were introduced to me by Sensei Kuda.

The first group is composed of those stances with the feet longer or wider apart. These are (1). Pinan Dachi or Forward Stance, (2). Renoji Dachi or "L" Stance, (3) Pai Sai Dachi, and (4) Naihanchi Dachi named after the Naihanchi Kata.

Pinan Dachi   **Renoji Dachi**

Pai Sai Dachi   **Naihanchi Dachi**

In these stances the feet are the same distance apart and they differ only in the angles of the feet. It is important to under stand that these are fighting stances and they are not used to strengthen the legs or other body areas. There is an adage that comes from American football: *"You practice like you play."* If you practice your kata with tachi kata that is impractical for actual combat; you may not be ready for actual combat when it happens.

"Practice does not make perfect….perfect practice makes perfect"
A lesson from a Chinese fortune cookie.

Tachi Nagasa and Tachi Haba

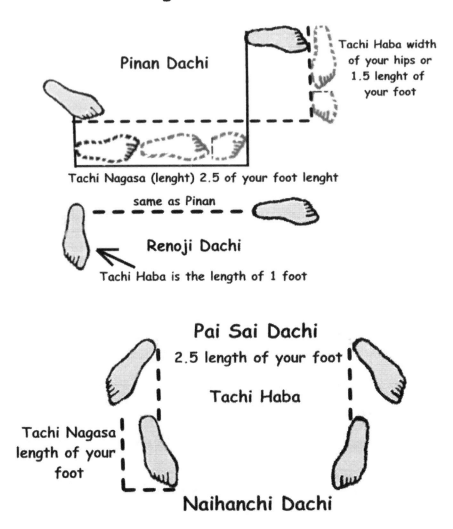

These are the tachi nagasa and haba that were taught to me in the late 1960's by Seizan Kinjo, Hohan Soken, and Fusei Kise. Yuichi Kuda's stances were a little wider and longer than were the stances of my other Shorin Ryu Matsumura Seito teachers.

The readers should also understand that stances will vary somewhat from person to person. Conditions of the ground will also cause a variation of stance width and length. There is a general rule that states your stance will be larger on wet, slippery ground and smaller on dry ground. The tachi haba and nagasa (stance width and length) should allow for the karateka to be mobile. Your stance should allow you to move in any direction at any time. You should have the ability to use both feet to kick in all directions at any time.

"If you can kick in all directions and jump straight up your stance is correct"
Quote from Fusei Kise during the 1960's.

258

TACHI KATA BASED ON THE YOI DACHI

Attention Stance or Musubi Dachi

Sensei Soken mainly used the Ready Stance or Yoi Dachi to practice fighting techniques. Unlike many other Shorin Ryu systems the old master did not begin kata from the Yoi Dachi. Rather he began kata from the Attention Stance or Musubi Dachi. Seisan Kata is the only kata started from the Yoi Dachi in Sensei Soken's system.

Sensei Soken's Yoi Dachi
Author's collection

The Yoi Dachi should allow you to move or kick in any direction. The Yoi Dachi is easily converted into several other stances; Sanchin Dachi, Neko Ashi Dachi and the short Pinan or Gojushiho Dachi.

Hohan Soken and his wife
Photo credit: Resources Unlimited

Stances based on the Yoi Dachi

Sanchin Dachi

Neko Ashi Dachi

Short Pinan Dachi
or Gojushiho Dachi

The Neko Ashi Dachi (cat footed stance)
used in Shorin Ryu Matsumura Seito has little or no
elevation of the heel of the front foot. This is the old style
cat stance. The Short Pinan Stance really has no name. This stance
is seen in White crane kata and in the kata Gojushiho.

Except for the Musubi Dachi the stances mentioned above are not widely used in most Shorin Ryu Matsumura Seito Karate/Kobujutsu Kata. The Short Pinan Dachi is not seen in kata until you learn the Gojushiho Kata.

The Sanchin Dachi in kata is unknown to most practioners of Shorin Ryu Matsumura Seito. The Shuri Sanchin or Matsumura Sanchin was once widely used. The Sanchin Dachi is very important in creating power as is the Neko Ashi Dachi. The Neko Ashi Dachi is seen in some versions of the Pai Sai Kata. But generally speaking Shorin Ryu Matsumura Seito does not use a Neko Ashi Dachi very often.

Drawing from "The Little Pictures of Japan" published by the Book House for Little Children Pictures by Katharen Sturges

Ready Stance or Yoi Dachi

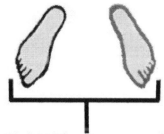

The Tachi Haba or stance width is
the same as the width of your hips

Sanchin Dachi

Short Pinan Dachi

Neko Ashi Dachi

From the heel of the back foot to the toes of the front foot
Tachi Nagasa for these stance is a little less
than the length of 2 feet. The Tachi Haba is the same as the
width of the hips or the lenght of 1.5 of your feet.

These are upright stances that play a major role in carrying out several of the most important principles of the Shorin Ryu family of styles (Matsumura-ha or Matsumura's lineage); the following adages explain these principles:

"It is not wise to:
Stress power over balance, strength over quickness and place recklessness over control.
Remember: softness over comes hardness."

These "new" adages are based on the principles learned from all of my teachers:
From the Author's collection.

STRENGTH AND WEAKNESSES IN YOUR TACHI KATA AND KAMAE

On of the reasons we learn kata is to understand the strength and weaknesses in our own form, once this is accomplished we will learn to see strength and weaknesses in others. The ultimate goal is to gain the advantage over your opponent in a self defense situation.

Drawing parallel lines from the shoulders through the hips and down to the feet is an important indicator concerning strengths and weaknesses in a stance. Forward stances such as Pinan (1) are strong against forces pushing from the rear or pulling from the front. Such a posture is less strong against forces from the sides. If the feet are outside of the parallel lines (2 and 3) than these postures are weak in the knees and weak against a push to the front or back but strong against these same forces being applied to the sides. These principles apply to all stances.
Photo credit: Author's collection

"Carelessness is one of your greatest enemies.

A lesson from a Chinese fortune cookie.

The alignment of the knee and the forward foot of the Pinan and Renoji Dachi and the alignment of the knee and both feet of the Pai Sai and Naihanchi Dachi play an important role in combat. In the Pinan Dachi, the alignment of the front foot in relation to the knee of the front leg deals with both balance and power.

The above photo illustrates two popular alignments of the front foot and knee. On the upper left the vertical line is in the middle of the instep. On the right the vertical line is forward of the front foot. Photo credit author's collection

The dot represent to position of the knee.
(1) This alignment of the knee in relation to the foot gives greater balance but less power.
(2) This alignment offer less balance but greater power.

Among karate styles and karate teaches there is always "controversy" as to which is most important "balance or power." Hohan Soken stressed balance first and power second. Sensei Kise stressed power first and balance second. Yuichi Kuda stressed balance over power but not to the extent that Hohan Soken did. As Sensei Kise grew old he began to place more importance on balance. The controversy between balance and power will change as one grows older and balance becomes more important.

BALANCE POINTS OF THE KAMAE

The most important point of the body's balance is the head. The old adage **ear, shoulder, hand, and hip** refers to the importance the position of the head as it relates to the body as a whole. This is an important key to maintaining and understanding balance.

Above left ...Ear, Shoulder, Hand and Hip alignment; above right
illustrates the frontal mid line alignment. Photo credit: Author's collection

The above photographs are indicators of balance. When the old masters looked at your kata; these are just some of the points that were used as indicators for balance and strength. If these lines are not vertical both mental and physical balance are lost.

Fusei Kise demonstrating "rolling the ball".
Photo credit: author's collection

If the head and lower parts of the body are not connected by the straight vertical lines the karateka is weak and can be defeated.

Sensei Kise practiced a technique that I call "rolling the ball". In this case the ball is the head. By pressing down on the muscles and nerve centers on the back of the neck; Sensei Kise would lower his opponent's head causing him to loose his balance and fall to the ground.

"Rolling the ball" can be a simple controlling technique or a deadly technique to use in truly dangerous situations.

"Practice this and all techniques only with a trained instructor."

"If you control your opponent's head, you will control both his physical and mental balance; then victory will be yours."

Controlling your opponent's head
Photo credit: Author's collection

We often hear the old saying that I attributed to Bushi Matsumura ***"steal your opponent's mind to defeat him".*** I believe this refers to causing your opponent to loose his balance by controlling his head.

At times it is difficult to gain control of your opponent's head because usually you have to go through his arms to reach his head.

There are several balance points that are easy to reach and by striking these points you will cause your opponent to loose his balance and he will ***"give you his head".***

Photos from left to right…striking the "girdle meridian, striking the large intestine meridian just above the elbow, and striking the inguinal crease will cause your opponent to bent forward and loose his balance to where you can control his head. .. Author's collection

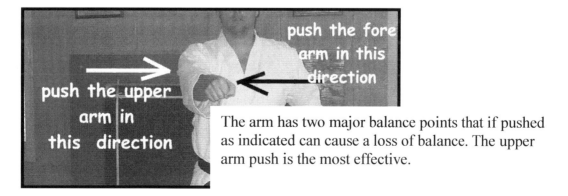

The arm has two major balance points that if pushed as indicated can cause a loss of balance. The upper arm push is the most effective.

Power can be gained by lowering the head and upper body and then striking upward with a powerful upper punch. Such a technique is often used by boxers and is an excellent example of being off balance and in weak position when you crouch down preparing to punch (above photo on the left); then suddenly changing to a strong position as you punch upward (above photo on the right). This is a working example of Yin and Yang.

An example of a boxer using an off balance position on the upper left and turning this disadvantage into an advantage by launching a powerful upward surging punch; upper right. Photo credit: Author's collection.

FRONT SHOULDER - HEEL ALIGNMENT

The alignment of the forward foot heel and forward shoulder is an excellent example of the ancient principle of Yin and Yang as it relates to the fact that with every plus there is a minus and with every advantage there is a disadvantage. This alignment is very important to consider as we learn the relationship between balance and power.

The photo on the right shows a vertical line connecting the shoulder of the forward punching arm with the heel of the forward foot.

If the shoulder does not extend forward of the heel of the front foot, balance is good but the power is less. If the shoulder of the punching arm extends forward of the heel of the forward foot power is increase but balance is less.

Shoulder and front foot alignment. Author's collection

266

UNDERSTANDING AND PROJECTING YOUR POWER

Too often the modern karateka gets wrapped up in "fads" and in doing so they neglect the truly important aspects their art. The grappling, throwing, and joint manipulation arts such as jujitsu, and aikido are found in arts that originally stressed hitting first and grappling second; Okinawan karate is the same.

Sensei Fusei Kise has his own method to stress this concept of hitting or striking first. He would say as he assume his fighting kamae *"You hit'em up";* meaning hit first. All of my Okinawan karate sensei all said that karate is a striking art and that techniques such as *tuite* play a secondary role in karate techniques.

Sensei Kise's fighting stance
Photo credit Authors collection

Generating power is largely about the understanding and utilization of those natural forces of gravity and moment that influences our ability to hit with power.

Nature has given each of us everything we need to develop powerful punches, strikes and kicks. All we need is our body mass or weight, the propellant (arms, legs, back and muscles) to propel this mass into motion. We also need our hands, fists, feet and other body parts to deliver this mass to a desired target. All we have to do is learn to deliver this force to the target as effectively and efficiently as possible.

The late heavy weight boxing great, Jack Dempsey, describes a powerful punch as having two parts (1) setting the weight in motion and (2) relaying the moving weight to a desired point on an opponent with a stepped up impact or explosion. Both karate and boxing follow these guidelines. [6-5]

Jack Dempsey Photo Credit Author's collection

267

The method that Bushi Matsumura made famous (speed x mass = power) is very famous and serves as the basis for almost all punches used in karate. Matsumura's hip twisting reverse punch uses a straight punch from the shoulder with the elbow of the punching arm brushing your side.

This is the power source for the Shaolin Tiger which is represented in Okinawa Shorin Ryu by the Pinan Kata.

This is one of the first power source to be studied in karate and must be thoroughly understood before the karateka can progress in the art.

Author's collection

Chinen Peninsula of Southeastern Okinawa as seen from the north during the 1950's. Photo credit: Mike Roberts Color Production

MAKE EVERY STEP A KICK

There is an old Chinese adage that states *"in kata practice every step can be a kick"*. In most styles of Okinawan Karate stepping forward in a Pinan or Forward stance is executed with the stepping foot moving forward with a *crescent step*. A kick is more powerful than a punch therefore, the skillful karateka will use a kick as often as the situation requires. The following illustrates the body mechanics involved in making each step a kick; this is Sensei Kuda's stepping methods:

Pinan Dachi crescent step

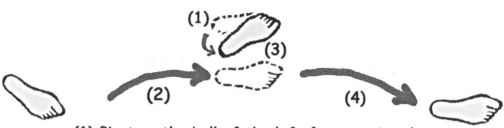

(1) Pivot on the ball of the left foot, moving the heel of the foot in the direction of the arrow.
(2) Step in a crescent with the right foot, brushing against the left foot. This relocates the center of balance to the left foot.
(3) The relacation of balance to the left foot allows the right foot to be kicked forward.
(4) Once the kick is complete the right foot steps down into a Pinan Dachi

Stepping from Pinan Dachi into a Pai Sai Dachi

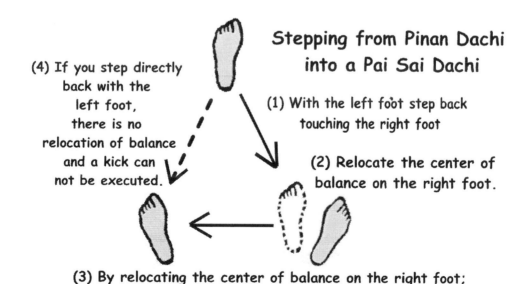

(4) If you step directly back with the left foot, there is no relocation of balance and a kick can not be executed.

(1) With the left foot step back touching the right foot

(2) Relocate the center of balance on the right foot.

(3) By relocating the center of balance on the right foot; the step outward with the left foot can be a kick.

SINKING POWER

One of the greatest "untapped" power sources in modern karate is gravity. This is especially true among those styles of a Shurite origin. Shurite is the type of karate that evolved around the Okinawan castle town of Shuri and includes styles such as Shotokan, Shito Ryu, Shorin Ryu and others.

These styles do a very good job of developing the hips as a power source; but most are somewhat lacking when it comes to developing "sinking power." Sinking power is one of the major techniques of the Southern Chinese White Crane Fist and is not very difficult to develop. All you have to do is relax; drop your weight suddenly by bending your knees and let gravity take charge. You also need to know when to use your sinking power

Sinking power does not work if your intended target is higher than your shoulder. So use this technique for targets shoulder high or lower. It is especially effective against your opponent's waist and will cause him to fall forward.

Sinking power; Photo Credit: Author's collection

It is simple to illustrate the delivery of power to the target by sinking lower. Our model for this demonstration is standing upright facing a vertical white line which represents a target. The karateka can touch the target merely by bending his knees.

Sinking power –Note the arms are straight-Yet He can reach the white line by only bending his knees. Photo credit: Author's collection

270

In the previous photos the arms are held straight outward so there is no moving forward of the fist. Yet the whole body is moved forward simple by bending the knees.

We know this is so because his arm did not get longer when he bent his knees and yet he can touch the target. If the dropping of the weight is quick enough, a great deal of the body mass can be used to hit the target. This is a powerful concept that enables the karateka to develop tremendous power simply by using gravity

SHIFTING THE BODY WEIGHT WITHOUT STEPPING.

Often, if not most of the time, things happen very fast in unarmed combat; you simple don't have time to set up in a "proper stance" and execute a "proper technique." You have got to respond to the situation from your position of the moment and make the best out of a bad situation. This is going to require that you master the art of shifting your body weight in order to dodge your attacker and to get your body weight into

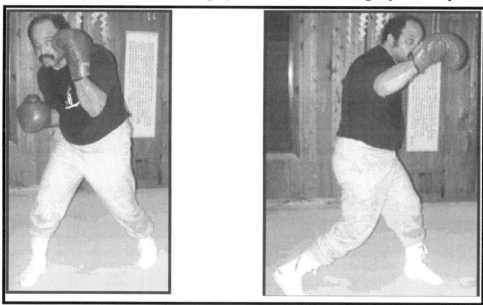

Surging upward Photo credit: Authors collection

your counter attack

One method Dempsey uses in his discussion of putting your body mass into motion in order to hit powerfully is "surging" upward to delivery an upper cut. This is an example of body shifting without stepping to gain power. This is an excellent technique made famous by boxers such as Mike Tyson.

Shifting from the Pinan Dachi into the Sanchin Dachi develops considerable power in a forward direction. Many modern karate styles no longer train in Sanchin. In the days of Bushi Matsumura most methods of Okinawan Karatejutsu used a Sanchin kata for training. It was a mistake to eliminate Sanchin kata as a training method.

271

Sanchin is essential to develop power beyond your physical ability. It is wrong to always be in a forward stance or Pinan Dachi and it is wrong to always be in Sanchin.

Learn to freely move back forth between the Pinan and Sanchin stance, this is a power source just waiting to be harnessed; but sadly many karateka, perhaps through ignorance, do not take advantage of this natural source of power.

Right Pinan Dachi

Changing your stance from
a forward stance to Sanchin Dachi
creates significant power.

Pivot on the balls
of your feet.

Sanchin Dachi

USING THE NEKO ASHI DACHI TO DEVELOP POWER

Too often among modern karateka the thought of using the Neko Ashi Dachi (cat footed stance or just cat stance) centers around "looking good in kata." Little thought is given to actually what this posture offers or has the potential to offer to the karateka engaged in combat. The truth is that the Neko Ashi Dachi can be a sound plan to add power to your technique that is achieved through natural forces not through an increase in your brawn. Such a combination of natural forces and technique is another example of putting Ki or Chi into your technique. Let us examine two such techniques.

*Drawing is from the
Author's collection*

On the left the karateka in a Neko Ashi Dachi the in the photo on the right the karateka put his foot down in doing so his body weigh is transferred forward to add power to his punch. Photo credit: Author's collection

In the first method, power is obtained by shifting your weight back into a Neko Ashi Dachi. Then shift this weight to the forward foot; coordinating the punch and the weight shift so that the shift occurs as the fist hits the target.

The second method is similar to the first; but is a little more complicated and more powerful. On the following page is a series of drawings illustrating this method of gaining power from the innocent looking cat stance.

Below…Scene from Naha late 1800's; photo credit: Author's collection

Getting power from the Neko Ashi Dachi
(Cat Stance)

Pinan Dachi

weight distribution
50% on each foot

Neko Ashi Dachi

Moving from the Pinan Dachi to the
Neko Ashi Dachi.

Slide the lead foot back with
the heel raised (1).

weight distribution
80% on back foot
20% on front foot

By sliding the front foot back into a
Neko Ashi Dachi; we have concentrated about 80%
of our body weight in one place (the rear foot). Now by
using the ancient formula for power (mass or weight x velocity = power)
we can transfer a great deal of force or power into an attack
on our opponent. To accomplish this we need to move forward
to create velosity.

Neko Ashi Dachi

(1) Schuffle step forward with
the front foot (still maintaining 20% of the
body weight on this foot).

(2) Schuffle step forward with
the rear foot (still maintaining
80% of the body
on this foot).

Coordinate a reverse punch...in this case with the left hand... just as
the schuffle step is completed. This technique has 80% of the body
weight behind it. Therefore, the technique can be more powerful than a
similar technique from a stance with a 50% weight distribution on each foot.
This is a core principle of Shuri-te Karate.

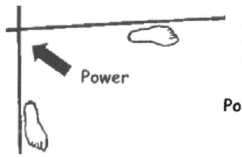

If we draw an invisible line from the outside of each foot and extend these lines well to the front and to the rear of the feet; these lines intersect is

Point the toes of the front foot outward to put power in the rear hand

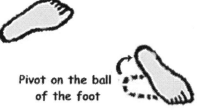

Pivot on the ball of the foot

where the potential power is stored.

Point the toes of the front foot outward to put power in the rear hand. This is one of the power principles of Hakutsuru (White Crane).

By pivoting the on the ball of the front foot and moving the heel to the inside and then moving our front heel to the outside we can adjust the power from the rear hand to the front hand according to the situation. This is one of Bushi Matsumura's principles of "Torque".

Turning the front foot straight will put the power back in the lead hand

Pivoting on the ball of the foot

This technique is found in the Matsumura Hakutsuru Kata and is an example of increasing power without becoming physically stronger. This is one of the principles of "Ki" flow. This is power that is from natural sources and does not require the development of a more powerful muscular body.

Drawing from "Little pictures of Japan" edited by Olive Miller and pictures by Katherine Sturges. Published by The Book House for Children

275

Hohan Soken demonstrating a special Nukite or spear hand attack from the Matsumura Hakutsuru Dai Kata. Techniques such as this can be made to be more effective once the karateka understands the foot work need to put power in the lead hand or in the rear hand as the situation requires.

Photo credit: Author's collection

Put power in the lead hand by pivoting on the ball of the rear foot. Move the heel of the rear foot in the direction of the arrow (2)

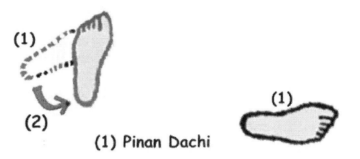

(1) Pinan Dachi

To put power back into the rear hand, move back into a (1) Pinan Dachi by pivoting on the ball of the rear foot and then moving the heel of the rear foot in the direction of the arrow (2).

to

In Matsumura Seito the pivot is on the balls of the feet. Other styles pivot on heels of the feet. Teachers of the Matsumura Seito system believe that greater balance is maintained by pivoting on the balls of the feet. Those styles that pivot on the heels believe that greater power is achieved by pivoting on the heels. This is a question of which is best…..placing balance over power or power over balance. This is Yin and Yang at work….there is no correct answer to this question.

"Seek and ye shall find…often the true answer lies hidden in ourselves."
A lesson from a Chinese fortune cookie

KICKING POWER

The position of the feet can greatly affect the power that can be applied to either the rear or front foot during a kick. The illustrations to the left and below are basic guidelines to understanding the methods of creating powerful kicks using body weight, momentum and body mechanics.

Point the toes of the front foot outward to put kicking power in the rear foot. This also improves balance when kicking.

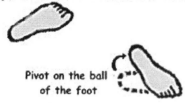

Pivot on the ball of the foot

As you execute a kick with the lead foot, turn the heel of the rear foot as indicated by the arrow (2) to increase power.

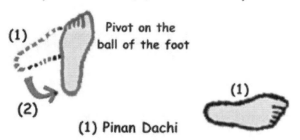

(1)

Pivot on the ball of the foot

(2)

(1) Pinan Dachi

(1)

As we pivot on the ball of the feet to increase power, there is a danger of raising the heel too high. This can cause a loss of balance

When kicking from a Sanchin Dachi, try to avoid kicking with the rear foot as balance is poor when using this method.

All of my Okinawan Sensei stressed using low kicks. They very seldom kicked any higher than the floating ribs. They also favored snap kicks over thrust kicks.

Kicking from the Sanchin Dachi results in a weak kick with the rear foot and a strong kick with the front foot.

Sanchin Dachi

In the Rohai Kata, which was once exclusively a part of Tomari-te karate; there exists a series of moves where you block low with a left Ge Dan Uke (low block) and then quickly strike upward with a right nukite (Spear hand) into the throat. As you execute the low block you are allowing your knees to bend and your weight to fall slightly. You are allowing gravity to pull you downward setting your body weight into motion downward.

The low block has a hidden technique attached. Following the low block there is a quick short jab with the blocking hand into the waist of your opponent. The jab is coordinated with the dropping of the weight and is surprisingly powerful. This causes him to bend forward; opening his throat area for an attack.

The spear hand to the throat is then executed with an up lifting action of the legs. This technique is found in the kata Rohai Jo Dan. This action insures that

Three photo illustrating power down and power up with a low block followed with a jab/punch to the girdle meridian to cause the opponent to buckle over and with a lifting motion of the legs hit the throat with a spear thrust. Photo credit: Author's collection

your body mass is behind the strike. This principle is found in a number of kata and is a very important concept of karate.

In the traditional Shurite karate styles of Okinawa there are two dachi or stances that play a major role in the karateka being able to focus his or her power upward or downward. One, the Pai Sai Dachi, focuses power downward. The other stance, the Naihanchi, focuses power upward.

Pai Sai Dachi on the left, Naihanchi dachi on the right
Photo Credit: Author's collection

Power up ---Power down
using the Pai Sai Dachi and Naichanchi Dachi

Pai Sai Dachi

Naihanchi Dachi

Pai Sai Dachi to Naihanchi Dachi

Naihanchi Dach to Pai Sai Dachi

Power up

Power down

By using both the Pai Sai Dachi and the Naihanchi Dachi and learning to change rapidly back and forth from the Pai Sai Dachi to the Naihanchi Dachi and back to Pai Sai dachi according to the situation; we can produces great power.

Two photos illustrate power up and power down; above on the left is a technique of punching upward from Naihanchi Kata; above on the right hitting down on the girdle meridian utilizing the Pai Sai Dachi power down technique. Photo credit Author's collection

Both the Pai Sai Dachi and Naihanchi Dachi can also generate additional power by rotating the pelvis area of the body up and down to produce power up or down as the situation dictates.

The rotation of the pelvic area of the body moving up and down is symbolic of the Shaolin Leopard climbing up a tree and then pouncing down upon on its prey or enemies.

In this way the leopard can use gravity to provide a great deal of power. The leopard then becomes a very powerful animal that has learned to use gravity to increase its strength.

Photo credit: the author's collection

GOJUSHIHO KATA INTRODUCES THE HALF STEP

The late Grandmaster Hohan Soken described the kata Gojushiho as lifting the karateka into a "new level". Sensei Kuda said the old martial arts text "Bubishi" describes Gojushiho as being the counter to the Hakutsuru or White Crane.

I personally believe that the Bubishi link between Hakutsuru and Gojushiho is based on the fact that the Gojushiho is the first kata in many Okinawan styles that introduces white crane principles. One of these principles is using the half step to generate power.

Famous drawing from the "Bubushi" showing the Hakutsuru on the left and Gojushiho on the right.

some weight remains on rear leg

The concept of the half step revolves around the fact that both of your feet bear weight. Usually each foot has 50% of your weight.

If we can get more of our body weight involved in the execution of technique we can produce more power. One way to do this is to coordinate the movement of the rear foot moving forward with the execution of the punch. If both the foot movement and punch end at the same instance; a large percentage of the body weight moves forward and forms the mass that combines with velocity to furnish the power.

Punching as illustrate with the photo on the left puts only 50% of the body weight into the punch. Photo credit Author's collection

Gojushiho Half Step

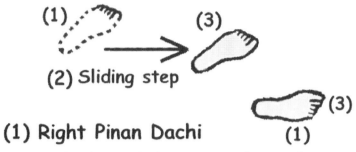

(1) Right Pinan Dachi

(2) Left foot sliding step foward
into a short Pinan Dachi (3)

The sliding forward step used in the Gojushiho kata creates a great deal of striking power.

Gojushiho Kata: Back foot moves up t o create power. Photo credit Author's collection

Moving the rear foot forward with a half step is one of the power sources for the Shaolin White Crane. Sensei Kuda said that over 80% of the body weight can be put into your technique using the Gojushiho half step. This is just one of the principles gives the crane the ability to be powerful without being strong.

力之所趨重心
隨勢轉移善
伐敵之重心者
盜伐其心也既
盜其心攻敵
必克

"Where your power goes so goes your balance.
To steal your opponent's balance is to steal his mind.
If you steal your opponent's mind, you will defeat him."

Poem by the Author
Calligraphy is Classic Chinese by Shifu Hwang.
Drawing by the Author: Author's collection

TSURU NO HANE
(WINGS OF THE CRANE)

DEVELOPING HANDS OF STEEL AND ARMS OF COTTON

Thus far in our study of Minari no Heiho we have studied the relationship of balance, projection of power and the tachi kata. In doing so, we have given our technique a foundation that is based on Ki or Chi. Ki is based on natural forces that are not dependent on great physical strengths. We now are going to expand this concept into developing our tools or weapons that can be used for self protection.

When Anko Itosu met with, Shintaro Ogawa, Okinawa's Commissioner of Public Schools to discuss the alteration of Okinawan Karatejutsu. They were setting out to make Okinawan Karatejutsu a safer and less combative art that would fit into the public school system. Itosu is alleged to have demonstrated various strikes and techniques and then discussed with Ogawa the suitability of these methods to be used as part of the Karate public school program.

Clearly some techniques were thought to be too dangerous for school children to practice and were eliminated from kata and were no longer taught. The reader should realize that Okinawan Karate was being converted from a "Jutsu" to a "Do" and that the combat effectiveness was no longer of primary importance.

Today, no one knows which techniques were eliminated. We can only make educated guesses about many techniques that may have once been a part of Okinawan Karatejutsu. The purpose of this article is to examine some of the hand and foot techniques found in Chinese and Okinawan White Crane styles. Since much of Okinawan Karatejutsu stems from the Southern Chinese White Crane systems; it is only natural to assume that many of the techniques of the Crane were once part of Okinawan Karate.

It is not enough just to be able to recognize these old weapons we've got to condition ourselves to use them. Our hands must be like steel and our arms like cotton to be effective at "Tode".

Drawing of Anko Itosu Photo credit:
Robert Teller collection

THE AWAKING OF YOUR TENDONS

The Obon Festival is one of Okinawa's rich cultural traditions. Associated with this festival is the cleaning of the ancestor's bones by the oldest daughter of a family. The cleaning of the bones occurs three years after the old family member dies. Over the years it has been noted that when the time came to clean the bones of many karate masters; their bones were more difficult to clean than were the bones of a normal person. This was because even though the flesh had decayed from the bones of the old masters, the tendons were still intact. The tendons were so developed that even in death they were still strong.

Many of these exercise and techniques that created the strong tendons of these old masters were not taught to those students learning the art in the Okinawan school system.

Developing hands of steel starts with several simple exercises to train the karateka to gain control of their tendons. Most modern karateka have been taught to use only a clenched fist. Even though their kata shows other hand strikes and techniques; training is done primarily with the **Seiken** or clinched fist. Their tendons are asleep and need to be awakened.

TENDON AWARENESS AND STRENGTHENING EXERCISES

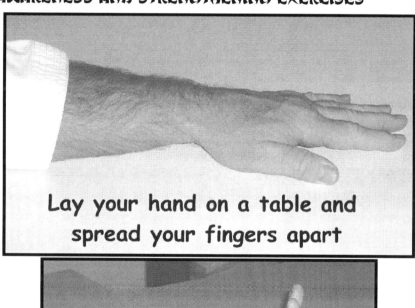

Lay your hand on a table and spread your fingers apart

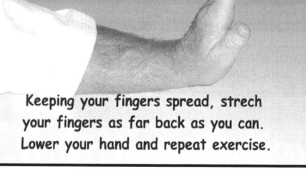

Keeping your fingers spread, strech your fingers as far back as you can. Lower your hand and repeat exercise.

285

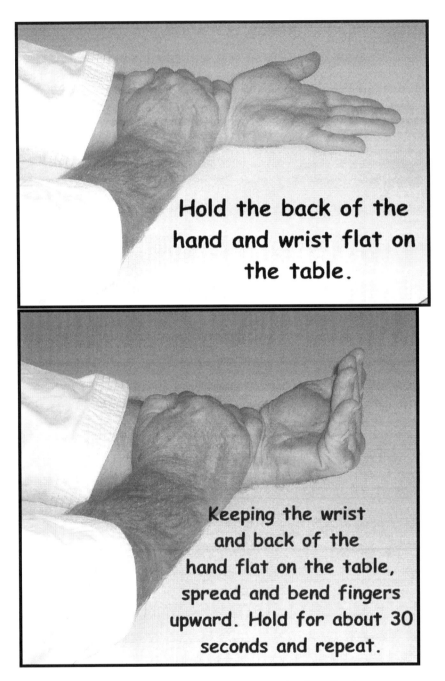

Hold the back of the hand and wrist flat on the table.

Keeping the wrist and back of the hand flat on the table, spread and bend fingers upward. Hold for about 30 seconds and repeat.

Previous four photographs… credit Author's collection

"Never be afraid to try something new.
Remember that Noah's Ark was built by amateurs."

A lesson from a Chinese fortune cookie.

Spread fingers open and point them upward at a
45 degree angle. Elbows are touching the ribs.
Point fingers back over your shoulders.

Push hands forward as you sink your chest inward
and round your back. Hold this position for 20 seconds
and return to starting position. This excercise is from the
Happoren Kata.

The previous two photos are from the Author's collection

The tendon exercises are to be practice slowly at first but gradually increase the time until you can hold these positions for 30 to 40 seconds. These simple exercises with time and practice will strengthen your forearms and fingers until you will posses arms of cotton and hands of steel. The karateka learns to tighten his hands fingers and forearms without tightening his muscles. Your fingers will emulate the point of a spear. Good results can be expected in about 6 months.

The atlatle or throwing stick was with little doubt developed thousands of years ago by primitive warriors and hunters. The men were probably influenced by unarmed men who learned the principle of relaxation and leverage to gain an advantage over their enemies in combat.

Atlatle...primitive man's throwing stick

The dart or spear is the projectile that stike the target.

The stick adds leverage

The arm and the body provide the relaxed whip like movement that propels the dart.

Modern karateka can learn much from studying this ancient atlatle. In order for the atatle to be effective the arm and hand and whole body must be soft and flexible in order for the atlatle to propel the dart forward with sufficient velocity to make the weapon effective. The karateka should learn to use his hands, arms and body in such a fashion as to emulate ancient man armed with the atlatle. The arm from the elbow forward to the finger tips should be hard and stiff with tendon techniques (not tight with muscle power) this becomes the dart that is propelled by the atlatle. The upper arm is soft and the entire body flexible (arms of cotton); with a whip like action of the upper arm and body, the forearm and hands are propelled forward just as the dart is launched by the atatle.

From the Author's collection

The karateka can throw his finger spear just as the primitive man "threw" his dart with the atatle.

The average karateka can perform this technique with little or no hand and finger toughening exercises.

"To understand the new; we need to study the old."
A timeless old martial arts adage.

EXPLODING FIST OF STEEL

The common karate punch is one of the misused of all karate techniques. Relaxation is perhaps the key to good punching skills. Hohan Soken said *"Form the fist as if you are holding a small rubber ball."* When the punch is executed tighten the fist by squeezing the rubber ball upon contact with the target. This creates a small explosion that makes the karate punch so effective.

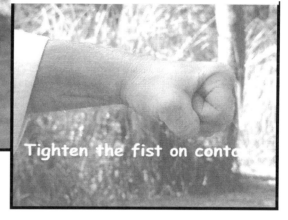

The Seiken or fist is the most common martial arts technique. Photo credit: Author's collection

Hold the punching hand open

Tighten the fist on conta

The two fisted vertical punch used near the beginning of the Gojushiho Kata is often called the "heart punch". John Wang a superb Chinese Martial Artist living in Austin, Texas; once told me that the vertical fist is about the same size as the human heart and many Chinese martial artists say that this weapon when used correctly with a punch to the heart can stop this organ from beating.

Therefore, the vertical punch is a very dangerous technique and should not be taught to children and should not be used in sporting contest. This like all techniques of karatejutsu (tode jutsu) are true fighting techniques that should be used only for self-defense.

Gojushiho Vertical punch
Author's collection

GOKENKI'S CRANE WINGS

Gokenki was a Chinese tea merchant living in Okinawa during the early 1900's until his death in the 1940's. There are different opinions as to which of the Fukein Chinese systems Go Kenki practiced. Some say his style was called "Kingai-noon" which is said to be a sister style to "Pangainoon" (Uechi-Ryu). Others say that his style was an offshoot of the "Shouting Crane Fist." Gokenki is known to have taught a number of notable Okinawan karate masters among these are: Chojun Miyagi, Kenwa Mabuni, and Hohan Soken. Gokenki's crane techniques were widely distributed and are very popular

Gokenki's crane wings can be seen in kata such as "Hakutcho." Using his method the hands and arms can be used for both blocking and striking. This method puts hard or "Yang" energy in the hands and soft or "Yin" energy in the arms. The fingers of the hand are in a strong position and can be used for finger thrust. This type of crane wing is used by many White Crane systems in China and Okinawa and is very effective.

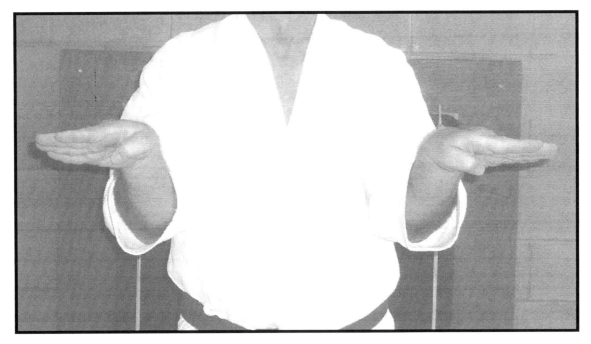

Go Kenki's crane wings
Author's collection

"Perhaps you will forget tomorrow the kind words you say today;
but the recipient may cherish them over a life time."

A lesson from a Chinese fortune cookie.

MATSUMURA'S CRANE WINGS

Perhaps the most famous White Crane Kata in Okinawa is found in the Shorin Ryu Matsumura Seito Karate Kobudo system of the late Grandmaster Hohan Soken. The reason for this fame probably goes back to a 1967 BLACK BELT MAGAZINE article that mistakenly referred to the Matsumura White Crane as "White Swan."

The Matsumura Seito system has several Crane kata that Sokon "Bushi" Matsumura is alleged to have brought to Okinawa after one of his many trips to China. The "Feeding or Eating Crane" system of Southern China is said to be a sister style to the Matsumura Crane.

Fusei Kise demonstrating a posture from the Matsumura Hakutsuru Kata. Photo credit: Author's collection

The wings of the Matsumura Crane are similar to those of the Gokenki system. However, the Matsumura Crane hand is relaxed and full of soft or yin energy. The thumb of the Matsumura crane hand is pointed downward. When the thumb is pointed downward the forearm is hard and full of yang energy while the hand is relaxed. This type of Crane wing is useful for blocking with the arm and grabbing or catching with the hand. This technique is most effective when used with dodging or evasive maneuvers. The two types of crane wing are best used in combination with the Matsumura wings used for blocking and the Go Kenki wings used for countering with finger strikes.

Go Kenki's crane wings
are finger strikes

Matsumura's crane wings
are blocks with grabs

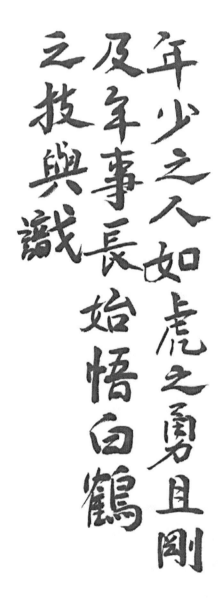

"When you are young, practice the boldness and strength of the tiger.
When you are old, practice the wisdom and technique of the white crane."

Calligraphy by Shifu Hwang

Poem by Chikin Akagawa

Author's collection

KOJO OR KOGUSHIKU CRANE HANDS

The Kogushiku family (also called Kojo or Koshiro) is one of Okinawa's famous Karate Families. This technique is not only limited to the Kojo Ryu style, it is also found in Uechi Ryu, and Shorin Ryu Matsumura Seito. It is one of the most useful techniques found in Okinawan Karate Justsu.

.The Swiss Army Knife is, with all of the small tools contained in the mechanisms of the knife, considered As one of the most useful items the outdoorsman can carry. The Kojo Crane hand can be considered as the Swiss Army Knife of karate's unarmed hand weapons. This hand

Kojo Crane hand Credit Author's collection

has many uses. This type of crane hand can be used a lot like a sai. In this case the thumb, middle, and ring finger resemble the prongs, foil or "tsume" of the sai. Like the sai, the Kogushiku crane wing does not grip the arm with muscle power. Rather the wrist and shoulders twist pressing the thumb and fingers in to your opponent's nerve centers the same way a sai accomplishes this task.

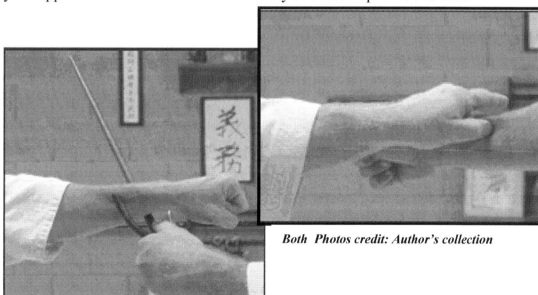

Both Photos credit: Author's collection

"The Kogushiku Bushi of Okinawa were once the most feared of all Samurai."

A statement by the Author based on historical facts.

HE TSURU HANE - FLYING CRANE WINGS

The main crane hand of the Flying Crane system is found in other crane systems as well. This is the "drooping" crane hand and it is very versatile and useful. But it is hard to develop.

The Flying crane wings appears to be soft; but appearances are deceiving as this hand is hard. Again this hardness comes from the control, development and "lining up" of your bones and tendons not from muscle power.

This type of crane wing is very special and is useful to use in executing hooking type blocks. The fingertips can be used in poking or in powerful finger strikes. This type of crane hand is very similar to the Bubishi technique called the *Iron Wing Hand.*"

He Tsuru Te Flying Crane Hands
Photo credit: Author's collection

When the little finger lines up in a straight line with the first joint of the thumb; the hand gains considerable hard or yang energy. When this alignment is obtained the fingers of the hand become very strong and will not collapse when used as downward finger strikes.

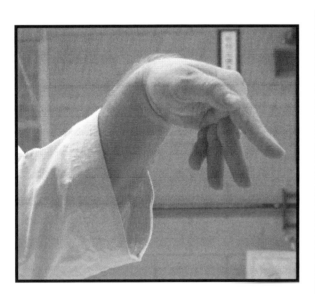
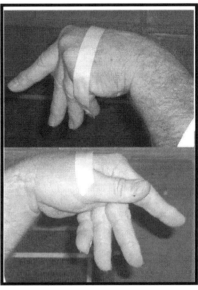

Above Left- He Tsuru Te (Flying Crane Hand) Above Right photo shows correct bone alignment for this technique. The tape on the hand shows the bone alignment. Photo credit: Author's collection

When the bones are lined up correctly as illustrated in the above photo the technique is very strong and the fingers will not collapse. Strong finger techniques are the results of correct bone alignment not conditioning.

294

THE CRANE'S BEAK

The first 'beak" technique is common to most styles of karate and this is the "Shi-Tsuki" or Beak thrust, this technique is commonly called the **Gojushiho Beak**. It is well known to many karateka as only a thrust with the fingertips. This is the most common way of using this weapon. However, the technique may be used to hook block or strike with the back of the wrist.

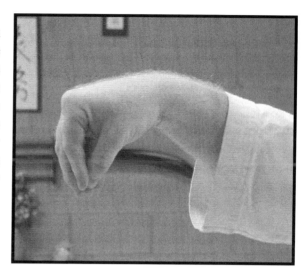

Gojushiho Beak… Photo credit: Author's collection

Another similar "beak hand" is a special hand that allegedly goes back to a long deceased master in Taiwan named "Nori." This hand presents a smaller striking surface than does the Gojushiho beak. However, Nori's Beak is difficult to form and offers no great advantage to the more common Gojushiho Beak.

There are other variations of the Gojushiho beak hand. There is a thumb and index finger beak and a thumb, index and middle finger beak. The more fingers involved in forming the beak, the stronger it becomes.

Also, the more fingers involved the greater the striking area will become. This lessens the "penetration" of the weapon and can make the beak less effective

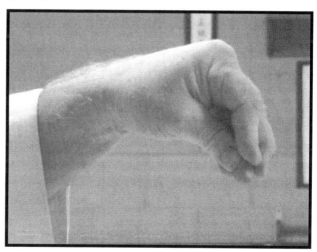

Above Nori's Beak below on the left Thumb and index finger beak, to the right the thumb, index and middle finger beak. Photo credit: Author's collection

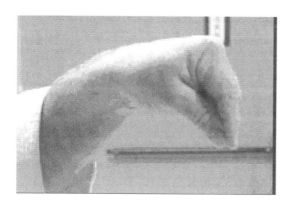
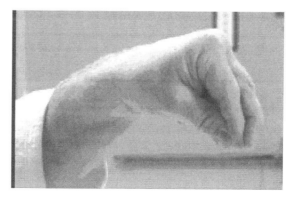

MATSUMURA NUKITE

I have given this name to a special spear hand or nukite that appears in some versions of the Matsumura Hakutsuru (White crane) Kata. This spear hand if formed correctly will not collapse. The hand is full of yang (hard) energy and yet the arm is relaxed. This is an easily formed and very useful weapon that should be in every karateka's arsenal.

Straighten the fingers and touch the index and ring fingers together, these forms Matsumura's nukite. The middle finger is placed on top of the index-ring finger junction. The little finger is placed on the side of the ring finger and the thumb is placed on the side of the index finger. The results are a very solid spear hand.

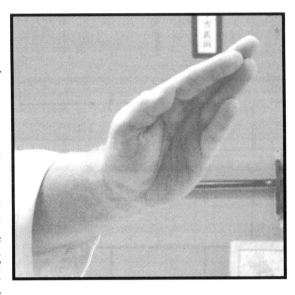

Fig. Matsumura Nukite Photo credit Author's collection

THE RAKE HAND

This technique is very common to many white crane styles. It is used extensively in the Flying Crane Fist kata and in the Matsumura Hakutsuru Kata. This technique resembles the "Iron Sand Hand" found in the Bubishi. It very closely resembles the Kaku Shi Ken found in Uechi Ryu Karate Do and is found in the Shorin Ryu kata, Pai Sai Sho This is a very hard hand that if formed and developed properly can be a very useful weapon. It is often used palm up.

Rake Hand…. credit Author's collection

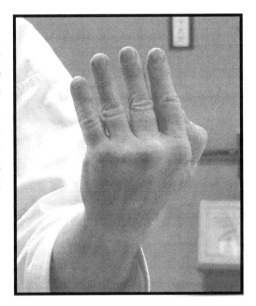

USING THE THUMB

Sean Connery, in the movie "Presidio", made the first Thumb Fist famous. This fist is neither hard nor soft; all you need to do is to line up the bones correctly and this technique can be devastating. Targets are the ribs and side of the neck. This weapon is delivered in the same fashion as a fist punch.

Most styles use a vertical fist or "Tate Tsuki", the use of this fist, as a fore-knuckle punching hand is obvious. However, the thumb brace on the top if the fist can be very effective in poking or in executing strikes in the fashion of a ridge hand This fist is neither hard nor soft. Correct bone alignment is all that is needed.

Two types of thumb fists
Author's collection

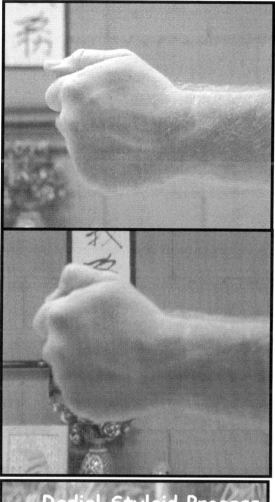

THE WRIST

The two Styloid Processes of wrist are among the most effective weapons that the karateka has in his or her arsenal.

The Radial Styloid process is used in a fashion similar to the ridge hand and the Ulna Styloid process is used in a fashion similar to a Shuto Uchi or Knife hand strike. These wrist strikes need very little preparation and with a little practice can become very effective.

Photo of the Styloid Processes are from the Author's collection.

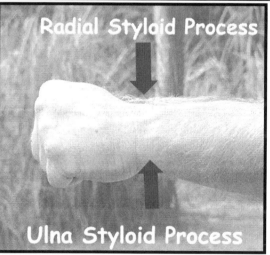

"If you fingers are broke hit with the fist, if the fist is broke, hit with the elbow, if the elbow is broke, hit with the shoulder, if the shoulder is broke, hit with the head, if the head is broke, hit with the hips."
From an old Chinese martial arts adage.

USING THE MATSUMURA SANCHIN CRANE WINGS

The strongest digit of the hand is the thumb; therefore, the strongest knuckle of the hand is the knuckle that attaches the thumb to the hand. Once this knuckle was widely used to punch with; yet it has disappeared from modern karate.

To execute this technique correctly the hand is held horizontally. However it is difficult to show this with a photograph.

The preferred target for this technique is a point just below the nipple of the breast, and the carotid sinus at the side of the neck. This is a dangerous technique that is found in true Okinawan karatejutsu.

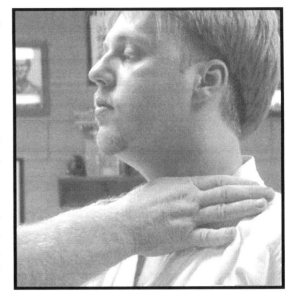

Using the Matsumura Sanchin Crane Wings; both photos: Credit: Authors collection

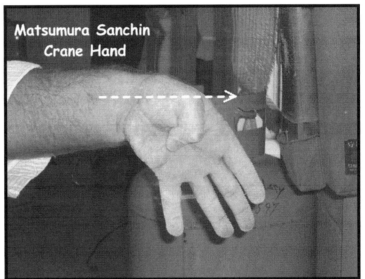

Matsumura Sanchin Crane Hand

Shore Bird... drawing by Charlie Dean Author's collection

PUTTING KI IN YOUR FOOT

Among the most powerful techniques the karateka has are kicks. Different styles of karate have similar yet different ways of "shaping" the foot for certain various types of kicks. The following are the methods I learned in Okinawa. These reflect most of the foot position used by my Okinawan teachers

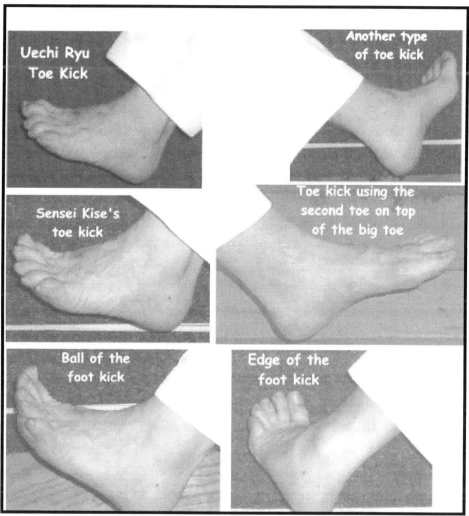

My Okinawan teachers stressed kicking with the toes. The more modern ball of the foot kick was used primarily to kick your opponent's knee cap and the pelvis bone protecting the bladder. Heel kicks were also used.

Snap kicks were used more than the modern thrust kick. All kicks were low; the highest kick was to the floating ribs. The instep of the foot was favorite targets for heel stomps or stomps with the edge of the foot.

"The art of effective kicking is found in the Niahanchi Kata."
Statement from the author based on experience.

SOURCES, ENDNOTES AND EXPLANATIONS

CHAPTER 6

Learning About Your Enemies

6-1   Source: Okinawan karate Folklore

A Lesson in Atemi Waza from Grandmaster Soken

Source: listed in text

The Bushi's Secret- -Developing Ki--The Key to Balance and Power

6-2   Source: "Championship Fighting" by Jack Dempsey, published by Prentice-Hall Inc.
6-3   Source: "Budo Jiten" by Fred Lovert, published by Taseki Publishing Co. San Diego, Ca. page 33
6-4   Source: Conversations with Sensei Fusei Kise and Yuichi Kuda

Tachi Kata of Shorin Ryu Matsumura Seito

Sources are listed in the text; specific source may be foot noted.

A Lesson from Seizan Kinjo

Ibid

The Dachi or Stances

Sources: My opinions based on teachings from all of my Okinawan Sensei.

Strengths and Weaknesses in your Tachi Kata

Ibid

Balance Points of the Kamae

Ibid

Understanding and Projecting Your Power

6-5   "Championship Fighting" by Jack Dempsey, published by Prentice-Hall page 24

Making Every Step a Kick

Source: John Wang, Austin Texas, a master if the Chinese Fighting Arts

Sinking Power

Source: Conversations with Sensei Fusei Kise

Shifting the Body Weight with out Stepping

Ibid

Using the Neko Ashi Dachi to Develop Power

Sources: Seizan Kinjo and personal experience

Power in the Front Hand-Power in the Rear Hand

Ibid

Kicking Power

Ibid

Power Up and Power Down

Ibid

Gojushiho Introduces the Half-Step

Ibid

Tsuru no Hane...Developing Hands of Steel and Arms of Cotton

Source: Personal experience gained through the teaching of my Okinawan Teachers

Awaking Your Tendons

Ibid

Tendon Awareness and Strengthening Exercise

Ibid

Emulating Primitive Man-Development Arms of Cotton

Ibid

Exploding Fist of Steel

Ibid

Gokenki's Crane Wings

Source: Conversation with Yuichi Kuda

Matsumura's Crane Wings

Ibid

Kojo or Kogushiku Crane Hands

Ibid

He Tsuru Hane-Flying Crane Hand

Ibid

The Crane Beak

Ibid

Matsumura Nukite

Ibid

The Rake Hand

Ibid

Using the Thumb Tips

Ibid

The Wrist

Ibid

Using the Matsumura Sanchin Crane Wings

Ibid

Putting Ki in Your Foot

Ibid

*Drawing from the
Author's collection*

302

CHAPTER 7
MAAI NO HEIHO
(STRATEGY OF THE COMBAT DISTANCE)

Maai no Heiho

(The Strategy of the Combat Distance)

Picture on previous page is from
the Authors collection

As we move into the last two Chapters of the **"Okinawa Bushi no Te"** we are going to deal with methods that I learned from my Okinawan Sensei. These are their methods and my discussion of these methods reflects on my understanding of their teachings. Other karateka who have studied with these same teachers may see things differently. This is the way of **"Suhari"** and the way of Okinawan karate.

When we deal with Maai no Heiho and Chushin no Heiho we are dealing with the Yang and Yin of Okinawan karate. Crossing the combat distance or the Maai deals largely with the attack and as such is of a Yang nature. Dealing with the Chusin is largely a defensive action and as such is of a Yin nature.

Both the Maai and Chusin are constantly changing and are actually only mirror images of each other. The need for flexibility is of great importance and mobility is a matter of life or death. The old samurai adage of **"henka ni tomu"** (be full of change) will govern the points involved in our discussion.

TOKOSHI NO HEIHO

Tokoshi no Heiho is the study of crossing a great distance. In this case it means a study of the maai or combat distance. In unarmed combat there are numerous maai that the combatants must recognize and control; each person in the fight has their own individual maai; therefore, if there are ten people fighting there are ten maai involved.

Any journey across a great or small distance has a beginning and an ending. Crossing the maai is no difference, the beginning is your position at the start of the journey; your position at the end is determined by wise or unwise strategy. This involves the study of the strategy of entering; the Japanese call this strategy **Irimi no Heiho.** Irimi is one of the most important strategies available to the warrior; it is one of the best known but least understood of all the fighting strategies.

To put it in simple terms, Irimi no Heiho is the study of methods used to reach the rear corner of your opponent. The rear corner of your opponent is one of the safest places in combat. Reaching the rear corner of your opponent sounds easy; but it is not easy. Your opponent has two rear corners and they are not the same.

Only a fool enters into combat, the journey of life or death, with out knowing where he or she is going. The art of Irimi as with all aspects of the fighting arts require considerable work and thought. The common man does not give this subject much thought. To enter with out a sound plan is no better than to enter with your eyes closed. Irimi can be your friend or foe; knowledge and training will determine what will greet you at the end of the maai.

> *"The best offense is a good defense;*
> *The best defense is a good offense."*

An old adage from American football

Understanding
Irimi no Heiho

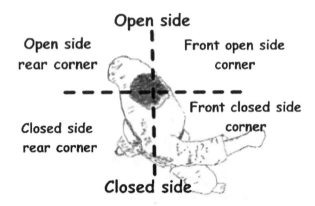

Open side

Open side rear corner

Front open side corner

Closed side rear corner

Front closed side corner

Closed side

To understand Irimi, in a quick glance you must see your opponent as a warrior not as a common person. In your mind divide him into four quarters, his forward foot will determine which his open side is and which is his closed side. His closed side is the side of his forward foot.

The wise warrior realizes that every thing in nature has its pro and cons; so it is with Irimi. Both the open side and the closed side offer advantages and disadvantages

If you enter the open side you have a greater opportunity to strike his vitals along his midline. However, your opponent can turn slightly toward his open side and then he can bring both hands and feet into action that can defeat you.

If you choose to enter his closed side, enter in such a fashion as to put your open side next to his closed side. This will cause him to have to turn toward his closed side to strike or kick you.

Entering his closed side with you open side facing his closed side offers the greatest safety and will open up the vital targets along your opponent's back for an attack.

In combat you need to pay special attention to your opponent's midline. This simple imaginary line is extremely important.

One of the unwritten principles of combat is to never cross your enemy's line of fire. Whether the fighting is armed or unarmed; when you cross his midline you are crossing his line of fire. Do not cross his mid line unless you have hurt him first. You may get by without injury

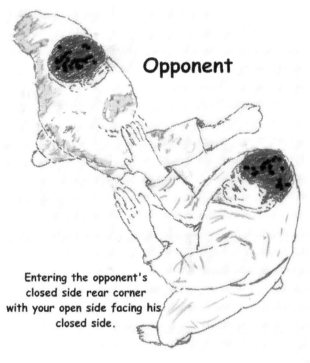

Opponent

Entering the opponent's closed side rear corner with your open side facing his closed side.

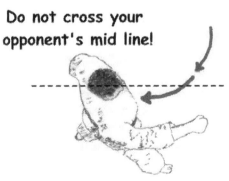

Do not cross your opponent's mid line!

by crossing the midline against a novice; but you will not be able to make such mistakes against a skillful opponent. This unwritten rule is applicable to both offense and defense.

THE MAAI

The maai consist of two parts (1) the outer circle, which is the range of your most long ranged weapon (which in karate is a side thrust kick) and (2) your inner circle which is the range of your more mobile and fast firing weapons (which in karate are your punches or other hand weapons). Most unarmed combat starts off at the outer circle and ends up with the combatants at the distance of the inside circle or closer. The reader must realize that the maai in combat is constantly changing in a very fluid situation with each side trying to gain an advantage. Our discussion here is not the last word on the subject of the maai; the information presented here is a mere introduction to the complexities of the maai.

The Shaolin Temple's Five Animal Fist involves the study of five animals; these are the tiger, leopard, snake dragon and crane. The snake's specialty is knowing the distance to strike. As such the snake is the expert at identifying the maai. The Okinawan equivalent of the five animals of Shaolin is Shorin Ryu. Okinawan Shorin Ryu's snake kata is Pai Sai. The snake is an expert in managing the maai.

We can use the Pai Sai Kata to identify the maai for most people in general. The opening series of moves in the Okinawan Pai Sai Kata identifies the outer circle for your self and your opponents in unarmed fighting.

Once we understand this general measurement; we then must use this information to learn simply to glance at your opponent and know with a great deal of accuracy just how far you can stand away from this person and be out of range from his most long range weapon. We can either take the defensive posture and wait to be attacked or we can seize the initiative and employ the strategy **Sente no Heiho** (the strategy of initiating); to do so we attack across the maai and defeat our opponent before he is ready.

We emulate the snake and position ourselves in such a way that we can touch our opponent and yet, he or she can not touch us. Once we have accomplished this we have won the contest for the maai and victory is ours.

Copy of an old Satsuma
Province Tsuba; made to
resemble St. George's Cross.
made of steel by the author.

Author's collection

307

Opening forward movement of Pai Sai Kata

From the Attention Stance (1)

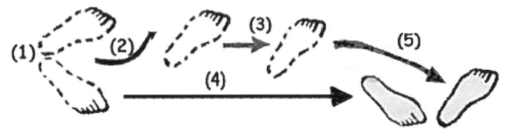

(2) Short cresent step with left foot (3) Short half step with left foot
(4) Long step with right foot (5) Short step with left foot

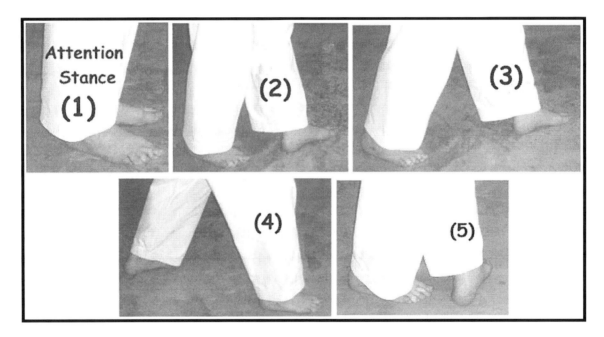

Photos corresponding to the above illustration
Both the illustration and photos are from the Author's collection

The above illustrations and photos give the karateka the distance of the outer circle of his or her personal maai. From *(1)* to *(5)* of the above illustrations and photos is the distance of the first forward set of moves of the Pai Sai Kata and is the distance of your outer circle. The ancient Shaolin snake is telling the karateka how far to stay away from his opponent.

Of course, you can not have your opponent stop the fighting then demonstrate the Pai Sai Kata; then measure the distance of the previous move and then determine the outer circle of the maai. However, you can learn from this principle and learn to identify your own outer circle and then learn to examine your opponent and stay just out of his or her reach.

In an actual situation you look at your opponent; in doing so, you learn to study your opponent with a quick glance. You look at the middle of your opponent's neck. In you mind, you draw an imaginary line from the middle of his neck, down to the surface on which your opponent is standing. Again in your mind, lay this line down in front of you from his lead foot to your lead foot or if you are standing in Yoi Dachi (ready stance), let the line extend from his forward foot to the toes of you feet. This is the outer circle of the maai for unarmed combat and this is the snake's secret.

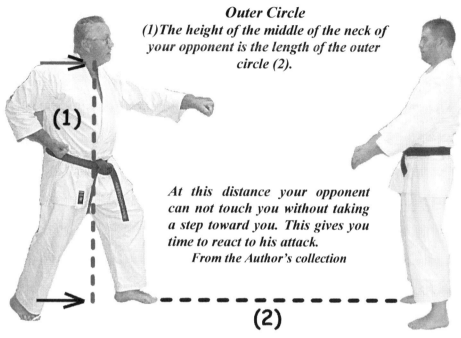

Outer Circle
(1) The height of the middle of the neck of your opponent is the length of the outer circle (2).

At this distance your opponent can not touch you without taking a step toward you. This gives you time to react to his attack.
From the Author's collection

Sensei Fusei Kise demonstrating the management of the outside circle of the maai. He stands just outside of the range of his opponent's side thrust kick. At this demonstrated distance the side kick range is about one foot too short. This gives Sensei Kise time to block the kick and execute a counter attack. Photo credit: Author's collection

Sensei Fusei Kise (on the left) demonstrates the management of the inside circle of the maai. Photo credit: Author's collection; Note the position of Sensei Kise's spar block (right hand).

To determine the **Inside Circle**, you mentally draw a line from your opponent's waist to the surface upon which he or she is standing. Mentally lay this line down in front of you as we did with determining the outside circle. At this distance both the attacker and defender can touch each other with their feet but not with their hands.

At the distance of the inside circles, it is difficult to block kicks. Therefore, the karateka must rely on koteaite or body conditioning to toughen the legs to be able with stand his kicks to obtain victory at this distance.

Sensei's Fusei Kise and Shihan Toma demonstrate the inside circle of the maai with Bo-Sai fighting. Photo Credit: Jerry Hobbs collection

CROSSING THE MAAI WITH GOJUSHIHO

Once we have identified both the outside and inside circle of the maai we then must learn to cross the maai to close in on our opponent and finish him. The kata that teaches the crossing of the maai is **Gojushiho.**

Oral traditions handed down through the practitioners of Okinawan Shorin Ryu Matsumura Seito state that the kata Gojushiho and Naihanchi are from the same source. As such these kata support each other with Gojushiho offering offensive long range training to assist with the crossing of maai from a long distance. Once the range is shortened; Gojushiho kata then switches to techniques from Naihanchi. The specialty of Naihanchi is in close fighting.

SHINKAGI NO HEIHO

The Gojushiho kata contains many techniques and utilizes many strategies that are utilized in crossing the maai. Almost all of these strategies deal with a major combat strategy called **Shinkagi no Heiho** or creating diversions. There are many sub strategies that can be used as "tools" to assist with creating these diversions.

KAIMON NO HEIHO

The first of these sub strategies is one called **Kaimon no heiho**. Fredrick J. Lovret in his book "The Way and the Power, Secrets of Japanese Strategy" describes this strategy as one that will force your opponent to "open the gate" of his or her defenses. I agree with Mr. Lovret's description and I would also describe Kaimon no Heiho as *"your ace in the hole"* which will enable you to defeat your enemies.

In many styles of Okinawan Shorin Karate the karateka while performing Gojushiho kata, goes down to the knee of the left leg and face the front right at a forty five degree angle. This move occurs just after the opening bow in the kata. At this point one of Gojushiho's secrets occurs that sets the stage of deceiving and creating diversions that will defeat your enemies. This is throwing sand in your opponent's eyes.

The three photos at the right demonstrate the sand throwing techniques of the Gojushiho kata. (1) Grab sand with the left hand, (2) The blocking posture found in the kata. (3) As the karateka stands up

he throws sand into his opponent's face with his left hand and counters with a right punch to the face......photo credit: Author's collection

You can use anything handy to take the place of the sand if sand is not available. Also you may use of a number of additional sub strategies to create other diversions.

The late Grandmaster Hohan Soken often referred to Gojushiho as a kata that lifts the karateka into a higher level of performance and understanding of karatejutsu. One of the strategies that Gojushiho introduces to Shorin Ryu karate is **Hanon no Heiho** or the strategy of the half step. The introduction of this technique divides Shorin Ryu kata training into two phases (1) Pre-Gojushiho and (2) Post-Gojushiho. Once the karateka has learned Gojushiho the influence of this kata will affect many of the kata the karateka has learned before Gojushiho. Let me explain with several illustrations of stepping at the beginning of the Pai Sai Kata:

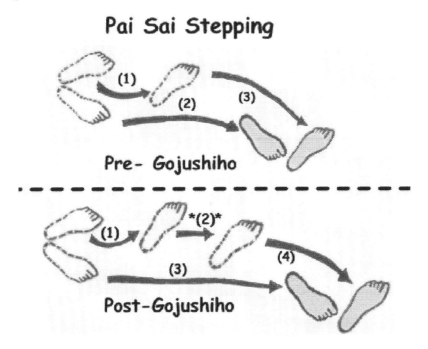

In the Pre-Gojushiho illustration of Pai Sai Stepping; simply move forward from the Musubi Dachi (attention stance) by (1) stepping with the left foot in a crescent pattern….delay the next step with a count of "one thousand and one" then step with the right foot as illustrated by (2). Follow quickly with a step with the left foot as illustrate in (3). This is the Pai Sai stepping I learned from Sensei Kise in the 1960's.

The Post-Gojushiho illustration of the Pai Sai Kata stepping includes a half step.
Moving forward from the Musubi Dachi with a left foot crescent step as illustrated in (1)….Hold this position for a count of "one thousand and one"; then with the left foot, step with a half step (marked *(2)*in the above illustration). After the half step, step with the right foot as illustrated in (3) quickly finish this series of moves with the left foot step as illustrated in (4). This is the Pai Sai stepping used by Sensei Soken in the 1960's.

The addition of the half step to the technique of stepping in the Pai Sai kata allows the karateka to rapidly gain enough distance with half step to kick the opponent with the right foot during the technique mark with step (3) of the **Post Gojushiho** illustration.
"Remember every step can be a kick."

The Gojushiho of Shorin Ryu Matsumura Seito Karate/Kobujutsu has two methods of stepping that the karateka uses to cross the maai and defeat his or her opponents. The first of these methods is called the *"3 step method"* and the second is the *"5 step method"*.

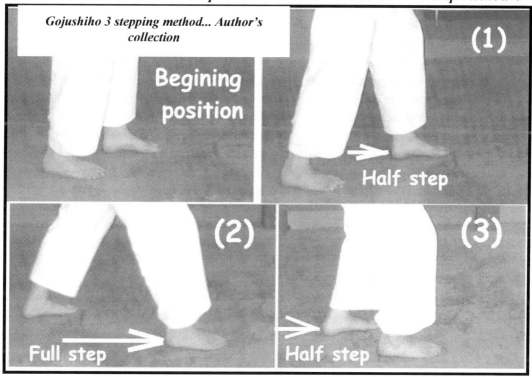

Gojushiho 3 stepping method... Author's collection

Begining position

(1) Half step

(2) Full step

(3) Half step

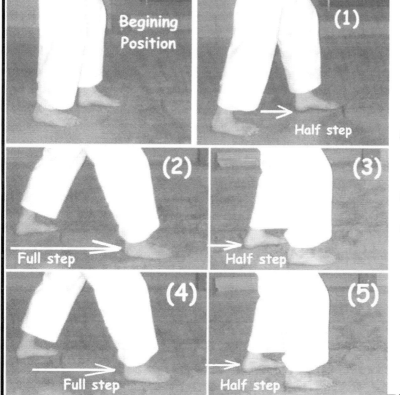

Begining Position

(1) Half step

(2) Full step

(3) Half step

(4) Full step

(5) Half step

Gojushiho 5 Stepping method is exactly the same as the 3 step method except that the 5 step method continues with two addition steps illustrated by (4) and (5).
Both methods share the same techniques and use the same Bunkai or interpretation.
I learned the three step method from Sensei Kise. In my opinion the 3 step method is more advanced as you have less distance and less time to cross the maai. You have less time for mistakes.

Photo credit: Author's collection

313

In both methods step *(1)* and *(3)* are half steps. The 5 step method has an addition half step at *(5).* It is these stepping methods along with the methods of the revolving the hands that gives the Gojushiho practitioner the ability to mesmerize his opponent with the established rhythm of the kata and then suddenly change the rhythm with both the stepping and revolving hands that enables the karateka to close in with his opponent and defeat him. This is the same principle that the snake charmers use in India.

Most Gojushiho kata do not use the revolving hands as the technique is preformed in the Shorin Ryu Matsumura Seito version of the kata. Relation is the key to learning this kata.

Gojushiho 3 step version....photo credit Author's collection

Every thing in the universe has a certain rhythm. This concept of rhythm and the use of this rhythm is called **Hyoshi no Heiho**. The karateka, with sufficient training, can learn to use hyoshi no heiho as a tool to cross the maai and just as we have learned to use sand to gain distance with the half step to "open" your opponent's gate; we can do the same thing with rhythm.   In the heat of battle you may not have the opportunity to pick up an object to throw into the eyes of your opponent; but once you have learned to use Hyoshi no Heiho this strategy will be instantly available.

Imagine the possibilities of deceiving your opponents by controlling the timing and rhythm of the revolving hands technique and stepping. First you establish the rhythm of either the three step or five step method. Perhaps the rhythm you've establish would be something like this: step 1...step 2...step 3; or in the case of the five step method step 1...step 2...step 3...step 3...step 4...step 5. Imagine that the dots following each number represent a small fraction of a second; therefore, with three dots following each number we have established an even rhythm with the same time lapse between each number.

We can change the rhythm by increasing or decreasing the time interval between each step. The count could go something like this: step 1..... step 2.. step 3 or 1..2....3..4......five.

Changing the rhythm in such a fashion can have the same effect on the rhythm of battle that the slow change of pace curve ball would have on a good batter facing a base ball pitcher with a good fast ball. The batter usually has a hard time adjusting to the first fast pitch and strikes too late to hit this first pitch. However, the batter can adjust quickly to the speed of the second fast ball and may tip the ball or hit a foul on the second pitch. The pitcher knows that the batter will hit his next fast ball so on his third pitch he throws a slow moving curve ball. The change of pace of this pitch may cause the batter to swing too quickly and miss the ball.

Both the three step and the five step method used in the Gojushiho revolving hands concept offer their own advantages and disadvantages. The three step method is quicker but covers less distance. This means that the first two steps of this method needs to happen quickly with a delay occurring between step two and three to throw your opponent off rhythm and gain an advantage over him. The three step version may work best on ground with poor footing.

The five step method is more slowly in its development. The two extra steps enable you to have more time to easily employ additional techniques that would be difficult to use in the three step method. The goals of these techniques are the same in each method; they are designed to steal your opponent's mind by controlling the rhythm of the battle and defeat him. It is obvious that the length of the maai would be the most important factor in selecting the three step or five step method.

There is an old adage that is used in warfare... *"If you wish to attack to the east, first move to the west".* Changing the direction or angle of attack could cause your opponent to become confused. His confusion could provide an opening in his defense that will allow you to penetrate his position and defeat him. Changing direction is an example of *"Henka no Heiho" (the strategy of change) and Gojushiho is full of change.*

Changing the direction of the attack is a useful tool that assists the karateka with the successful crossing of the maai. While crossing the maai the attacking karateka must be aware of the best way to finish the conflict.... *The longer a fight lasts, the greater chance you have of being defeated; so, end it fast....* The finger or spear attack feature in the kata at the end of the stepping and revolving hands move should be sufficient to defeat your foe. However, be ready to continue your attack.

"In combat be unpredictable."

Altering moves from the Gojushiho kata to Change Directions:

From the opening posture of Gojushiho...Instead of stepping forward with a left foot half step: (A) step forwards a full step to the left front with the left foot. Quickly follow the left foot step with a long right foot step that brushes against the left foot at (B) and then moves toward (C). The movement of the right foot brushing against

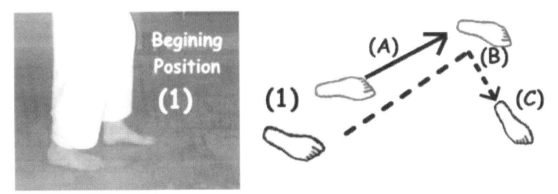

the left foot at (B) relocates the body weight on the left foot. This enables the move toward (C) to be a kick or step. You are now on the right front of your opponent....you have exposed his right flank. At this point you can attack his flank to finish him.

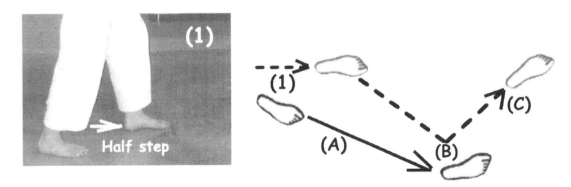

From the left foot half step that starts the "revolving hand technique" that is unique to the Gojushiho kata; instead of stepping forward with the right foot after the left half step...step with a quick long right foot step to you front right (A). Then quickly step with your left foot brushing against your right foot at (B), with your weight relocated on your right foot you can kick or step toward (C). You are now on your opponent's left front; you have exposed his left flank. You can press toward the left side of his body to finish him.

These two short examples of crossing the maai with Gojushiho should give the reader an idea how to use the kata stepping technique along with the revolving hands to move forward while changing direction keeping your opponent confused and "off guard" as he tries to figure out your next move.

KIAI NO HEIHO, METSUKI NO HEIHO, KAGEUGOKASHI NO HEIHO

The strategies of **Kiai no Heiho** (strategy of shouting*)*, **Metsuki no Heiho** (strategy of eye contact) and **Kageugokashi no Heiho** (strategy of feigning) are three very important concepts that can give the warrior and edge over his opponent by creating diversions.

It is difficult to separate these heiho in a combat situation. If used together they become more effective than if they are used separately. Nevertheless, I will introduce each of these strategies separately; it will be up to the reader to learn to use these heiho together.

My four year old grandson, Carson, attends a Christian pre-school class. One day he came home singing an old spiritual that he had learned in school. The old spiritual that he sang was *"The Battle of Jericho".* The old song was once very well known to children all over the world. Sadly this is not the case any more. But there are some that still know it and part of the lyrics go sort of like this….*"Up to the walls of Jericho, he marched with a spear in his hand…Joshua commanded the children to shout and the walls came tumbling down".* My grandson and his class mates did not know it, but they were reciting a Biblical account of *Kiai Jutsu.* Call it Kia jutsu or *Kiai no Heiho*; the ancient battle cry still has a place in modern warfare just as it did thousands of years ago at the Battle of Jericho. This is especially true when it comes too unarmed fighting.

The shout or cry is a weapon of warfare that is as old as the human race and perhaps is as old as the animal kingdom. The shout is animalist, it is historic, it is Biblical and it is found in every culture. But there is not a single type of shout. The kiai or shout is a very complicated technique and as such is used for many purposes with each purpose having its special type of shout.

Let's discuss three types of kiai that are found in the fighting arts. The first kiai is similar to the roar of the tiger or the bellowing of a bull, it is used to frighten the enemy as well as boost the courage and confidence of those doing the shouting. This shout can serve either the individual or a group. This is a long shout that can be executed throughout the length of the charge or through the length (distance or time) of a situation. An example of the use of this kiai would be using a loud powerful roar through the length of the stepping associated with the revolving hand technique used in the Gojushiho kata.

The second method is the silent kiai that is meant to expel air from the lungs of an attacker. This will lessen the chance of getting the "wind knocked out of you" if you are hit with a counter attack in the solar plexus and this kiai can also increase the power of your attack by lowing your center of gravity and focusing your strength on one point.

The third kiai is a short high pitch cry that resembles the yelp of a dog when you accidentally step on its tail. This type of kiai can cause to your opponent to "freeze" for a fraction of a second. This gives you the opportunity to close in and defeat him. This type of kiai is the same as the short, shrill, piercing cry of the white crane. The shout of the crane can be heard for a long distance. The old Southern Chinese style of the *"Shouting Crane"* is based on this type of kiai. All three of these kiai are useful in combat.

However, with the exception of the silent kiai these shouts are not executed just as you execute punch or kick; rather these shout are executed before you kick, strike, or punch your adversary.

Correct eye contact is a strategy that should accompany all strategies dealing with the crossing of the maai. ***Metsuke no Heiho*** is the strategy of using eye contact or more accurately the lack of eye contact to gain an advantage over your opponent in combat.

There is an old adage that plays an important role in fighting. "***Look at nothing but see everything***". This is the adage that best explains correct eye contact. There are certain simple practical rules to learn correct eye contact; (1) Avoid eye to eye contact, do not give your opponent the chance to "out stare you". (2) Your eye contact points change with the distance between you and your opponent.

Eye contact at the out side circle distance of the maai

Sensei Kise using correct eye contact. Photo credit: Author's collection

Eye to eye contact is a contest to see if you can mesmerize your opponent. This could be dangerous and cause you to loose your concentration. Look at two points above each breast. Looking at these two points will allow you to look at nothing but see everything.

As you get closer to your opponent your eye contact changes; but again avoid eye to eye contact. The following illustration offers simple guidelines for correct eye contact at the inner circle of the maai.

Eye contact at the distance of the inter circle of the maai

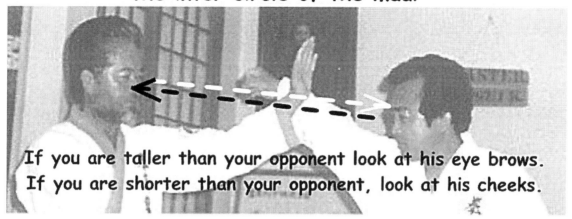

If you are taller than your opponent look at his eye brows.
If you are shorter than your opponent, look at his cheeks.

Correct eye contact… Photo credit: Author's collection

Correct training in Metsuke no Heiho should occur very early in the student's career. Mistakes learned early in one's training become very difficult to correct later.

Kageugokashi no Heiho is the strategy of feigning. The Gojushiho kata movements that we are calling the "revolving hands" contain a very important feint that is a ***kakusareta waza*** or hidden technique. This hidden technique is very important to the successful crossing of the maai.

Both the Gojushiho 3 step and the 5 step method contain feints. One of which occurs in the move preceding the right hand finger thrust at the end of the maai.

The feint at this point causes the opponent to concentrate on the left hand feint which allows the right hand finger thrust to succeed.

It is also wise to kiai with a crane shout at the point of the

Gojushiho 3 step method last two moves showing the feint….Author's collection

feint. The sharp, shrill piecing cry of crane is unsettling and will cause you opponent to loose his concentration; you then can penetrate his defenses and defeat him.

319

教化雖費而無不識之病

"*Education will never be as expensive as ignorance.*"

A lesson from a Chinese Fortune Cookie.

Calligraphy by Shifu Hwang

From the Author's collection

HANASHI NO HEIHO AND KADO NO HEIHO

As we cross the maai events may occur that go contrary to your plans; this is the way of war and combat. One of the major differences between the senior and the novice is that the senior is experienced in **Hanashi no Heiho**, the strategy of letting go. The novice on the other hand lacks a workable knowledge of this strategy and will try to stick to his original technique and will try to make this technique work by adding muscle power. Usually the novice's attempts to "prop up" a failing technique are unsuccessful.

The senior on the other hand has developed a certain feeling and instinctively knows when his technique is beginning to fail. He lets go of his first technique; he blends with his opponent and employs **Kado no Heiho,** the strategy of taking what ever you can get. He finds another technique that will be successful.

Using these two strategies together is very similar to a good running back in football. Ideally you would like to score each time you carry the ball. But as the running back breaks through the defensive line; he many times will be forced to make a decision ….should he make that cut and just maybe he can score…. or should he lower his head and shoulders and get the first down. The good back will go for the sure thing which in this case is the first down. The successful warrior in battle will go for the sure thing and stay alive and win the battle.

Hanashi and Kado often are two strategies that are over looked in the modern dojo. Much too often in the modern dojo the techniques being taught are too dependent on physical strength alone. Perhaps the strategy of the correct use of strength in the fighting arts can best be explained by the following adage:

"You can not be stronger than every one.
On any day you will meet many people who are stronger than you.
If you train to defeat your opponent with only strength;
then you can be defeated many times.
Regardless of strength, train to defeat your opponent and you
may never know defeat."

MAGIRI NO HEIHO AND MATSUMURA HAKUTSURU

As we finish crossing the maai with the Gojushiho Kata as our guide; we need to pay special attention to our posture (tachi kata and kamae) at the end of the "revolving hands technique" that we have used to cross the maai.

At this point we have closed the "gap" called the maai. We are in a position that is neither offensive nor defensive, for a small amount of time we are like a car in neutral. If our closing technique did not hurt our opponent we could be in danger.

Our position is extremely important. Our closing technique at this point in the kata must leave us in a position from which we can remain mobile, and flexible. We can change our technique and renew our attack or we can retreat. We may wish to employ *Magiri no Heiho*. This is the strategy of continuing our attack; we can employ a variety of techniques to follow through and completely defeat our opponent.

The final position of Gojushiho's revolving hand and stepping moves leaves the karate in a very good position to continue the attack with number of techniques. The most obvious would be a front foot snap kick to the opponent's groin.

If the Gojushiho finger thrust is blocked, follow up with a front kick to the groin.
Photo credit: Author's collection

Comments on Kata from my Teachers:

"How can you have karate without kata?" Sensei Fusei Kise
"Only through kata can you rise above your physical ability." Sensei Seizan Kinjo
"Practice your kata and you will learn karate." Sensei Hohan Soken
"Only the old Bushi kata have value." Sensei Yuichi Kuda

The Gojushiho Kata is strangely "silent" when it comes to continuing the attack with **Irimi no Heiho.** As with many karate kata, Irimi attacks are implied even though they are not "seen" in the kata. Irimi after the front kick would easy to execute.

Gojushiho Irimi technique
Author's collection

After hurting your opponent with a front kick you will have the opportunity to move to your opponent's rear corner. Once you have entered into your opponent's rear corner opportunities will present themselves that will allow you to finish your opponent with a variety of techniques.

A technique from Gojushiho

Author's collection

Gojushiho's signature technique when it comes to the employment of "*Magiri no Heiho*" is the throw about mid way through the kata. However, before we discuss this technique I would like to share with the readers several personal stories that relate to Okinawan karate throws in general.

Over the last 40 years or so, I have had the opportunity to ask three Okinawan Grandmasters the question: *"Why the Okinawan masters do not teach falling as do many of the Japanese masters?"* This question was asked to Grandmasters Fusei Kise, Yuichi Kuda and Zempo Shimabukuro. This was their answer: Grandmaster Shimabukuro said that any competent Okinawan karateka can do throws and falls and that these same karateka did not need to practice these arts.

From left to Right: Dan Smith, Zempo Shimabukuro, Ronald Lindsey: Photo credit Author's collection

Both Grandmasters Kise and Kuda said that the throws used in the older Okinawan arts are very dangerous and in fact it does no good to practice falls as the old Okinawan method of throwing is done in such a fashion as to severally injure the person being thrown before he or she hits the ground.

The author with Fusei Kise on the left and Yuichi Kuda on the right
Both photo credits: Author's collection

As you can well imagine this got my interest up and I asked Sensei Kise and Sensei Kuda to show me these throws. They replied with laughter and said "you do them all the time". They then said that throws were not important and that Okinawan karate is a kicking, punching and striking art and that to be successful in defending yourself these are your primary techniques. They then agreed to show me Okinawan Throwing.

I was expecting something very difficult and complicated but what I found were techniques that were simple and effective. Sensei Kise and Sensei Kuda were correct, I did do throws all of the time; my kata was full of throws. The turns in kata were the throws. ***The turns in kata are the secrets to Okinawan karate throws!***

Several years ago I was performing in a master martial arts show in Morgantown, West Virginia. I do not remember what technique I was doing but my ***"uke"*** for the event was a very good karateka named Scott Anderson. Before it was my turn to go up on the stage; Scott and I were covering a few points as to what we were going to demonstrate.

During the course of this quick discussion; I told Scott that I was going to throw him to which Scott replied "Oh I am not worried about your throws because they are soft." Upon hearing Scott's word I remembered my discussion with Sensei Kise and Sensei Kuda about the throws of Okinawan karatejutsu. I knew full well that Scott was right; the throws I was compelled to demonstrate at this master's show were not going to hurt Scott. The real throws of Okinawan karatejutsu would have left Scott badly injured before he could carry out his falling technique.

The ***signature throw of the Gojushiho kata*** occurs after the first revolving hands/stepping sequence. Once this sequence is completed ***(in the following photo #1)***; with your right foot stomp on the top of the right foot of your opponent ***(#2 in the following photo….in practice only lightly step on your opponent's foot)***. You then grab his right arm with your left hand and with your right hand fingers press against the nerves under his jaw and pivot counter clock wise to your left ***(#3 in the following photo)***. If this move is carried out until your opponent is completely on the ground; he or she will have dislocated their hip and knee. ***In practice you must realize that this technique is very dangerous and you must not let you practice partner actually fall or even if they loose their balance, he or she can be injured.***

Gojushiho's signature throw…photo credit Author's collection

The secrets of the Gojushiho kata are many and the kata is truly a gem to be practiced and cherished by all karateka. The following is true of Shorin Ryu Karate:

"If you do not practice Gojushiho; you do not practice Shorin Ryu."

Gojushiho teaches you to be a master of Henka no Heiho; to master the maai you must master Henka. Change is the essence of karate jutsu. These are just a few of the lessons from Gojushiho as I understand them. It is my sincere hope that these explanations of *"crossing the maai with Gojushiho"* will inspire the reader to study this ancient kata and accept this kata as a gift that the old Bushi of Okinawa have given us.

"Happiness is enjoying what you have. Happiness is never from what you want."

A lesson from a Chinese fortune cookie.

SOURCES, END NOTES AND EXPLANATIONS

The names of the various strategies or heiho used in Chapter 7 are from Fred Lovret's book
"The Way and the Power, secrets of Japanese Strategy" published by Paladin Press
All other sources are explained in the text

View of Itoman Port…..Tools of the fisherman…boats and nets
Photo by Mike Roberts Color Productions
Author's collection

CHAPTER 8

CHUSHIN NO HEIHO

Chushin no Heiho

The Strategy of managing the Center
Credit the Author's Collection

Picture on the previous page is a computer generated drawing by the Author; it is based on a picture taken from the "Little Picture of Japan" edited by Olive Beaupre Miller; pictures by Katharine Sturges…published by <u>*The Book House for Children*</u>

Chushin is the heart of the self protection arts; it is the art of managing the center. Like the other heiho studied by the warrior, Chushin no Heiho is a strategy of change. It is an art of deceiving the attacker. While Maai no Heiho deals with the offense; Chushin deals with the defense. The offense and defense in combat are constantly changing back and forth; this is a realm where time is measured in fractions of a second and time is not your friend.

The old strategy of **Suigetsu no Heiho** sets the stage for our discussion of Chushin no Heiho. Suigetsu, as we are using the term, means the moon reflection on water. The term, Suigetsu, also means solar plexus. To protect the center you can present your center as a target. As your opponent attacks your center, the target, your center, disappears. Instead of victory, he is met with defeat. Our discussion in this chapter will be about developing the skills, knowledge and strategies needed to make Suigetsu successful.

To accomplish this task, it will be necessary to repeat the use of several strategies that

The moon's reflection on water, reach for it
and your hand gets wet.
Strike at the Bushi and you hit only air.

Drawing from the "Little Pictures of Japan" edited by Olive Miller, pictures by Katharine Sturges
Published by the Book House for Children
Poem is by the author....credit: Author's collection

have been used in previous chapters. The Heiho of Henka or change is always of major importance; my Okinawan teachers did not use the term Henka very often. They just simply called the concept **"Change Body"**.

THE INVISIBLE WALL

Back in the late 1960's when I was on Okinawan; I was told by several older American service men and Okinawans that the Okinawan karate looked different when they fist saw the art back in the 1950's. These older gentlemen described the karate practioners as looking more like "old time" boxers.

After I started training in Shorin Ryu Matsumura Seito; I realized that fighting stances of Grandmaster Hohan Soken and other practitioners of Matsumura Seito did indeed resemble the boxers of the old bare knuckle fighting days.

Fred Lovret in his book "The Way and the Power, Secrets of Japanese Strategy" writes of a technique of the older classical karate where karateka stood with their arms in front of their bodies with their fist at their midline.

Above: John L. Sullivan Heavy Weight Champion of the 1890's; to the left, fighting with hands in front of the Invisible Wall (white line). Photo credit: Both photos are from the Author's collection.

In Okinawa this type of karate posture was still widely practiced in the 1950's. For a lack of more proper term I call this method the *"using the invisible wall"*.

I, often when teaching the concept of the invisible wall, will tell my students that I am the fastest man in the world. I tell them that I can out run anyone in the 100-meter dash. Of course I always get this confused look of doubt on most of their faces. I then add a special condition. I am the fast man in the world in the 100-meter dash if and only if you give me a 90 meter head start!

Using *the invisible wall technique* your hands stay out in front of you and never are brought back behind the invisible wall. Therefore, you have that "head start" and you can counter attack more quickly; even if you are slower than your opponent.

Using the Invisible Wall to hit your opponent first. Photo Credit: Both photos are from the Author's collection

Modern boxers use concepts very similar to the *invisible wall technique*. In order for this concept to be effective you must learn to relax. Since your counter punches are not moving very far before they hit their target. Your fist or hand must accelerate very quickly to build up to the critical velocity that will provide much of the power in your punch; this more effective when you are relaxed.

UKE WAZA/BLOCKING TECHNIQUES

POWER OF THE TRIANGLE

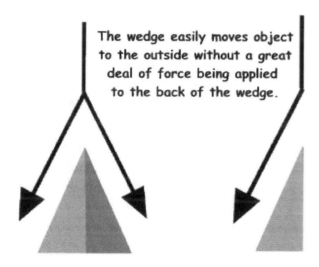

The wedge easily moves object to the outside without a great deal of force being applied to the back of the wedge.

The Shorin Ryu Matsumura Seito Karatejutsu concept of blocking is to simply redirect the direction of the force or weapons of the attack. One of nature's most perfect designs for turning or redirecting a force is a simple triangle or wedge. If this concept is used with the acceptance of the fact that ki is a force of nature; than the use of the wedge or triangle in any aspect of fighting arts can be described as using ki.

Since in general terms the use of ki indicates a natural force that can be harnessed by anyone (both the strong and the weak); than we can say the use of the wedge is a great equalizer and can give you the edge over any opponent.

The wedge moves objects to the outside without a great deal of force being applied to the back of the wedge. The wedge is strong when moving resisting forces from the inside to the outside and vice versa. Half wedges are used as if they were a complete wedge.

Learn to think of your blocks as wedges and let the natural strength of the wedge to provide much of the force behind your blocks. Photo credit: Author's collection

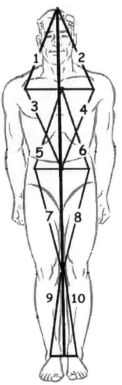

Karate blocks and strikes are very strong when they are made to resemble a wedge. ***Those blocks moving force away from your body can readily adopt the power of the wedge.***

Your blocks are stronger when moving a force from your inside to your outside than blocks that are moving the same force from your outside to your inside. When you move away from the wedge concept you are generally weaker. This wedge concept can be applied to blocks against attacks to all parts of the body.

Many martial artists are familiar with various drawings of man with two or more overlapping triangles on the front of his body. I have asked several senior martial artists if they knew the meaning of these drawings with the triangles. Each time I received a vague answer.

Using the drawing on the right, the 10 lines forming the sides of the triangles (marked 1, 2, 3, 4, 5, 6. 7, 8, 9, and 10) represent the angles which according to my teachers are the strongest for blocking and are the sides of these natural wedges that become powerful blocks. Note: the points of the wedges are all on the mid line.

When you shape your hands and arms like wedges; you are able to block high (1), middle (2), and low with great efficiency (3). The block illustrated in (4) of the above group of four wedge techniques is a combination of a low and middle wedge that works good to block many types of kicks. Using the wedge allows you to keep your hand in front of you and allows you to hit your opponent before he can hit you.

KATA BLOCKS/HONTO WAZA BLOCKS

Honto Waza refers to techniques which could be called "real fighting techniques." We need to understand that there is a kata block and a version of this same block that is used for actual fighting techniques. The kata block is usually performed in a stylistic and formal method. The actual block in a fighting situation can be executed utilizing the concepts of the *"invisible wall"*, the wedge and the use of natural forces such as gravity and momentum to provide much of the power used in the blocking technique.

Also, in both kata and kumite or actual fighting training; blocks are executed with two hands. This is important to explain that since the mid 1970's or so, a number of Okinawan Shorin Ryu Matsumura Seito Masters have started to teaching blocking with only one hand and this leaves out the important concept of protecting your center. This has resulted in a lack of understanding of "Honto Waza" (real fighting techniques) for a great many of Shorin Ryu Matsumura Seito practitioners.

The old kata of Okinawa are deceptive; they are arranged and performed in such a fashion that some one observing your kata could not easily learn your fighting secrets. The technique you see on the "surface" in kata is very misleading and is very different from what you actual use in a real situation.

The kata is also a complete exercise, in other words techniques performed in the kata are not only teaching actual self protection techniques but they are also strengthening muscles and tendons that allow you to actually use the kata concepts in a real situation.

The Ge Dan Uke (lower area block), Chu Dan Uke (middle area block) and Jo Dan Uke (upper area block) taught in the kata of Shorin Ryu Matsumura Seito Karate as taught to me in the late 1960's were some what different than that which were being taught in similar Shorin Ryu styles and different than that which has been taught in Shorin Ryu Matsumura Seito Karate after about 1972.

All of the blocks I have learned are really three fold, **(1)** lining up the blocks on the body's natural wedges as it relates to the midline for strength, **(2)** placing the "tools for blocking" (arms, hands, legs etc.) on the sides of these wedges to actually perform the blocks and **(3)** moving your midline to increase the effectiveness of the block *(Suigetsu no Heiho or Change body)* and to place yourself in a position where you can touch your opponent and he can not touch you. None of these "three folds" happens first; rather they all happen simultaneously.

Starting with the upper block or Jo Dan Uke, *which corresponds to the sides of the triangle or wedge marked (1 and 2)*. We will proceed to the downward to the Chu Dan *(3, 4, 5 and 6)* area and then to the Ge Dan *(7,8,9, and 10)* area blocks. (See drawing on page 332.)

We will examine both the kata and basic honto waza blocks for each area and then we will take a look at what is really happening in your kata as it relates to protecting your center and defeating your attacker. These are the basic blocks of the Shorin Ryu Matsumura Seito System.

The Jo Dan is perhaps the first area of the body that man learns to protect. Babies instinctively know to turn their heads to protect their eyes and face. In Shorin Ryu Matsumura Seito Karate the kata Jo Dan Uke is performed as indicated in the below photos:

Kata Jo Dan Uke Block (High Block)

The High kata blocks teaches "good habits;" the technique helps you to line up your bones and tendon that will enable your "real fighting techniques to work. The above series of photos show a series of moves that carry out the kata block; **(1)** the left arm is placed across your chest with the left hand just above the right breast. Your left arm is the width of one fist away from your body. At the same time **(2)** the right fist is chambered on your right hip. As we move through the photos from left to right at **(3)** the right fist quickly moves upward in an almost vertical line…the fist is held palm toward your body about 6 inches away from your body, at the same time you left fist **(4)** move toward your left hip chamber position.

At the position of **(5)** the palm of the right hand is rotated outward and the palm of the right hand is snapped out ward and the arm is extended upward until it is almost straight. This result in a powerful whip movement of the right wrist allowing the Ulna Styloid Process of the right blocking arm to strike the tender underside of the attacker's forearm. The left moves into a chambered position on the left hip **(6)**.

The final position of the Jo dan Uke is obtained by moving the blocking arm back down to where the wrist of the blocking arm is at the height of the fore head **(7)**.

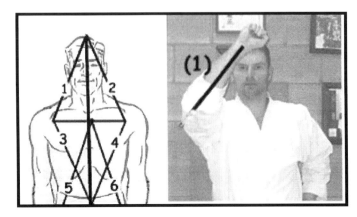

The Jo Dan Uke in its final position is the angle # 1 represented in the drawing at the far left. This is a strong block that is not easy to collapse.

The Honto Waza (real fighting technique) equivalent of the Jo Dan Uke kata technique utilizes the concept of the *"invisible wall"*

Photos and drawing on the upper left and left are from the Author's collection.

Fighting with your hands out in front of you enables you to counter quickly and allows you to "beat your opponent to the punch."

There several techniques that are called kata **Chu Dan Uke** (middle area block). One of the most common is called **Soto Uke.** This block moves from your inside to your outside.

Assuming you are going to execute a right arm bloc; **(1)** move your left arm slanting upward to where your fist is in front of the right upper chest about the distance of the width of your fist from your chest.

At the same time move your right arm across your body parallel to the surface. Keeping the right arm parallel and about the width of your fist from your body; move your right arm across and forward to position

(3) with the fist of the blocking arm at you mid line about the width of one fist from your body. The left fist moves to a chamber on your left hip *(4)*. This block strikes your opponent's attack with the Ulna Styloid process of you right wrist.

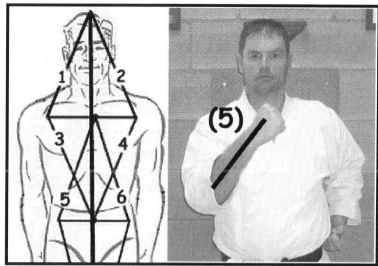

The actual Soto Uke block that is used in real fighting can be very much different than the block seen in kata. Sensei Kise's taught me the following bunkai for the Soto uke seen in many kata. This is just one interpretation of the kata Soto Uke.

The above series of two photographs represents the Soto Uke bunkai that I learned from Sensei Kise. Looking from left to right in the first photo we see that the Soto uke found in kata is actually a series of several blocks along with several strikes or controling techniques.

The move identified as *(1)* is the first block; at this point the left hand deflects your attacker's punch toward the attacker's midline. At the same time you counter strike the attacker hitting him with your right hand to the his solar plexus *(2)*. You then push his upper arm to his inside *(3)*; forcing him off balance as you strike his head in the temple area *(4)*. Using Sensei Kise's bunkai you are performing your technique with the strategy or count of one.

Today many of the Shorin Ryu Matsumura Seito practitioners use a Chu dan Uke that is commonly called the *"Double Bone Block"*. The Chu Dan Uke performed with the block previously described as the Soto Uke that is performed with the fist of the blocking hand at the mid line is not widely taught to Shorin Ryu Matsumura Seito practioners any more. This mid line block is generally practiced by people who learned the art prior to about 1972 and their students. Sadly the more modern practitioner of Shorin Ryu Matsumura Seito know little or nothing of the midline Soto Uke.

Drawings from the 1960's clearly showing the mid line block. Credit the Authors' collection.

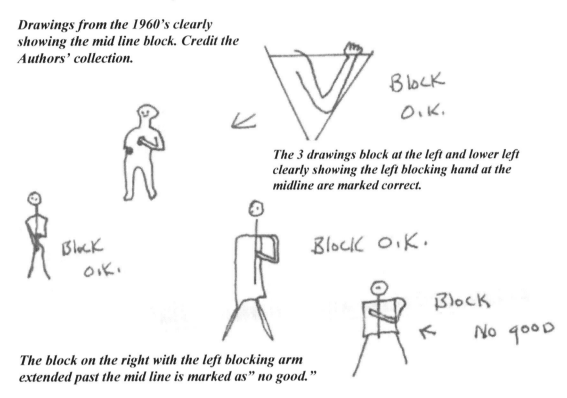

The 3 drawings block at the left and lower left clearly showing the left blocking hand at the midline are marked correct.

The block on the right with the left blocking arm extended past the mid line is marked as" no good."

I never saw the double bone block used in kata until 1976 when I visited with Sensei Kise at Jim Coffman's Dojo in Silver Springs, Maryland. I learned to use the double bone block in Okinawa as a block to use against an attacker armed with a club or Bo. During the 1960's this block was called the "*Old Man's block*."

*Double bone block
"The old man's block"
Photo credit Author's
Collection*

338

The ***Uchi Uke*** or hitting block is actually several techniques that appear as one block in kata. In photo *(A)*, we see that the right arm is held out ward to the right front and the fist is held slightly open *(1)*. This move could be a block to an attack coming from your right front or it could be a hammer fist striking at a target to the side as seen in the Naihanchin Kata.. The left arm is held across the body *(2)*.

Naihanchi Kata Author's collection

The blocking arms strikes across your body blocking an attack aimed at your chest *(photo B)*. In this case the blocking arm is the right arm and it moves across the body as a vertical line. By keeping the arm vertical you are able to block an attack to the upper chest with the right *(3)* Ulna Styloid Process *(Sensei Kinjo called this the "top bone")* or block an attack to the solar plexus with the *(4)* hard bones just forward of the elbow *(Sensei Kinjo called this the "bottom bone")*.

Okinawa Mountain Village....Credit: Paul Bystedt collection

The below photos illustrate the real fighting techniques of Uchi Uke; *(1)* the defender's left hand is held in front of his chest. As the attacker delivers his punch to the chest the defender's right arms strikes the punching arm of the attacker with the ***top bone block*** at the same time the defender's left hand grabs the right wrist of the attacker *(1)*. The defender counters with a right inverted fist to the face of the attacker *(3)*. As the counter is made the defender is still holding on to the attacker's right wrist there by denying him the use of his right hand *(4)*. The technique is swift and efficient and is in keeping with the old adage: ***"Give your opponent one and only one encounter."***

Hitting block from Soken's one steps; author's collection

Our next middle block or Chu Dan Uke is the Shuto Uke or knife hand block. In Okinawa we called this technique the ***"hand block"***. The shuto or knife hand block I learned in Okinawa was very effective but is it really a block? The answer to this question is both yes and no.

Author's collection

To execute the Shuto Uke that I learned in Okinawa; you first raise the shuto hand in this case the right hand to where the palm of the hand is about as high as your fore head and slightly to the left of your mid line with the palm facing the left side of your for head *(1)*. It is important to note that the blocking arm is vertical and is not pulled back to the head but remains about five to six inches to the right front of your face

At the same time the left hand points outward toward your opponent's solar plexus *(2)*. You then strike outward to the side of your opponent's neck. Striking with the Pisiform Bone of the wrist *(3)*. Among many karateka this technique is called Seiryuto or the "ox jaw". The left hand then *(4)* moves to position that Sensei Seizan Kinjo called the "Spar block".

Good advice for teaching Kata:
"Be definite now, worry about precision latter."
A lesson from a Chinese fortune cookie.

Demonstrating real fighting techniques with the Shuto Uke. (1) Block across your body with the right open hand. At same time stick you fingers into the attacker's ribs (2). Then strike into the side of your opponent's neck (3) and at the same time (4) the left hand moves back into a spar block position. This is a dangerous technique that should only be used for self protection.
Photo credit: Author's collection

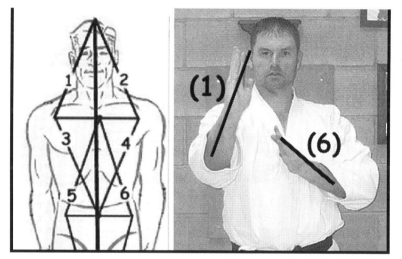

It is easy to see the triangles in the photo on the left.

Shuto Uke with the lines of the triangle.
Author's collection

The Ge Dan Uke is often misunderstood as to the real technique being taught. Let me explain with a little story. Several years ago a student of mine who was studying "Hakutsuru" under me was attending a seminar in which Grandmaster Shugoro Nakazato was one of the feature instructors. My student was a black belt in Grandmaster Nakazato's style of Shorin Ryu Shorinkan Karatedo.

During the course of the seminar the Grandmaster had an opportunity to observe my student demonstrate a low block followed very quickly with a low punch with the blocking hand.

Upon seeing the technique Grandmaster Nakazato asked my associated how he learned this technique. My student told Nakazato Sensei that I had taught him this technique and that it came from O'Sensei Soken in Okinawa. Grandmaster Nakazato told the young man that this was a good technique and to keep practicing it. Even though Grandmaster Nakazato did not teach this technique, he understood it and approved if its usage.

"Don't give into cynicism."
A lesson from a Chinese fortune cookie.

取勝之道必以全
爭曠日持久自取
滅亡速戰速決

"In battle, victory belongs to those who get there first with the most.
The longer the battle lasts, the greater are your chances for defeat.
Win quickly with a strategy of one."

Computer generated drawing by the Author….Poem by the Author
Calligraphy is old classic Chinese by Shifu Hwang
Credit: Author's collection

Kata Low Block/Gedan Uke
Credit: Author's collection

The sequence of the low kata block is as follows: *(1)* the left arm is held the width of your fist away from your body; the left fist is on your mid line. The right fist is on your left elbow. *(2)* As the right arm moves toward your lower right it blocks an attack at the mid line of your lower body. The blocking arm continues moving to the right until it reaches its final position at *(3)*.

In kata the complete sequence from (1) to (3) is very smooth; it is almost like a sword cutting downward. Using actual kata techniques the following photos gives the reader a better under standing of what Grandmaster Nakazato saw when he commented on the my student's technique. When the attacker *(1)* punches low, the defender *(2)* blocks the punch with a low block. At his point the defender need to counter attack as quickly as possible. His right hand is about one foot from the attackers body...***remember the old adage...***"***victory belongs to those who get there the first with the most***"...he counters with his right hand and defeats the attacker.

Author's collection

"Life is a school; why not try taking the curriculum?"

A lesson from a Chinese fortune cookie.

343

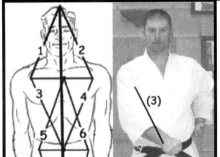

I learned several types of low blocks or **Ge Dan Uke** from my Okinawan teachers. First of all Grandmaster Soken, Sensei Fusei Kise and Seizan Kinjo used kata low block where the blocking arm is one fist away from the upper thigh..

Sensei Soken, Kise and Kinjo's block

Blocking Arm is held one fist away from the upper thigh

The above photos are as follows....on the left is the starting position for low blocks....the middle photo shows the low block being one fist width from the upper thigh....the photo on the right shows the final position of this block. This block is best used with a dodging or "change body" move.
From the Author's collection.

Sensei Kuda taught a low block where the blocking arm was held farther away from your body than the low block taught by Grandmaster Soken, Sensei Kise and Sensei Seizan Kinjo.

Sensei Kuda's low blocking arm was held father away from the body then were Sensei's

Soken, Kise and Kinjo's block. Sensei Kuda's block was held one fist width from the body.

It is my opinion that Sensei Kuda's low block is more versatile then the low block where the blocking arm is held closer to the body.

Photos L to R...block is held one fist away from body...R. final position for the block. From the Author's collection

The signature low block that is used in many Shorin Ryu Matsumura Seito kata is a powerful two fisted *"knuckles down block"* low block. There are many types of these powerful blocks that hurt. In Okinawa, these were called "knuckles down blocks; we had no other named for these blocks.

"Knuckles Down Low Block" It is seen in many of Hohan Soken's Kata. Photo is from the Author's collection

"Avoid senseless contradictions with others."
A lesson from a Chinese Fortune Cookie.

The *"Hakutsuru"* or white crane influence in Okinawan karate can be seen in the numerous types of leg blocks. Each of these blocks emphasizes standing on one leg and blocking with the opposite leg.

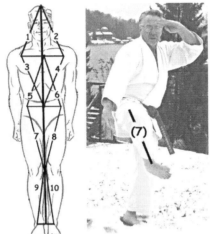

Author demonstrating a leg block from the Rohai Kata' The Photo was taken in the mountains of West Virginia.

It is easy to see that this leg block is one side of a triangle.

This frees the hands and arms to perform other tasks than blocking; the leg blocks are somewhat difficult to develop but can be effective. The down side to leg block is that any time you stand on one foot your balance is poor.

Leg blocks from the Naihanchi Kata
From the Author's collection

Credit: Author's collection

346

SUIGETSU NO HEIHO

To become effective in **Chushin no Heiho** we must learn to coordinate blocks with body movement or dodging. Imagine your body being the moonlight reflecting on water. Then imagine your opponent's attack being the same as some one reaching for the reflection of this moon light on water. When the hand reaching for the reflection and touches the water; the reflection disappears. You must learn to be like the moon light. When your opponent attacks your body; your body disappears before he can strike you. Sounds easy doesn't it.

Like many things involved in the study of Bujutsu; the skill of **Suigetsu no Heiho** appears to be very difficult. However, Suigetsu is not difficult once you understand the methods of the old masters.

You must understand that these Okinawan masters appeared to have super human quickness. I will agree that they may have been quicker than most people; yet many well trained athletes are as quick or quicker than the fastest karate master. The old Okinawan Karate masters new how to cheat and gain the advantage in combat. *They understood the importance of time as it relates to combat and that the longer a fight last the greater their chances were of being defeated.* Their methods seemed magic but they were based on sound strategies and techniques. My teachers called their Suigetsu methods *"Change Body."* Change body seem very difficult to the novice...the truth is that it is based on simplicity. Remember *"KISS".....Keep it Simple Stupid!*

CHANGE BODY....SUIGETSU.....HENKA....IT IS KNOWN BY MANY NAMES

I once asked Sensei Yuichi Kuda how he, Fusei Kise and others could change body so quickly. The following information is based on what he told me and what I have observed and the methods I have put to good use in my almost 50 years of practicing of Bujutsu.

In combat there are at least two people involved, you do not know what type of techniques your attacker is going to use. *You can only know what you are going to do and what you are not going to do.* Take advantage of this fact!

Both you and your opponent have mid lines. Your first act is observe your opponent, see him completely....it will take years for you to learn to "see" your opponent. Notice his Chushin or mid line as it will be the key point for your actions.

Shidai no Heiho is the strategy of managing the battlefield. Yes, even combat between individuals has a battlefield and in order for you to be victorious you must know how to manage it. One aspect of battle field management is choosing your own terrain; one aspect of this is learning to take advantage of your opponent as you prepare to face him.

Mentally extend his mid line forward to your own position; then adjust your position to where your mid line is to the right or left of his mid line. You do not line up mid line to mid line. You want to be just to the right or left of his extended mid line. A "rule of thumb" is to line up to where your mid line lines up on the shoulder crease of either your opponent's right or left shoulder. You are standing with your feet parallel in a ready stance. You are off center just slightly but your opponent does not realize this. You now have the potential to take advantage of him.

***"Give your opponent one and only one encounter;
win with the strategy of one."***

Whether you choose to be off center to the right or left of his mid line depends on a number of factors. If you are right handed you may wish to line up to your right. The opposite is true if you are left handed. Look at the immediate terrain factors that can affect the battle. Look for obstacles such as wall or some other factor that can cause you to become "boxed in" or influence the battle in some other way. Never loose your ability to be mobile. Learn to see your opponent and make up your mind what you are going to do before your opponent makes his move.....**this is your head start**....you make your move just as your opponent begins his move. Therefore; you will be able to move with almost magical quickness; this is my teachers' secret to their change body technique.

Let us assume you have chosen to line up to your left of his mid line and you have made up your mind to *change body* by moving your right foot backward and around into an "L" stance. For demonstrational purpose you are called the Uke and the attacker is called the Uchi.

The Uchi attacks with a powerful right hand punch. As the Uchi approaches the mid point of the maai, the Uke steps quickly with the right foot back into a left Renoji Dachi. As soon as the Uke's right foot touches the ground, he counters with a finger thrust to the Uchi's neck. All of this was done in a twinkling of the eye and victory is yours. The secret of change body is how you position yourself and knowing what you are going to do before your opponent starts his attack.

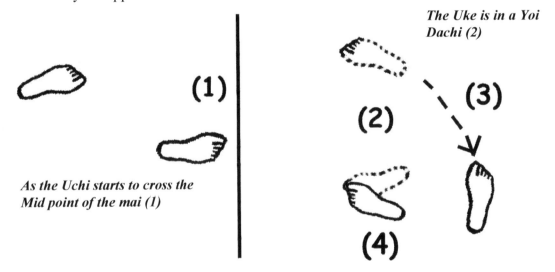

The Uke is in a Yoi Dachi (2)

(1)

(2) **(3)**

(4)

As the Uchi starts to cross the Mid point of the mai (1)

***(3) The Uke steps back and around into a Renoji Dachi. At the same time the Uke pivots
on the ball of his left foot pointing his left foot at the Uchi (4).***

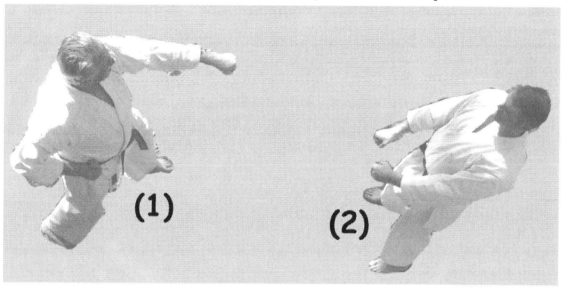

In this scenario the Attacker or Uchi (1) prepares to attack the Defender or Uke (2) The Uke lines up to his left which put him slightly to the Uchi's right front.
Photo credit: Author's collection

As the Uchi attacks; the Uke steps back into the Renoji dachi and counters with his left hand.

Suigetsu or Change body is not difficult. The technique like all techniques takes practice. Many times students will try and learn change body with out knowing that they must decide on what to do before the fight ever starts. These students wait until the Uchi actually begins his attack. They try to be quicker than the Uchi. They give the Uchi the head start. There is little chance that the student will be able to make the change body technique successful. The student becomes discouraged and believes that change body will not work. It is not the student's fault. The teacher is to be blamed!

There are many principles and techniques that assist the Uke in making his or her change body technique successful. Yin and Yang are at play here, there are pro and cons to every thing and change body is no exception. I will pass on to the readers the knowledge my teachers gave me about the skill of change body. I hope that this will help you avoid many "pit falls" and helps you to be a better karateka.

Indeed the kanji for rice is one of the major points of *"Bujutsu"* and becomes the foundation for very important principles involved in the fighting arts.

Bei... the kanji for rice is a symbol for several fighting principles. The first that comes to mind is from Kenjutsu (Japanese Sword fighting)...the basic kata "Happo giri" or cutting in eight directions teaches the basic cutting moves with a Japanese sword. Bei the symbol for rice becomes almost synonymous for eight.

Bei- Rice
Author's collection

Happo means "eight directions or eight steps"; if we look at the kanji you see marks or lines that go out or come in from eight directions. Happo becomes a guiding term for the martial arts. *Happo ayumi* means stepping in eight directions. *"If you can step in eight directions your stance is correct. If you can react to a situation in eight directions your strategy is correct." Happo ayumi becomes the strategy that we employ to use change body techniques . These principles are from my Okinawan Sensei.*

The Kanji for Bei inside an octagon
Author's collection

Another method used to teach change body or Suigetsu is to explain the moves and techniques as if they were occurring inside an octagon.

Sensei Kise's method of explaining change body was to use a square; Sensei Soken, Sensei Kuda and Sensei Kinjo used an octagon.

When designing a logo and patch for the *"Kokusai Kobujutsu Hozon Domei"* *(Alliance to Preserve the Old Fighting Arts)* I experimented with various designs to used in the center of the logo. I tried cranes, different weapons and so forth. Finally, I used a copy of an old Japanese sword tsuba that resembled the kanji for rice for the logo.

In my opinion the relationship between the kanji for rice and the fighting arts is very important and the knowledge of this relationship must be taught if we are to preserve the old combative forms of karate.

Kokusai Kobujutsu Hozon Domei logo....Author's collection

MANAGING THE OCTAGON

There are many change body methods; all have their disadvantages and their advantages. Generally speaking all of my Shorin Ryu Matsumura Seito teachers were alike and yet they all were different. I am going to explain the change body methods they used as they began teaching their students these types of techniques. These are only a few of the basic techniques they taught to introduce change body.

Let us start this discussion with your opponent (Uchi) attacking with a powerful lunge punch as you (Uke) prepare for his attack from a ready stance. This will be the introduction to "Change Body" technique used by Grandmaster Soken, Sensei Kise and Sensei Kinjo.

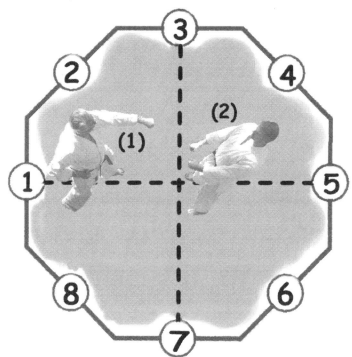

We will start each of our body change scenarios' with the Uchi *(1)* preparing to attack the Uke *(2)* with a powerful right fist lunge punch.

Before the Uchi attacks the Uke decides to change by stepping back and around with his right foot toward the octagon flat #6. This is a safe change body direction and offers good protection, but decreases the range for the Uke's counter attack.

As the Uchi attacks, the Uke move as soon as the Uchi makes the slightest move. As the Uke moves; he only needs to move a few inches before he is out of the way of the Uchi's attack.

I believe that Grand Master Soken, Sensei Kise and Sensei Kinjo taught this method as an introduction to change body because it was safe and the student could experience some success early in his or her development toward learning the change body strategy.

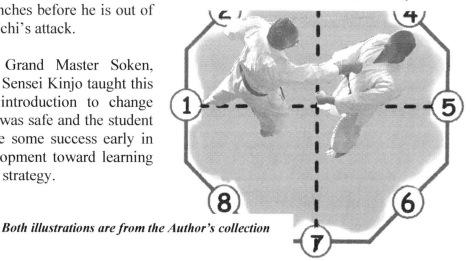

Both illustrations are from the Author's collection

351

The Uke ends up on the right front of the Uchi. In this position the Uchi is almost out of range for the Uke's counter attack.

In this scenario the Uke chose to use to take the out side position in this brief battle with the Uchi.

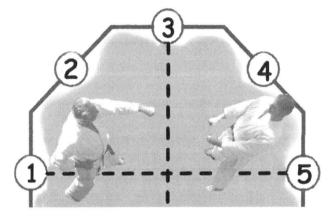

Change body… the outside position offers safety; but the technique may leave the Uke out of range for his counter attack. From the Author's collection

Below: Taking the inside position, the Uke lines up on the Uchi's left front. Author's collection

The outside position in my opinion is safer than inside position. Never the less the karateka must be skillful in changing body in all directions.

Below: the Uke blocks the Uchi's punch from the inside position. Both illustrations credit Author's collection

In our next scenario the Uke lines up slightly on the Uchi's left front *(above)*.

As the Uchi attacks *(1) illustration on the right, the Uke steps back and around (2) toward Octagon flat #4.*

This move to the Uchi's inside is not as safe as moving to the outside because the Uchi can

quickly strike the Uke with his left hand. However, the Uke's right hand is closer to the Uchi's vital areas than the Uchi's left hand is to the Uke's vital areas. The Uke has the head start and can hit the Uchi before the Uchi can use his left hand. *The Uke can get there first with the most…*therefore victory belongs to the Uke.

"The longer a battle last, the greater are your chances for defeat".

All of the change body techniques employed by my Okinawan Shorin Ryu Matsumura Seito Sensei depend on several very important principles these include: *making the body smaller, making the arm longer, and always use a cover force.*

"Making the body smaller and the arm grow longer"....When using the "L" stance or Renoji Dachi the heel of your feet line up on a straight line. There fore, when you are facing your opponent and you are standing in the Renoji Dachi, the side of your body is facing your opponent.

Making the body smaller

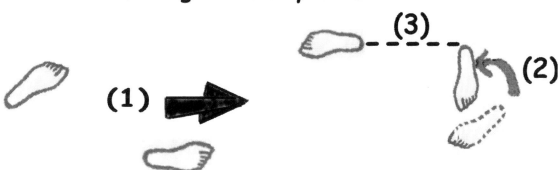

Imagine if you will an attacker moving rapidly in from the left as represented by *(1)* in the above illustration. The Uke responds by stepping into a Renoji Dachi or "L" Stance *(2)*. The heels of the Uke *(3)* intersect forming the "L". The right side of the Uke' body is facing the Uchi (attacker); this means that the Uke is facing his narrow side of his body toward his attacker. Since the front of the body is wider than the side of the body, the Uke is reducing his target profile by facing his side toward the Uchi.

By facing his side toward his opponent, the Uke is also increasing his reach with his right arm thus he is *"making his arm grow longer"*.

When the Uke turned the side of his body toward the Uchi, he was adding the length of his right shoulder to his right arm reach. In photo on the left it is easy to see how the Uke gained the advantage over the Uchi by increasing his reach through his change body technique.

From the Author's collection

353

Sensei Kise is not very tall even by Okinawan standards. His arms are not very long. Yet, he would often demonstrate his ability to *__make his arm longer__*; he would touch tall American military men before they could touch him. When demonstrating his command of the maai or combat distance, he left little doubt in the minds of everyone viewing his demonstrations that in spite of being smaller he could easily defeat his taller opponents.

He used the "L" stance technique which we have previously discussed. He also manipulated the length of his 'L" stance to gain reach over his opponent. His experiences with the actual use of short stances in real fights caused him to alter his kata by making his stances shorter than those of his teachers.

__Both of the above photos are from the Author's collection.__

In each of the above photo, the Uchi is on the left…. The photo on the left demonstrates that if the Uke steps back with a long stance to avoid the Uchi's attack; the Uke's counter will lack sufficient range to strike the Uchi. The photo on the above right demonstrates that by stepping back with a shorter stance the Uke will have sufficient range to strike the Uchi.

When performing your change body technique always step with your arms in front of you. Your arms will serve as a *__"covering force"__* and will enable you to block those techniques which you were not expecting.

*__From the Author's
collection__*

Sensei Kuda once told me that one of my teachers, Seizan Kinjo really liked performing the Shorinji Ryu version of the *Ananku Kata.* This makes sense because Sensei Kinjo taught a change body technique that was some what risky but with much practice it could be a very effective technique. This technique was from the Ananku Kata.

The illustration on the left shows the start of Sensei Kinjo's Ananku technique. The Uchi *(1)* prepares to attack the Uke *(2)* with a right hand punch.

The Uke has lined up to almost

Both illustrations are from the Author's collection

directly in front or slightly to the left front of the Uchi. As the Uchi attacks, the Uke steps forward with his left foot to where the heel of his left foot lines up with the heel of his right foot *(Illustration on the right).*

The Uke makes his move as soon as the Uchi makes the slightest movement. In doing so the Uke is able to move very quickly and control the mid line of the Uchi from the inside position. At this point the Uke can touch his opponent but the opponent can not touch the Uke.

Sensei Kuda's beginning change body technique was somewhat different than the technique taught by Grandmaster Soken, Sensei Kise, and Sensei Kinjo.

The illustration on the left shows the Uke is standing in a Yoi Dachi *(ready stance).* The Uke has line up in such a way that he will be positioned on the Uchi's right front as the attack occurs.

From the Author's collection

As the Uchi attacks, the Uke steps to his front left with the right foot, he is stepping toward octagon flat #8.

This move is somewhat dangerous as it involves stepping forward toward the Uchi's attacking hand.

The Uke must have his arms out in front. His arms acting as a cover force can block the Uchi's technique. In my opinion Sensei Kuda's technique is too difficult for beginners; but, it is very effective once the karateka become skillful with the concept of "Change Body."

Foot Work of Sensei Kuda's "Change Body".

Middle of the Maai

Uchi's position

(1)

(2)   Uke's initial positoin

Uchi's Mid Line

Uke's final position

(3)

(1) Direction of the attack
(2) Uke's right foot steps toward Octagon flat #8.
(3) At the same time, the Uke pivots on the ball of his left foot, pointing the foot toward the Uchi.

GRANDMASTER HOHAN SOKEN'S IRIMI

Several years ago I was visiting with a friend of mine named Steve Davis. Steve had been a marine stationed on Okinawa during the mid 1970's. Steve knew that I taught karate. During the course of our conversation; Steve told me about an old gray headed Okinawan Karate master he had seen demonstrating karate at Kadena Air Force Base on Okinawa during the 1970's. According to Steve the old master would almost magically evade the attacks by much younger karateka and suddenly the old master would be standing behind the attacking young karateka.

Steve did not know the name of the old man and he was quite surprised when I told him that the old master's name was Hohan Soken and that I had known him and had studied under him.

Sensei Soken's technique that Steve Davis had seen was based upon some of the change body techniques we have already discussed. Sensei Soken's technique was simple he changed body with one step and with another one or two steps he was behind his opponent. His change body was defensive; the addition steps to reach his opponent's rear corner were offensive and in the martial arts world this is called *Irimi no Heiho (the strategy of entering).* Grandmaster Soken was an expert in Irimi.

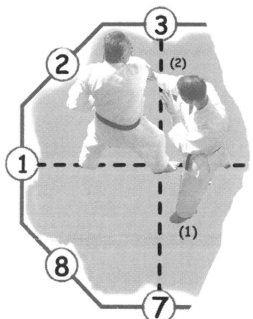

The illustration on the left shows the change body and Irimi technique that Steve Davis saw Grandmaster Soken demonstrate in the 1970's.

The illustration on the left picks up the action just as the Uchi *(karateka on the left)* attacks the Uke *(karateka on the right)* with a lunge punch. The Uke is in a Yoi Dachi *(ready stance);* he side steps with his left foot toward octagon flat #7 *(1)*. At the same time with an open right hand, the Uke blocks the Uchi's punch and he then pushes the Uchi's right elbow across the Uchi's chest *(2)*.

The pushing of the elbow turns the Uchi's upper body to the left and exposes his right rear corner to a counter attack from the Uke.

At this point in the action the Uke can counter attack to numerous targets on the right side and back of the Uchi. The Uke can also enter into the Uchi's right rear corner by taking one or two additional steps.

When the old Grandmaster performed this technique his action was very smooth and effortless. To the novice he seemed to move by magic. To the trained karateka the simplicity of his technique and the wisdom of his strategy left an ever lasting impression.

Grandmaster Soken technique was actually in two parts. Part one was the change body or dodging technique. The change body technique *(step 1 and 2 illustration on the previous page)* is the most important phase of Sensei Soken technique. At this point the "fight is over."

Part two, the Irimi technique, puts the finishing touch on the situation and puts the Uke behind the Uchi. From this position the Uke can use the Uchi as a shield if the situation involves more than one attacker. *(Illustration on the left)*

Photos and illustrations on this page are from the Author's collection.

Foot Work Soken's Irimi Technqiue

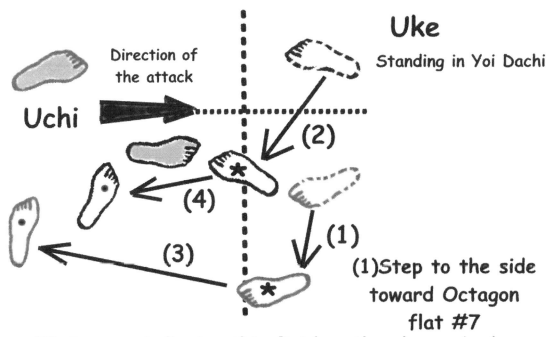

Uke
Standing in Yoi Dachi

Direction of
the attack

Uchi

(2)

(4)

(1)

(3)

(1)Step to the side
toward Octagon
flat #7

(2) Step as indicate: this finishes the change body stepping. Change body position is marked with a star *.
Step (3) and (4) as indicated; final position is marked with a dot ●.

358

DEALING WITH MULTIPLE OPPONENTS

Grandmaster Hohan Soken once said that dealing with opponents you imagine them to be children and you then lead them around as if they were some type of domestic animals. Sensei Kise and Sensei Kuda told me that dealing with multiple opponents is the same as fighting individuals. You position yourself to where the multiple opponents are in a single line; then you can fight them one at a time.

Sensei Kinjo once told me that when fighting a group of people use one of the individuals as a shield and push this person into the others this will give you the opportunity to stick your finger into their eyes. I once had an old street fighter tell me that when dealing with multiple opponents, you run in quick and hit one real hard and the others will quit.

Shinpan Shiroma (1889-1954)
Author's collection

There are many theories and many good ideas, however, in Okinawan karate history and folklore there is a story about one master whose must be considered the Island's resident expert when it comes to fighting a group of people. This story comes from Sensei Ernest Estrada, Mr. Estrada sent me this on are about 1985. Since this time I have lost the printed copy. So I am relying on my memory and I may have forgotten some of the details of the story

This is a story about Shinpan Shiroma who was also known by his Okinawan name Shinpan Gusukuma. He was born in 1889 and he died in 1954. He was a student of Anko Itosu (Shuri-te) and Kanryo Higashionna (Naha-te). Shinpan Shiroma was a member of a famous old Shuri Samurai family. He was a school teacher and a karate master.

It seems that a group of about ten farmers were investigating the possible theft of some missing chickens; for some reason they believed that Shinpan Shiroma may have been involved. The farmers went to Shiroma's house to question him about the missing chickens. The farmers knew of Shiroma's skill in karate and they believe that since there were ten of them, they doubted that Shiroma would present a problem.

One thing led to another and an altercation broke out; Shiroma retreated from his front yard into his house, the farmers, full of misguided confidence, charged into the house. In the house Shiroma knew how to even the odds. He fought with his back to the wall, he fought behind furniture, he fought in the hallways and in the door ways. Soon the ten farmers were trimmed done to one or two who could still fight. Those still able gave up and along the injured and "walking wounded" they beat a hasty retreat out the front door. As they left Shiroma shouted at them.... ***"ten is not enough, next time bring fifty"***.

A few weeks went by and Shiroma had forgotten about his challenge to the farmers about bringing fifty men the next time they wanted a confrontation with him. A commotion in his front yard quickly renewed his memory as he looked out the window and saw fifty farmers ready to charge into his house. Quickly Shiroma retreated into the rice field behind his house.

The rice fields had recently been flooded so the only way to walk in the rice field was to walk on the rice paddy dikes or get bogged down by the thick mud in the flooded rice field.

Shiroma had chosen his terrain wisely. He ran fifty feet or so on the paddy dike before turning and facing fifty anger farmers. Shiroma had lined up the farmers in a neat single file line that was only as wide as the rice paddy dike (about three feet). He could now fight them one at a time.

As the farmers charged on to the paddy dikes after Shiroma, they found themselves fighting a skillful warrior that they could not best in spite of their superior numbers. Those that chose to wade out into the mud found that they could not move fast enough to get behind Shiroma. With their numbers rapidly being reduced, they beat a hasty retreat out of the rice paddy and headed for their homes. As they left Shiroma shouted *"fifty is not enough…next time bring one hundred."*

Shinpan Shiroma the little school teacher had played the part of a brilliant strategist. His "heiho" had been correct. He chose his terrain wisely; he stayed mobile and fought only when he was in a position of strength. He did not fall to the ground and wrestle with the farmers. Such action is not realistic and would have led to Shiroma's defeat. Mobility is what gave Shiroma his victory.

"Scene from Okinawa"
From Lithographs from the 1853 Cmd.
Perry Expedition
Author's collection

虎知曉地勢鶴則知天
知地知海虎怒嘯而
逸戰鶴已輕翔遠逝

"The tiger knows only the earth.
The crane knows the earth, the sky and the sea.
The tiger roars with anger and defiance.
The crane merely flies away."

Classics Chinese Calligraphy by Shifu Hwang
Drawing and poem are by the Author
Credit: the Author's collection

THE BUS DRIVER

Sensei Ernest Estrada sent me an interesting story in the mid 1980's. This is about an unnamed Okinawan karateka who was a student of Shinpan Shiroma. This unnamed karateka may not have been Okinawa's strongest or it's most famous warrior. But he certainly would be a candidate for Okinawa's wisest warrior. We will call him the bus driver.

The time era for this story is unclear; this story may have taken pace just before World War II or a few years after World War II. As the story goes, the bus driver was driving his bus full of people in the Naha area of Okinawa. He stopped at one of the many bus stops in the area and picked up several more passengers. One of the people that boarded the bus was very drunk. It did not take too long for every body aboard that bus to realize that the drunken man was also very belligerent and wanted to fight.

All peaceful attempts to calm the drunk down and to behave properly failed. The drunken man wanted to fight some one, any one and he would not take no for an answer. After a few minutes the bus driver agreed to fight the drunk and begin looking for a safe place to pull the bus over to the side of the road.

The drive pulled the bus over to the side of the road and opened the door…the drunk, loudly cussing and threatening all aboard the bus, stepped out through the door and turned to face the driver. Once the drunken man was out of danger from a moving vehicle; the drive shut the door and drove away. The wise Bushi wins without fighting.

"The tiger roars with anger and defiance.
The crane merely flies away."

This ends my book, it is my hope that you will:

"Light the way….carry the torch….be a leader... and help preserve the art that the
Okinawan Masters have given us.

"Practice your kata….listen to your body…. and you will learn karate."

ABAYO

Sources, End Notes and Explanations

Sources for the information presented in this chapter are listed in the text. Those sources not list in the text are from my teachers and own personal experiences.

GLOSSARY OF TERMS USED IN THE STUDY OF BUJUTSU
(Both old and modern terms used in this book and in the language of Bujutsu)

abayo............ Japanese slang for good bye

abumi...........Stirrup of a saddle, the term is also used instead of tetsuko (iron fist) a weapon developed from the abumi or stirrup.

abunai..........dangerous

age..............upward

aiki..............united spirit, short for aikido, aikijutsu

aite..............together-hand, an opponent

Aji...............A social rank of the old Okinawan Kingdom that would be just under the rank the Okinawan Royal family

ayumi...........walking

ayumi-ho.......The study of walking also called ayumi waza.

batto.............The act of drawing the katana from the obi and cutting in one motion.

batto jutsu......the art and study of batto

bo................a wooden staff

bogu kumite... Karate sparing with the use of kendo like protective equipment.

bugei............old Japanese name for martial arts

bugeisha........student of a martial art

bugi.............martial arts technique

bujin............warrior or soldier

bujutsu..........War or fighting art the primary goal of which is self protection or preparation for real combat.

buke..............A military or samurai family, literal translation is "war house" in this case the house refers to the people or family living the house, in the Okinawan dialect the term would be *"buya"*.

bushi.............warrior

bushi-te or ti....warrior's hand an old name for karate

bunkai............practicing parts of the kata as kumite

cha................tea

chu...............middle

chudan...........middle level

chuden...........The level of learning mid level of techniques.

chushin.......... mid line, heart

chushin dori..... controling the center or mid line

dai................generation, large,

dai sho...........a pair of swords one long and one short

dake..............the word for mountain (Okinawan dialect)

dan...............a black belt rank

deshi............. a disciple

dojo.............. a training hall for the martial arts

dojo kun..........the moralistic guiding maxims for a dojo

Edo...............the old name for Tokyo

enbusen..........the pattern or performance line of a kata *fuchi*............The metal band around the front or forward end of a Japanese sword handle.

fudo.............immovable

fundoshi....... A loin cloth, prior to World War II it was often worn while practicing karate.

furi..............To swing something such as a nunchaku or suruchin.

futon.......... a quilt

gaijin............the Japanese term for a Caucasian

gakusei........ student

gendaito.......modern Japanese sword

geta............wooden clogs or sandals

gunjin..........soldier

gyaku..........reverse or opposite

.

ha...............cutting edge of a sword, also means a sect or clan

Hakutsuru....white crane one of the five animals of Shaolin.

hanbo.........a three foot bo also call a sanshaku bo

hancho........a leader of a group or province or municipality

hanko.........a stamp or seal

hajime........the command to begin

happo.........Eight steps, an important term for martial artist as it indicates the ability to function in all directions.

hara...........abdomen also refers to "inner" or spiritual strength

hiden..........the level of learning secret techniques

hojo undo.....supplemental training

iaijutsu........The drawing of a sword and cutting in one motion same as batto.

inazuma.......lightning

ippon ....one strike one point, finish the fight with one technique

ishi.............a rock

itai.............pain

itto.............one sword

jissen..........a real fight

juken jutsu...the art of using a bayonet

jutte ....An iron truncheon used by police in feudal Japan similar to the Okinawan sai.

kaden..........hereditary family fighting secrets

kaeshi waza...counter techniques

kai/kyokai.....an organization or association

kaicho.........the leader of an organization

kaiden.........final level of teachings

kamiza.........the shrine area at the front of a dojo

kata............prearranged formal exercises taught in martial arts

keimochi.......Okinawa noble class

kenpo..........fist law, Chinese Boxing, kung fu or quan-fa

kime...........focus

kobujutsu......Old war art, does not necessarily refer to Okinawan weapons training; but refers to all old fighting art including karatejutsu; kobudo refers to old war way.

koryu......... old style or old method or old concepts

koteaite........body toughening exercises

kumite........actual fight training either prearranged or free practice

Kyoshi..............A special title of honor given to outstanding individuals of the rank of 7 Dan to 8 Dan

Kyu................pre-black belt temporary grades

mai................Okinawan term for young woman in Shorin Ryu Matsumura Seito it often refers to Bushi Matsumura's wife

Menko Kaiden .A certificate or diploma recognizing that the recipient of this document has received the final teachings of a Ryu. This is a Japanese tradition not an Okinawan custom or tradition.

mon................Okinawan or Japanese family crest or "coat of arms"

Naha-te...........Term that came into general usage after the 1920's, means the hands of Naha and refers to the karate styles descending from the teachings of Kanryo Higashionna.

ninja.............groups of outcast in served as spies and assasins in feudal Japan.

nito...............Two swords, refers to the Nito Ryu sword fighting method developed by Musashi Miyamoto

O.................prefix meaning large or great

Okuden...........the level at which hidden techniques are taught

Oni...............A goblin or demon, these mythological beings are often blamed for stealing cloths off the cloths line.

O-sensei..........great teacher

Os!.................An abbreviation for ***"Ohayo-gozaimasu"*** or "Good morning", also a "can do positive greeting or respond to a request or order, this term is of a Japanese origin and not widely used in Okinawa before the 1970's.

Oyakata......... A high ranking court official of the Okinawan Kingdome, also called Uekata.

Peichin......... A Bushi Class title given to an officer in the service of the Okinawan King.

Rei............... a bow of respect

Rengo Kai...... a federation also called Remmei made up of one or more associations

Renshi...........an honorary title given to outstanding 4 Dans, 5 Dans or 6 Dans

Ryu...............a method or style of an art

Ryu-ha...........The lineage or branches of a specific Ryu, similar to a family clan.

sakura............cherry tree, a favorite symbol of the samurai

samegawa........The skin of a type of sting ray used to wrap around the handle of swords to add strength to the handle.

Sappushi.........Chinese envoys to the old Kingdom of Okinawa.

sempai............senior members of a dojo

sensei..............some one who points the way; a teacher

Shihan...........a licensed instructor

Shizoku...........The noble class of the Okinawan Kingdom.

Shodai............First generation, a title given to one who founds a martial arts style, Ryu or organization.

Shurite........... "Shuri-hands" the karate style or styles that developed over 500 years ago in Shuri, Okinawa.

Soke................. The inheritor of a traditional Japanese bujutsu system or "Ryu." This term does not refer to one who has founded or developed their own martial arts style.

Swiss Army knife.....A popular style of military knife that has several blades and different types of tools which makes this knife very useful.

tanbo............... half Bo, a 3 foot Bo

Tan Me...............An unofficial title of respect awarded by Okinawan society to certain individuals.

touti.............. Okinawan Hogan (dialect) term for tode meaning Chinese hand. One of the old names for Okinawan karate.

tetsu.............. iron

Tomarite........... "Hands of Tomari" the karate style that developed in the port city of Tomari.

tsuka............... sword handle

Uchi...............a strike or hit....one who attacks

Uchinan............old name for Okinawa

Uchinan guchi.....old name for the language of Okinawa

Unanti..............One of the old names for karate; means Okinawan Hand.

Udun................This term means a castle in the Okinawan Hogan (dialect) and refers to a high ranking family (royal family or Aji family).

Udunti............. Udun means a castle or palace, ti means hand. It refers to the "hands" or a fighting art of a particular fighting style of a high ranking Okinawan family. For an example the *Motobu Udunti* refers to the fighting style of the Motobu family.

uke.................a block, one who receives a technique... your partner in fighting drills

waza...............technique

ya.................. An Okinawan term...ke in Japanese actually means house or house hold or family. When used with a surname; for example Machimura-ya the term means Matsumura house or family.

yakko...............samurai street gangs

yakuza.............Japanese organized criminal gangs similar to the mafia

yari.................spear

zen.................all

zoku............... clan

zori.............. sandals

*"Think not that I am come to send peace on earth;
I came not to send peace, but a sword."
Holy Bible
Matthew 10:34*

INDEX OF PEOPLE'S NAMES

A.J. Advincula, 145

Aburaya Yamashiro, 80

Admiral Nagumo, 214

Agena, 75, 79

Akacho, 71

Akahachi Oyakata., 24

Akahito, 71

Akamine, 61, 80, 169

Amawari, 21

Anbun Takuda, 111

Anea Shosho, 53

Ankichi Arakaki, 115, 118, 119, 121

Anko Asato, 105

Anko Itosu, 61, 70, 80, 82, 92, 93, 105, 107, 108, 112, 123, 126, 150, 284, 359

Anko Itosu,, 70, 82, 107

Anthony Sandoval, 92, 126, 189

Anya Masaharu, 46, 53

B. H. Liddel Hart, 212

Bill Hayes, 124, 189

Bob Herten, 234

Bodhidharma, 31, 32

Brandon Pender, 169

Brunei, 20

Bucho, 89, 91, 106, 126, 142, 144, 204, 205, 207, 218, 222

Budo no Bugei, 207, 208

Bushi Matsumura, 34, 61, 67, 70, 72, 80, 89, 91, 92, 93, 94, 97, 98, 99, 101, 104, 105, 107, 108, 113, 125, 126, 134, 135, 136, 137, 140, 141, 142, 143, 144, 151, 152, 172, 189, 202, 204, 205, 207, 208, 211, 236, 265, 268, 271, 275

Bushi Takemura, 72

Bushi" Matsumura, 31, 134, 141, 291

Carson, 317

Ch'in Shih Huang Ti, 9

Charles Garrett, 169

Chatan Yara, 39, 42, 43, 82, 84

Chikin (Tsuken) Shitahaku, 71

Chikin Kraka, 143, 144

Chikin Seinori, 71

Chikin Seinori Oyakata, 71

Chinen, 75, 80, 82, 105, 121, 179

Chinen Mahsanra, 105

Chojun Miyagi, 53, 61, 62, 63, 64, 121, 123, 290

Choki Motobu, 56, 70, 111, 119, 121, 123, 152, 154

Chokuho Agena, 75, 79

Chomo Hanashiro, 53, 56, 105, 111

Chorin Yamakawa, 111

Choshin Chibana, 80, 112, 114, 115, 123, 161, 162

Chosin Chibana, 111, 139, 159

Chotoku Kyan, 79, 105, 107, 111, 117, 118, 119, 120, 121, 123, 145, 158, 172

Chotoku Makabe, 169

Choyo Oshiro, 111

Choyu Motobu, 73

Chozo Nakama, 115

Chuck Chandler, 85, 92, 125, 137, 189

Chuen Yuan Shangjen, 32

David Mauk, 169

David Shelton, 169

Dempsey, 271

Dutch Meyers, 222

Ed Gingras, 169

Ed Thompson, 169

Eiichi Miyazato, 162

Eiso, 18, 19

Eisuke Akamine, 83

Eizo Shimabukuro, 118, 123, 124

Emperor Meiji, 102

Emperor Seiwa., 12

Emperor Wei, 31

Emperor Yung Ching, 33

Ernest Estrada, 125, 137, 148, 158, 189, 359, 362

Ernest Estrada's, 137, 158, 189

Fred Lovret, 326, 330
Fred Sypher, 169
Fredrick J. Lovret, 194, 311
Fujiwara family, 12
Funakoshi, 82, 111, 113, 143
Funakoshi Gichin, 111
Fusei Kise, 25, 70, 85, 92, 99, 117, 125,
    126, 156, 163, 169, 170, 175, 176,
    189, 194, 242, 254, 258, 267, 300,
    322, 324, 344, 347

Gabai Zenni, 34
Gary Stanfield, 156, 169
Genghis Kan, 12, 14, 28
George Kerr, 28, 126
Gichin Funakoshi, 111, 112, 113
Gihon, 18
Gima Seichu, 46
Go Ken Ki, 46, 47
Gokenki, 52, 53, 84, 114, 144, 145, 149,
    290, 291, 301
Gordon Hansen, 169
Gosamaru, 20, 21
Grandmaster, 35, 54, 56, 57, 58, 63, 74,
    119, 124, 133, 137, 139, 143, 146,
    148, 152, 154, 155, 157, 158, 162,
    163, 164, 166, 169, 170, 179, 184,
    187, 189, 190, 213, 246, 253, 281,
    291, 300, 312, 324, 330, 341, 343,
    344, 345, 351, 355, 357, 358, 359
Grandmasters Soken, 156
Greg Ohl, 146, 158
Gusukuma, 108, 109, 359

Hakugyo Ku Hou, 34
Hashi, 20, 26
Henry de Bohun, 218
Hideo Nakazato, 169
Higashionna Kanryo, 31
Hina-san, 147
Hohan Soken, 53, 73, 91, 93, 94, 125,
    133, 134, 135, 136, 137, 138, 139,
    140, 141, 142, 143, 144, 145, 147,
    148, 149, 151, 154, 156, 158, 159,
    161, 162, 163, 166, 168, 169, 170,
    179, 188, 189, 190, 193, 194, 207,

213, 225, 228, 236, 246, 253, 254,
    258, 281, 289, 290, 291, 312, 322,
    330, 357, 359

Irimaji Seiji, 68, 85, 170
Ishimine Shinchi, 105
Isshin Ryu Karatedo, 122
Itoman Bunkichi, 60

Jack Dempsey, 267, 300
James Longstreet, 212
Jhuhatsu Kyoda, 61
Jim Coffman's, 338
Jim Corbett, 202
Jim Louge, 231
Jimmu, 10
Jimmy Coffman, 169
Joen Nakazato, 118, 121
John L. Sullivan, 202
Jushin Kohama, 169
Jyoei Kushi, 162
Jyokei Kushi, 158

Kamato Toyozato, 46
Kamiya Jinsei, 82, 83
Kamura, 145
Kana Kinjo, 145
Kanamura, 145
Kana-san, 147
Kanbun Uechi, 46, 47, 49, 50, 51, 84
Kanei Uechi, 49, 50, 51, 52, 126, 162,
    166
Kang Kanashiro, 145
Kanryo Higashionna, 61, 62, 63, 64, 85,
    113, 114, 125, 359
Kantoku Uechi, 46
Katsume Murakami, 71
Katsuya Miyahira, 115, 125, 162
Katsuyuki Shimabukuro, 115
Ken Cohen, 163
Kenji Nakaima, 55
Kenko Nakaima., 55
Kensu Yabu, 56, 105, 111, 113
Kenwa Mabuni, 53, 54, 61, 111, 112,
    114, 144, 290
Kenyu Kudenken, 111

Kimo Wall, 64
Kinjo Matsu, 59, 61
Kiyohide Shinjo, 203
Kiyuna Pechin no Tanmei, 105
Ko Ishigawa, 137
Kobashigawa Kyosho, 105
Kobayashi Ryu, 105, 114, 115
Kogushiku, 67, 133, 201, 293, 302
Kojo, 47, 61, 67, 68, 85, 201, 293, 302
Kojo family, 67, 68
Kojo Kaho, 68
Koki Shiroma, 61
Komesu Ushi, 143
Kosaku Matsumora, 70, 117
Kosei Nishihira, 169
Kublai Khan, 19
Kuda family, 179
Kukushi no Bugei, 207
Kusanku, 39, 40, 41, 42, 56, 72, 91, 94,
   117, 119, 139, 142, 189
Kushi Bushi, 207
Kushigawa Uehara, 98, 126
Kyan (1870-1945), 105, 117

Lord of Nakajin, 19
Lord Ozato, 20

Machimura-ya, 142
Maeda Pechin, 117
Makabe Chojun, 91
Manataka Tsuken, 143
Mark Gracey, 63
Masami Chinen, 72, 80
Masamitsu Oshiro, 169
Master Azato, 108, 109, 113, 245
Matsuda Michiyuki, 45
Matsuda Toksabudo, 46
Matsuda Tosaburo, 46, 47, 84
Matsumora Kosaku, 31
Matsumura, 67, 71, 75, 80, 89, 91, 92,
   93, 94, 95, 97, 98, 99, 100, 101, 102,
   104, 105, 106, 107, 108, 109, 117,
   125, 126, 133, 134, 135, 136, 137,
   138, 139, 140, 141, 142, 143, 144,
   145, 147, 149, 158, 170, 171, 172,
   179, 189, 190, 194, 204, 205, 207,

   208, 211, 218, 222, 230, 246, 255,
   258, 260, 261, 268, 275, 276, 291,
   293, 296, 298, 300, 302, 311, 313,
   322, 330, 331, 334, 335, 338, 345,
   351, 353
Meiji Era, 75, 103, 133
Meimoko no Bugei, 207
Mike Farrell, 227
Mike Muller, 75
Mike Tyson, 271
Minamoto, 12, 16, 17
Mitake Higa-san, 147
Mitsou Enoue, 169, 170
Mitsugi-san, 147
Moden Yabiku, 82, 83, 111
Motobu, 46, 47, 54, 67, 70, 72, 73, 74,
   133, 134
Motobu Udundi, 73
Motokatsu Inoue, 83, 99

Nabe Matsumura, 105, 107, 126, 134,
   136, 137, 139, 143, 144, 149
Nabe no Tanme, 143
Nabeshima Naokira, 104
Nakagoshi Chogo, 46
Nakaima Bushi, 55
Nakaima Kenri, 31, 55
Nakamoto Kiichi, 81
Nakamoto Masahiro, 28, 71, 85, 137,
   152, 158
Nakasone, 25
Nakazato, 121, 161, 341, 343
Nishimae Jinji, 169
Nita, 169
Nomura, 100, 101, 126, 211
Nori, 145, 295

Ogushiku, 57, 111, 133
Oh Irei, 79
Oh o So, 146
Oshiro) no Tanmei, 57
Oyadomari, 72, 113, 117

Pimeku, 9
Prajnatara, 31
Prince Mutsuhiro, 102

Richard Ewell, 213
Richard Kim's, 59, 84
Rick Rose, 125, 169
Rison, 34
Riyu, 18
Robert E. Lee, 212
Robert Teller, 27
Robert the Bruce, 218
Ronald Lindsey, 3, 28, 133, 169
Roy Osborn, 169
Roy Suenaka, 169
Ryosei Kuwae, 105, 205
Ryosei Kuwei, 105
Ryusho Sakagami, 83
Ryuyu Tomoyose, 49, 52

Saburo Uehara, 63, 162
Sakayama Ketoku, 55
Sakihara Pechin, 105
Sakugawa, 39, 40, 41, 42, 56, 67, 80, 84,
  89, 91, 94, 218, 234
Sanda Chinen, 80
Sanda Kanagushiku, 80, 81
Satto, 19, 20
Scott Anderson, 325
Sean Connery, 297
Seiki Arakaki, 92, 169
Seiki Itokazu, 162
Seikichi Odo, 56
Seikichi Toguchi, 64, 65
Seikichi Uehara, 72, 73, 74
Seiko Chinen, 75
Seiko Fukuchi, 64
Seiko Higa, 64
Seishin Kan, 117, 170, 171
Seisho Arakaki, 46, 47, 54, 84
Seito Higa, 61
Seito Ishigawa, 115
Seitoku Higa, 72, 73, 74, 158
Seiyu Oyata, 56, 57, 59, 63, 179
Seiyu Shinjo, 52, 194, 203, 215
Seizan Kinjo, 98, 101, 125, 126, 155,
  169, 175, 189, 194, 216, 246, 254,
  255, 258, 300, 301, 322, 340, 344,
  345, 355
Sekichi Odo, 194, 231

Sensei Kinjo, 101, 155, 175, 255, 339,
  350, 351, 355, 359
Sensei Kise, 25, 70, 117, 146, 156, 157,
  163, 170, 171, 172, 174, 175, 176,
  177, 187, 189, 190, 264, 324, 325,
  337, 338, 345, 350, 351, 354, 355, 359
Sensei Kuda, 73, 97, 155, 179, 189, 190,
  236, 256, 269, 281, 282, 324, 325,
  345, 350, 355, 356, 359
Sensei Kuda's, 179, 190, 269, 345, 355,
  356
Sensei Soken, 140, 144, 146, 154, 155,
  156, 157, 158, 163, 164, 166, 184,
  189, 228, 246, 259, 341, 350, 357, 358
Sensei Yuichi Kuda, 73, 137, 151, 155,
  164, 168, 179, 236, 242, 347
Shian Toma, 56, 74
Shigeru Kojo, 68
Shigeru Nakamura, 55, 56, 57, 179, 184
Shigeru Tamaya, 62, 85
Shimabukuro, 120, 122, 123, 124, 145,
  324
Shimazu clan, 27, 102, 103
Shimazu Clan, 99, 103
Shimpan Shiroma, 61, 111
Shinchin Matayoshi, 79
Shinei Kyan, 162
Shingi Matayoshi, 79
Shinken Taira, 82
Shinkichi Kuniyoshi, 55
Shinko Matayoshi, 79
Shinpo Matayoshi, 79, 148, 158, 189
Shintaro Ogawa, 284
Shinyei Kyan, 81
Shinyu Isa, 81
Shiroma, 108, 359, 360, 362
Shirotaru, 26
Shishu, 106, 108, 205
Sho Gen, 71
Sho Nei, 27
Sho Shin, 20, 113
Sho Shitsu, 70, 114
Sho Tai, 89, 102, 104, 134, 135
Sho Taikyu, 21
Sho Toku, 27
Shosei Kina, 81

Shoshin Nagamine, 118, 119, 158, 162
Shugoro Nakazato, 115, 162, 341
Shumba-junki, 18
Shunten, 16, 17, 18
Shushiwa, 47
Soeishi Ryotoku, 72
Soken, 73, 91, 94, 133, 134, 135, 136,
    137, 138, 139, 140, 141, 142, 143,
    144, 145, 146, 147, 148, 149, 152,
    154, 155, 156, 157, 158, 162, 163,
    164, 166, 168, 169, 184, 185, 187,
    189, 190, 193, 213, 228, 253, 259,
    300, 344, 345, 351, 355, 357, 358
Soko, 72
Sokon Matsumura, 75, 89, 91, 94, 98,
    100, 117, 137
Steve Davis, 357
Sueyoshi, 72
Sun Tsu, 245
Sun Tzu, 198, 218

Taira, 12, 16, 17, 82, 83
Takahara, 39
Takaya Yabiku, 68, 85, 91, 92, 145, 146,
    152, 169, 170, 189
Takaya Yabiku., 68
Takayuki Kinjo., 55
Taketo Nakamura, 56
Tamagusuku, 19
Tametomo, 16, 17, 18, 19
Taro Shimabukuro, 118, 119, 121
Taru Kise, 46
Tatsuo Shimabukuro, 118, 121, 123
Tawada Megantu, 80
Tawata Shinboku, 80, 105
Ted Lange, 169
Teiichi Nakamura, 56
Tengu, 227
Teruya Kanga, 39

The Last Samurai, 133
Tokugawa Shoguns, 103
Tokumine, 56, 70, 117
Tom Belamy, 169
Tongushi Kansaburo, 48
Toyama, 52, 72, 111, 112, 113, 123
Tsuguo Sakumoto, 55
Tsuyoshi Chitose, 54

Uechi Kanbun, 46
Uhuchiku, 81
Untura, 24, 25
Ushi Tanme, 144

Vincent Wiegand, 169

W. C. Fields, 214
Waishinzan, 54
William Dometrich, 54, 84
Wong Chung-Yoh, 43

Yabiku Moden, 82
Yamachi, 72
Yamagusuku Andaya, 80
Yasuhide Tamaki, 64
Yazusato, 108
Yonamine Tsuru, 94
Yoshitsune no Minamoto, 12
Yuchi Kuda, 190, 194
Yuchoku Higa, 115, 162
Yuichi Kuda, 84, 85, 92, 125, 126, 154,
    169, 179, 189, 254, 255, 258, 300,
    301, 322, 324

Zaha, 169
Zempo, 120, 324
Zenryo Shimabukuro, 118, 120, 121,
    123

"When a strong man keepeth his palace,
his goods are in peace."
Holy Bible
Luke 11:21

AUTHOR'S CONTACT INFORMATION

Ronald Lindsey
P.O. Box 689
Bastrop, Tx 78602

Email: kobudomei@yahoo.com

The above photo is an old Shinshinto Japanese Samurai Sword that I have owned and practiced with for nearly 40 years. At the request of my students I am having copies made of this fine sword. The unsigned sword dates back to the 1860's; the blade has a cutting edge of 30 inches (76.2 cm.). I call the sword "Smokey". If you would like a copy of this sword please contact me.

"Then he said unto them.
But now, he that hath a purse let him take it and like wise his scrip: and he that hath
no sword, let him sell his garments and buy one."

Holy Bible
Luke 22:36

苦難有時
而盡爭戰終
有止時

*"For all the bitterness in man must cease
and every battle must be ended."*

**The closing lyrics (third verse) from the "Minstrel Boy"; an old Irish Patriotic Song
written by Thomas Moore (1779-1852).**

Classic Chinese calligraphy by Shifu Hwang

12735466R00216

Made in the USA
Lexington, KY
24 October 2018